*Charles Ludlam and
the Ridiculous Theatrical Company*

Charles Ludlam and the Ridiculous Theatrical Company

Critical Analyses of 29 Plays

by
Rick Roemer

McFarland & Company, Inc., Publishers
Jefferson, North Carolina and London

Excerpts from the following plays are printed by permission of Samuel French, Inc.:

The Mystery of Irma Vep by Charles Ludlam
Copyright ©1984 by Charles Ludlam
Copyright ©1987, 1989 by the Estate of Charles Ludlam

The Artificial Jungle by Charles Ludlam
Copyright ©1986 by Charles Ludlam
Copyright ©1987 by the Estate of Charles Ludlam

Reverse Psychology by Charles Ludlam
Copyright ©1989 by the Estate of Charles Ludlam

Stage Blood by Charles Ludlam
Copyright ©1976, 1979 by Charles Ludlam

Bluebeard by Charles Ludlam
Copyright ©1971 by Charles Ludlam
Copyright ©1987 by the Estate of Charles Ludlam

CAUTION: Professionals and amateurs are hereby warned that The Mystery of Irma Vep, The Artificial Jungle, Reverse Psychology, Stage Blood and Bluebeard, being fully protected under the copyright laws of the United States of America, the British Commonwealth countries, including Canada, and the other countries of the Copyright Union, are subject to a royalty. All rights, including professional, amateur, motion picture, recitation, public reading, radio, television and cable broadcasting, and the rights of translation into foreign languages, are strictly reserved. Any inquiry regarding the availability of performance rights, or the purchase of individual copies of the authorized acting edition, must be directed to Samuel French Inc., 45 West 25 Street, NY, NY 10010 with other locations in Hollywood and Toronto, Canada.

Excerpts from Ridiculous Theatre: Scourge of Human Folly, edited by Steven Samuels, copyright ©1992 Estate of Charles Ludlam, appear by permission of Theatre Communications Center.

British Library Cataloguing-in-Publication data are available

Library of Congress Cataloguing-in-Publication Data

Roemer, Rick, 1956–
    Charles Ludlam and the Ridiculous Theatrical Company : critical
analyses of 29 plays / by Rick Roemer.
        p.   cm.
    Includes bibliographical references and index.
    ISBN 0-7864-0340-3 (library binding : 55# alkaline paper) ∞
    1. Ludlam, Charles — Criticism and interpretation.
2. Homosexuality and literature — United States — History — 20th
century.   3. Avant-garde (Aesthetics) — United States.   4. American
farces — History and criticism.   5. Ridiculous Theatrical Company.
6. Ridicule in literature.   I. Title.
PS3562.U258Z86   1998   97-43335
812'.54 — dc21   CIP

Manufactured in the United States of America

McFarland & Company, Inc., Publishers
    Box 611, Jefferson, North Carolina 28640

This book is lovingly dedicated to Bruce Lane Holbrook

Acknowledgments

I would like to gratefully acknowledge the support of the following: Carl Mueller, for his invaluable insights and encouragement; Leon Katz, who first steered me in the direction of Charles Ludlam; Mel Shapiro whose guidance, support and friendship has been, and continues to be, truly inspirational; the staff at the Billy Rose Theatre Collection at the New York Public Library for the Performing Arts for their patience and guidance; Dr. Bert Thomas and Dr. Roy Meals of the UCLA Medical Center and physical therapist Jan Stone for reconstructing and rehabilitating my shattered left wrist in the middle of writing this book, enabling me to finish; my parents, Richard and Beverly Roemer, who have always lovingly and unconditionally supported my endeavors; and most importantly, Bruce Holbrook — without his constant love and support, this book would never have been completed.

Table of Contents

Introduction

The chief enemy of creativity is "good" taste.
— Pablo Picasso

As a rebellious, artistic, long-haired youth of 1960s New York City, Charles Ludlam and friend Stuart Sherman would often join the "blue-rinse" set at Wednesday matinees on Broadway.[1] This was the cheapest way for them to see shows. One Wednesday, during the run of *Conduct Unbecoming*, Sherman told Charles that he would pay for two front-row seats if Charles would agree to arrive dressed as a woman. Undaunted, the bearded Ludlam appeared on the appointed Wednesday in a lovely frock, sporting a string of pearls and a tiny handbag filled with tissue paper. Sherman met him out front and they leisurely strolled down the aisle, arm in arm, totally aware that every eye was upon them. They quietly took their front-row seats and prepared for the afternoon play. One by one the actors, when required to be downstage, would peek down in astonishment, often doing double takes at this bearded man in a dress, holding his dainty little clutch. It was obvious that when each actor left the stage they ran to tell the others backstage to be sure to get a glimpse of *what* was sitting in the front row. The expressions of astonishment and disbelief were many as Ludlam sat thoughtfully with his chin perched delicately on his finger, never acknowledging that he, in fact, had become the show that afternoon. It seemed completely natural for him to be the center of attention. While most audience members clicked their tongues, considering this display to be in bad taste, Ludlam saw the irony and humor in how ridiculous he must look. He also knew that most matrons in the audience that afternoon would be oblivious to the commentary his parody would provide.

Throughout his career Charles Ludlam was often accused of presenting bad taste on stage in the guise of serious comic art. As a playwright he relished in reviving and revamping discarded genres, using bad jokes, corny lines, and nonsequiturs. As an actor, he had as many overt facial expressions as could be mastered by one person and possessed the ability to be completely in character and, simultaneously, to let himself, Charles Ludlam, be revealed. As a designer, he would recycle any and all discarded items he could find from trash cans and sidewalks, find a use for them and use them in his shows. As a director, he was kind, fun, tough, wild, erratic and prolific. Many, including some critics, gave him a mere passing nod, not crediting what he was doing with any degree of significance. They would, undoubtedly, be dumbfounded when asked to explain why and how Ludlam was able to keep a core of actors together as an ensemble in an actual repertory atmosphere for twenty years, a feat shared by few, if any, other theatre companies in or outside New York City. Not only did Ludlam maintain an ensemble of actors, he wrote, designed, directed and starred in almost every play performed under the Ridiculous banner. He was not just running a theatre, he was pursuing a mission. Charles Ludlam wanted to create the premier American comic theatre, and often dreamed and talked of being handed the keys to the Vivian Beaumont Theatre in Lincoln Center by the mayor of New York. Ludlam confessed in an interview once that "What I'm trying to do is bring the classical tradition to the modern era."[2]

Charles Ludlam died at the age of 44 after being hospitalized with pneumocystic pneumonia and other complications resulting from the deadly disease AIDS. He left a legacy of twenty-nine excessive and outlandish farces that might combine any or all elements of Jacobean tragedy, French farce, burlesque, Warner Brothers epics, "B" movies, Wagnerian opera and Victorian melodrama. It has been written that "not since Molière have we been blessed with such a playwright, and it may be several centuries more before we see his like again."[3] For this reason it is imperative that Charles Ludlam and his ridiculous theatrics be studied and documented so that in the future, actors, directors, scholars, playwrights and fellow farceurs can profit in their own searches for artistic identity and expression by studying one who remained so faithful to his own.

The ridiculous has validity as an aesthetic genre because, as we shall see in future chapters, it blossomed in a unique period, the 1960s, but it actually has a direct legacy as far back as the previous century in Europe. The romantic movement, to which Ludlam was constantly drawn, gave rise to a different societal voice and altered the collective literary consciousness in Europe. As Victor Hugo professed in his famous doctrine, "There are no rules or models, or rather there are no other rules than the general laws of nature, which extend over the whole domain of art, and the special laws which, in every composition, result from the conditions peculiar to each subject."[4] What Hugo was declaring was that the content of art is guided by rules not necessarily mandated by the *form* of the art. Also, the romantics stressed individual expression over conforming with societal authority, often at great personal risk. Until that time in Europe, most novels, plays, poetry, symphonies, ballets, operas, concertos, sculptures and paintings were confined by uniform rules that, more or less, determined their content. Ludwig van Beethoven burst through the boundaries of classical music when he composed his 3rd Symphony, the *Eroica*. He divorced himself from the strict classical structure of tempo and rhythm, and wrote heroic and sweeping phrases. Playwrights began breaking the unities of time, place and action, so long entrenched in the dramatic community, and wrote vast epics encompassing many years and various locations. What was once deemed noble in the classical mode soon became passe with the romantic iconoclasts.

Although the romantic movement itself was short-lived, its impact on future artistic expression was immense. At the end of the 1890s, an avant-garde movement began in France that stretched the frontiers of art even further. This was the time when cubism, surrealism, expressionism, Dadaism and futurism took hold, a time when artists were not only displaying their own voice in their works, but delving even farther into the psyche and the soul. Rules were forever broken and the sky was the limit.

An avant-garde movement in America did not take hold until the 1950s and early 1960s. Within the context of the tumultuous decade of the sixties, when Ludlam began his artistic career, American avant-garde art was expanding beyond the defined boundaries of form and exploring the limitless soul of content. In the theatre a new institution, Off Off Broadway theatre, emerged out of a discontent with standard, commercial Broadway fare. Playwrights and directors feverishly explored the "plotless" drama and emphasized the experiential. What was being redefined was the very nature of performance, including the space in which it was presented. Audiences were often included in the performance as another character. The "fourth wall" was definitively broken.

This is all briefly discussed to show that Ludlam's ridiculous aesthetic was actually a continuation of already established conventions. Certainly one can observe similarities between Charles Ludlam and the Dadaist movement when, in his *Manifesto: Ridiculous Theater, Scourge of Human Folly*, Ludlam writes what could easily be the creed for the absurdist Alfred Jarry and his Ubu plays:

> This is farce not Sunday school. Illustrate hedonistic calculus. Test out a dangerous idea, a theme that threatens to destroy one's whole value system. Treat the material in a madly farcical manner without losing the seriousness of the theme. Show how paradoxes arrest the mind. Scare yourself a bit along the way.[5]

As critic and scholar Richard Schechner notes in *Public Domain*, "The greatest playwrights of the Western tradition (and it would seem of every civilization), stole from each other, from the public domain, from the existing work, from other cultures, from history. They worked as craftsmen, not 'poets.' They organized events, performers, and things."[6] Charles Ludlam, as playwright and actor, aptly fits this description, only he referred to it as "recycling the culture."[7] He was, indeed, a cultural scavenger, looking back into forgotten and often ignored genres and breathing new life into them.

Ludlam was not necessarily without precedent in his aesthetic approach to theatre, but he flavored his version with a level of indulgence that betrayed the credo of what had become the standard avant-garde; minimal sets, minimal lights and minimal words. Ludlam was quoted as saying, "I hate minimal art. I hate conceptual art. I am for *execution*. I am for *maximal* art. Minimal art is inflationary art: less for your money."[8] Any person who doubted this claim needed only to attend a production of the Ridiculous Theatrical Company and witness that, indeed, Ludlam strove for virtuoso maximalism, the polar opposite of minimalism. He seemed to redefine the concept of excess on stage, and presented it in a light which shone like a beacon for other artists to follow.

Ludlam hated being referred to as avant-garde, when in fact what he was attempting to do was help revive a stale and lackluster commercial theatre by bringing it back to some of its traditional roots. He is quoted in a *New York Times* interview as saying, "All I'm doing down here is working within a comic tradition using character types that have been around for centuries. I'm just trying to make them live again in a way that's funny and thought-provoking."[9] That was his intent, clear and simple.

Since Ludlam's death in 1987, only one of his twenty-nine plays, *The Mystery of Irma Vep*, is consistently performed in regional theatres. Although not his final play, *Irma Vep* may well be the epitome of Ludlam's quest for the ridiculous. It is a masterpiece of parody and recycled theatrical and cinematic melodrama, with two actors playing all the roles, male and female. It is the intention of this book to explain the ridiculous so that more of Ludlam's plays will become familiar and, thereby, be incorporated into the American repertory. As more critical work is written about Charles Ludlam and the Ridiculous Theatrical Company, directors, designers and actors will come to understand the genre and his intent, critics will begin to understand how to review the work, and a wider audience will be exposed to what, except during the occasional tour, only New York audiences enjoyed for twenty years.

In spite of its importance and influence, the Ridiculous Theatrical Company has virtually been ignored by major scholars. It gets only a passing mention in a few theatre history books and texts dealing with experimental theatre. As of yet, critical scholarship on Charles Ludlam has been limited to a chapter in Stefan Brecht's *Queer Theatre*, Calvin Tomkins' 1976 *New Yorker* article, "Profiles: Ridiculous," and various published articles, reviews and interviews. A complete volume of Ludlam's plays was not published until 1989 — two years after his death. In 1992, Steven Samuels, company manager for the Ridiculous Theatrical Company for ten years, compiled and edited a sampling of Ludlam's prose entitled *Ridiculous Theatre: Scourge of Human Folly*. There has been one doctoral dissertation, written in 1985 by Robert Thomas Wharton and titled *The Working Dynamics of the Ridiculous Theatrical Company: An Analysis of Charles Ludlam's Relationship with His Ensemble from 1967 through 1981*, but this work is simply a compilation and attempted synthesis of personal interviews. Very little, if any, analysis of theatrical style is undertaken and its primary contribution to critical scholarship is simply the body of interviews as a source of primary research material. Since the plays were not published until 1989 and were therefore inaccessible to Mr. Wharton, they were not included for analysis.

Ludlam's style is one that is performance oriented; in other words, the style of a Ludlam play cannot be ascertained merely by reading it. His true genius manifested itself in performance: the quick glance of shared insight to the audience, the inane bits and gags performed with aplomb, the outrageously tacky costumes and sets, the gregarious and uncensored use of language. These are all elements of the ridiculous that must be experienced and digested viscerally to be fully comprehended. However, the publication of his plays has now made it possible to examine the raw material of works that eventually developed into something outrageous on the stage.

Because Ludlam's work is visually oriented, and with no critical works to guide, it is difficult to construct critical research and document the performance style. One is limited to the individual reviews, but considering the immediate pressures and deadlines of modern critics and their individual biases, it becomes impossible to take those writings at face value. That which inspires one critic to clarify and describe may either completely escape or fail to merit another's attention.

The most illuminating materials are the articles and interviews that, luckily, took place throughout Ludlam's career. From these it is possible to dig more deeply into Ludlam's creative spirit and begin to understand his mission.

Also available for the scholar, and the public as well, are videotapes of various Ludlam plays in performance. At the New York Public Library for the Performing Arts, the Charles Ludlam archives were catalogued and made available in 1992. This writer was the first to comb through the archives in the summer of 1992. Included among these materials are videotapes of Ludlam's last nine plays. It is unfortunate that Ludlam came to video late in his career, but the ability to view even his later work gives scholars and critics a window into the remainder of the other twenty plays, especially the visual and performance aspects of the ridiculous style. Having the published plays only makes for a more thorough and concrete examination.

In this book I hope to introduce the reader to Charles Ludlam, his work, his mission and his artistic sensibility. Chapter 1 is a brief biography of Ludlam from his childhood years up through his college graduation. Chapter 2 traces the roots of the ridiculous, including its early ancestors, Aristophanes, commedia dell'arte, and Molière. It explores the counter-cultural movement of the turbulent 1960s and the gay liberation movement, the influence of Andy Warhol and his pop art explosion, Ronald Tavel and John Vaccaro and their original Play-House of the Ridiculous, and Jack Smith and the underground experimental film movement. Chapter 3 is an examination of the theoretical components, the underpinnings, that comprise ridiculosity, including the inspirations of homosexuality, films, camp, drag and gender, opera and theatre artifice. Chapter 4 looks, in general terms, at how Ludlam's canon of plays and performance reflect his sense of ridiculous theatre artifice, including the elements of acting, playwriting, directing, language and design. Chapter 5 is a more detailed examination of Ludlam's plays from 1967 through 1980, when his artistic vision underwent various significant changes. Beginning with Ludlam's early "collage" period (*Big Hotel*, *When Queens Collide*, *Turds in Hell*, and *The Grand Tarot*), this chapter explores Ludlam's source materials and his recycled versions, concluding with his rendition of Charles Dickens' *A Christmas Carol*. Chapter 6 continues this exploration of Ludlam's plays from 1980 through 1987, after Ludlam redirected his efforts toward presenting only new works, many of them original farces. Although he struggled artistically and financially in the beginning of this period, in his last five plays, *Le Bourgeois Avant-Garde*, *Galas*, *The Mystery of Irma Vep*, *Salammbo*, and *The Artificial Jungle*, Ludlam finally struck the balance between the level of theatre artifice and dramatic structure he had worked so diligently to achieve. When his final production, *The Artificial Jungle*, was forced to close due to Ludlam's battle with AIDS, the era of Ludlam's ridiculous vision came to an end with his death shortly thereafter. And in the final Chapter 7, Ludlam's legacies will be synthesized, including his work with puppets and his venture into theatre for children, *Professor Bedlam's Educational Punch and Judy Show*, and *Anti Galaxie Nebulae*, a science-fiction, serial puppet thriller, and his involvement in various non-ridiculous projects. This chapter also will detail titles and short synopses of some of Ludlam's unfinished projects and, finally, will summarize Ludlam's impact on theatre and his legacy of lunacy. Following this chapter is an appendix revealing Ludlam's *Manifesto: Scourge of Human Folly*.

Finally, I would like to propose that a new word be entered into theatrical terminology: ridiculosity. Because this style did not develop in a vacuum, but rather is an extension of previous art movements such as absurdism, expressionism and romanticism, I feel that this unique style deserves a category of its own. And it would be an injustice to brand this excessive style with a commonplace, uninteresting version of the other "-isms." So I chose a truly ridiculous word to denote a truly ridiculous theatrical fashion — ridiculosity. The excess of the word itself does credit to the excesses abounding in the plays and performances of Charles Ludlam and the Ridiculous Theatrical Company, and gives the scholar and critic a definitive term to use in reference to the peculiar stamp Charles Ludlam has put on the nature of theatre and performing.

— 1 —
Charles Ludlam
in the Beginning

One bright summer day in 1949, a shy little Charlie Ludlam, six years old, and his mother were having a grand time at the Mineola Fair on Long Island. Although Mrs. Ludlam seemed to be wearing out, Charlie was becoming more and more energized with each passing hour. There was something about all of the bright lights, the loud music, people in costumes, the big rides, and the stage-like booths that captured his young, vivid imagination. Earlier in the day, while strolling around, he had noticed a sideshow exhibition with a sign that read "Freak Show." He wondered what that could be about and vowed to somehow sneak through the entrance sometime during the day and see for himself. When Mother finally had all she could take and demanded to sit down for a well-deserved rest, Charlie put up a stink, whining that there was still so much to see, so much to do. Seeing his wide-eyed enthusiasm, Mother Ludlam gave Charlie some money and told him not to wander off too far. They planned to meet in a half-hour by the Ferris wheel.

Charlie took the money and ran. Mrs. Ludlam, her motherly acuity overwhelmed by aching feet and tired eyes, didn't even notice in what direction he went. Charlie, of course, headed straight for the Freak Show. What could possibly be in that tent? What could a "freak" conceivably be?

Charlie entered cautiously and beheld sights that would, undoubtedly, influence his life forever. In the tent there sat a fat lady weighing over 600 pounds, a fire-eater, armless black dwarfs painting portraits with their toes and a freakishly thin man weighing a mere 75 pounds.[1] Afterward, wide-eyed and fascinated, young Charlie wandered around, digesting all the odd sights, sounds and smells he had encountered in this bizarre sideshow. So absorbed was he that he failed to notice a tall wooden structure until he banged into it. He looked up and saw two puppets, a man with a huge, pointed nose and clownish hat, and a woman in a nightgown and cap, arguing and hurling insults at each other. He also observed that they both carried sticks and thought nothing of bopping each other over the head. He sat down and began watching his first Punch and Judy puppet show.

After the show he drifted back outside in a daze, to find his mother beside herself with worry. She had the police searching for him. He was not at all aware that he was lost.[2]

Little could he have known at that young age how the reverberations produced by this enchanting day at the fair would echo throughout his entire future creative life.

Charles Ludlam was born on April 12, 1943, in Floral Park, Long Island. His parents, Joseph and Marjorie, were both strongly indoctrinated in the Catholic Church by their parents, specifically Charles's two Irish Catholic grandmothers who had even managed to convert their Protestant husbands to Catholicism. It was, as Ludlam himself put it, "a puritanical Protestant tradition with a *very* puritanical Catholicism glued on."[3] This would prove to be an invaluable influence for Charles while his own personal creativity was blossoming. The grand and theatrical ambience of the Catholic Mass can later be glimpsed in much of his work, as he later confessed in a personal diary: "The whole imagery in my way of thinking is Catholic — icons, incense; sensual, theatrical; theatre as an essential part of life, which the Mass was; theatre as sacrifice, as a form of a ritual sacrifice; theatre as life, really integrated into the life."[4]

While he was a young child, Ludlam's family moved to New Hyde Park, right across the street from a movie theatre. While sitting in his room reading any and all comic books he could get his hands on, he waited for the movie marquee to change twice a week, knowing his mother would take him. As a very young child, Ludlam saw almost every movie made in the 1940s. Like the misadventure at the Mineola Fair and the theatrical Catholic upbringing, these trips to the movie house would gestate in Ludlam's young, fertile imagination, waiting for the right time to emerge.

While his imagination was brewing, young Charles began to unleash his creativity by putting on puppet shows in his basement, influenced by his experience at the fair. He would usually corner his bright-eyed and willing young brother, Donald, to be the audience — sometimes making him don a hand-puppet himself when their mother would venture down to see what was going on, thus capturing an entirely new audience. Although young Charles Ludlam was withdrawn and a loner at school, he seemed to come alive with just his voice and a puppet on his hand. He was also "the boy who shone only once a year, when he starred in the class play at school."[5] He learned to live and cope in the world of his imagination.

Another strong influence on Ludlam was the burgeoning new medium of television. When not voraciously reading comic books or sitting in the movie theatre, Ludlam sat in front of the little, gray, snowy family television absorbing every cartoon and puppet show. His two favorite shows were *Howdy Doody* and *Kukla, Fran and Ollie.* He would later reminisce that "animated cartoons and puppets shaped my life, along with movies. I learned to read from comic books."[6]

Not only was Ludlam's youthful inventiveness heavily influenced by these visually theatrical impressions, but there was something else that set him apart from most other children in his neighborhood world. Young Charles found that he was mysteriously attracted to his male teachers and various young male friends. Not fully understanding the ramifications of this discovery, he somehow knew that this was something he must keep to himself, thus plunging him further into the security of his already vivid fantasy life. As most pubescent homosexuals growing up in the late 1940s and 1950s knew, these strange feelings were intense and strangely seductive, but utterly taboo, given all of the wholesome, heterosexual images surrounding them in films and on television. These early powerful erotic feelings in Ludlam fueled all of the other influences in his life; the more secretive he became about his "other" fantasy life, the more he absorbed himself in his imaginative life of comic books, movies and puppet shows, and thus the more withdrawn he became. He admitted himself that:

> If I hadn't discovered theatre early on, I would almost certainly have become a juvenile delinquent. I think I was expected to settle down in Greenlawn, Long Island, marry a somewhat homely girl and produce lots of children. But if I had done that and not what I wanted to do, they would have found me hanging in the garage one day.[7]

As we shall see in later chapters, Ludlam's homosexuality would be at the very root of his developing aesthetic, aided heavily by his cartoon-like visions of 1940s melodramatic movie heroines caught up in the ritualistic dramas of forbidden love. One element of his developing homosexuality that enticed him was the wearing of girls' clothes. Unknown to him at the time, this affinity for exploring the limits and boundaries of gender would be a cornerstone of his theatrical expression. His favorite holiday was Halloween because he loved dressing up as a girl and going trick-or-treating. Although he often caused a bit of a scandal each Halloween, he was hardly fazed because people often mistook him for a girl anyway. As a child, Ludlam was small and slight, so it is not surprising that he preferred his own inventive world of fantasy to the more typical world of playing army and football with the neighborhood boys. As he grew up, it seemed perfectly natural that he pursue a career in the theatre, which his family seemed to support.

In 1958, at the age of 15, he was hired by William Hunt as a summer apprentice at the Red Barn Theatre, a local summer stock company in Long Island. This was Ludlam's first introduction to the inner workings of a professional theatre, and it would prove to be an invaluable lesson in running what he called a classical stock company. This was also the first time that he met real actors and realized there was a world outside his small Long Island neighborhood. He confessed in an early interview in *The New Yorker* that "[I] met people who had a different concept of sexual morality from anything I'd been exposed to before."[8] Although Ludlam played no major roles in any plays that summer, he always seemed to make his presence known, even while in the chorus. It was clear to most everybody, none more so than Charles himself, that he was not an ensemble player. He was then, and would remain throughout his life, a renegade, even wearing long hair that summer at the Red Barn before it was the hip thing to do. No matter what he did, he invariably stuck out. But this summer of stock reinforced in Ludlam the idea that the theatre would be his life, and that one day he would have his own theatre company. After this highly energized and creative summer, Charles began to venture into New York City to see how real professional New York theatre worked.

One of the first shows he saw on these self-prescribed field trips was *Tonight We Improvise*, performed by the Living Theatre under the tutelage of Julian Beck and Judith Malina. He was so enthralled by this production that he immediately returned to see *The Connection*, another piece performed by the Living Theatre. These two performances provided Ludlam with an earth-shattering revelation — that theatre could be expressed in many ways and could be, ultimately, a personal expression.[9] He idolized the Becks and was determined to start and run his own theatre based on their standards. Even at this point in his life, Ludlam was turned off by what he saw as strictly commercial theatre which tended to play to the lowest common denominator. He also was disenchanted with avant-garde and experimental playwrights like Samuel Beckett and Jean Genet, whose works he felt were too minimal. He longed for the exotic. He felt aligned with the Becks and wanted to stretch the boundaries of his theatrical expression. He became immersed in the plays of Pirandello, Strindberg and Aeschylus, and, once again, dreamed of starting a theatre that was more than just an entertainment medium. He wanted to create a new theatre.

This dream began emerging at Harborfields High School in Greenlawn, Long Island, where Ludlam began the Students' Repertory Theatre with the cream-of-the-crop actors from his and neighboring high schools. He vowed to be neither commercial nor avant-garde, like his idols the Becks. His first season, in a thirty-two seat theatre in an abandoned meeting hall atop a liquor store, he staged *Madman on the Roof* by Japanese playwright Kikuchi Kahn, *Theatre of the Soul* by Russian avant-garde playwright Nikolai Niko-laivich, Eugene O'Neill's *Great God Brown* and August Strindberg's *Dream Play*. "I searched out oddities like a pig sniffing truffles," Ludlam reflected in an interview.[10] It was clear from an early age that Ludlam was rejecting naturalism in his theatrical expression. This rebellion was to remain a guiding force in his entire body of work for the rest of his life. "The whole idea of something being natural becomes a very oppressive concept; it's shallow," he said in an interview in *Performing Arts Journal.* "Gradually, through training with Stainslavsky teachers, I realized they wanted me to behave in a civilized manner in a room, and not to do anything extraordinary. But everything I'm interested in is extraordinary."[11]

Twenty-three years later, in an interview in the *New York Times*, Ludlam was still clearly nurturing the seeds that had been planted in high school when explaining that he wanted "to go beyond a merely literal representation of reality and search for greater expressive possibilities."[12] As an astute young businessman, Ludlam even offered a season pass which included a reduced price for agreeing to see all the shows. This was all just a hint of what was to follow. After only two seasons, however, the Student's Repertory Theatre closed because Ludlam, its guiding force, was off to Hofstra University on Long Island to major in theatre.

Thanks to a strong recommendation from his high school acting teacher William Baden, Ludlam was granted an acting scholarship to Hofstra University where he performed in and staged many of the classics. He also continued his intense fascination with Strindberg, especially the expressionistic plays, and began experimenting with plotless dramas.

Ludlam's teachers at Hofstra did not understand his broad and emotive acting style and suggested he stick to writing and directing. They thought his style of acting hammy, aggressively expressive and not at all appropriate for the student actor attempting to seriously unleash Ibsen, Shakespeare, or Corneille. This style, however, seemed natural to Ludlam himself; it was a blend of the melodramatic movie-stars of the 1940s films he had spent hours digesting, comic book adventure heroes, cartoon buffoons, and the comically sarcastic, two-dimensional puppets he had been weaned on from an early age. He became progressively outraged, battling with his professors and rebelling against almost everything they tried to teach him. This antagonistic relationship struck a tender nerve with Ludlam, who had been told a few years earlier by William Hunt at the Red Barn that "[he] had effeminate mannerisms that would destroy [his] career."[13]

Ludlam, however, was listening to his own instincts which were guiding him in a completely different direction from that of his educators at Hofstra. He was beginning to uncover and express his artistic voice and, luckily, was astute enough to realize it. So he finished college on his own terms, switching his major from acting to dramatic literature. This afforded him the freedom to explore and develop his own projects while at the same time studying and absorbing many wonderfully powerful and significant plays from the theatrical canon.

Before his senior year at college, he had experimented with writing a couple of expressionistic one-act plays and a romantic tragedy in verse. During his senior year, though, he wrote a full-length, semi-autobiographical, plotless play called *Edna Brown*, based loosely on his family history. Although he destroyed the only copy in a fit of melancholy, there were reportedly in this play hints of things to come: a character named Exotica A La Carte, who lived on the proceeds of a string of pay toilets, and another character who spoke entirely in song titles.[14]

It was also at Hofstra where Ludlam first met Susan Carlson, immortalized in the Ridiculous Theatrical Company as Black-Eyed Susan, who would remain with him for most of his life. A young and inexperienced Carlson, captivated by this energetic, bold young artiste who dared to be different and reveled in defying the authorities, recalls that:

> I was in a play he directed called *The Solid House* — it was a Mexican play he'd found somewhere, about people after death. It was set in a tomb. The play was twenty minutes long, and we rehearsed it for three months. When we performed it, Charles wouldn't let us take curtain calls — he locked us in the dressing room. It was partly a joke and partly the fact that we were all supposed to be dead. Oh, Charles was the bright spot in that school for me.[15]

Although difficult at the time, Ludlam's victories and defeats at Hofstra would prove to shape and influence his entire creative career.

> Those four years at Hofstra were a very turbulent period for me. I was rebellious against my teachers, many of whose ideas I found offensive. I had an idea of the theatre that I wanted to create — I'd made a rough start on it with the Students' Repertory Theatre in high school. Somehow, I felt I had to create a new theatre, but I didn't completely realize what that meant.[16]

After graduating from Hofstra University in 1965, Ludlam moved into Greenwich Village on the island of Manhattan in New York. Greenwich Village had been the hot-bed of Bohemia since the 1920s and was the center of the 1950s beat generation. The explosion of artistic movements of the 1960s, coupled with the counter-cultural youth movement, made the

Village yet again a mecca for artistic exploration and trendiness, with Ludlam now strategically and energetically positioned at its core. It was an obvious and natural move for Ludlam, who was dissatisfied with any academic or literal approach to theatre. This move into Manhattan would prove to be the beginning of Ludlam's imprint on the newly blossoming Off Off Broadway theatre movement, and his radical style fit in perfectly with the spirit of the 1960s. Ludlam was truly at the right place at the right time, and was intelligent enough to see it and to take complete advantage of it. As critic Michael Bronski reveals about this time period in New York:

> Off-off Broadway brought the movements for social change of the 1960s to mainstream theater. With its beginnings in social unrest, the new theatrical temperament evoked and provoked social and cultural change. As the whole culture became more permissive — with a deeper understanding of the personal and political in people's lives, whether it was black liberation, feminism, youth movements, leftist politics, anti-war activities, or gay liberation — Off-Off Broadway promoted and presented the changes.[17]

— 2 —
The Roots
of Ridiculosity

Ridiculosity as a theatrical form emerged in New York City in the mid–1960s. However, as mentioned earlier, this sensibility has many illustrious ancestors. From classical Greece to 1960s America, ridiculosity hails from an impressive and influential lineage. It could certainly be argued that the genuine father of ridiculosity was the classical Greek comic poet-satirist Aristophanes. Not only did he make use of parody, burlesque, caricature, satire, "bits" and sexual innuendo in his plays, he also painted them onto the canvas of ancient "pop" culture, ridiculing everything from politics to social mores.

As Charles Ludlam was a unique reflection of his era, so too was Aristophanes. Ludlam was influenced by and responded to the turbulent cultural revolution that took place in America in the 1960s and 1970s. In classical Greece, Aristophanes was reflecting upon and ridiculing the already corrupted politics of the very beginnings of democracy, social roles, including transgressions of traditional gender and sexuality, the maddening urge to war with neighboring states, and any and all institutions which he felt were less than fair and impartial. In short, Aristophanes was the mouthpiece of the people, reflecting their unspoken desires and frustrations, which is not only why he was so immensely popular in his time, but also why his plays are still performed today. He touched a nerve within his people.

We begin the discussion of ridiculosity with one of its most basic tenets, artifice. Charles Ludlam was unequivocally not mirroring reality as prescribed by realism or naturalism, rather he was commenting upon it and criticizing it through his ribald and extravagant farces. Critic and theatrical journalist Gerald Rabkin notes that:

> Ridiculous theatre, reacting against both the naturalism that has dominated mainstream American theatre for half a century, and the metaphysical

17

abstraction of Absurdism and its heirs, responded to images and imperatives closer to home: a world on the brink of sanity and survival, of speed-freaks, drag queens and would-be superstars, a parochial world which nonetheless spoke metaphorically to the perilous state of the human condition in the mid 20th century.[1]

This statement, with obvious alterations, could easily be applied to Aristophanes and Athenian society of the fifth century B.C.

Two thousand years before Walt Disney imbued animals with human qualities in his legendary cartoons, Aristophanes had already portrayed a menagerie of human dogs, pigs, donkeys, frogs, beetles, wasps and birds in his repertoire of satire and social commentary. Although Ludlam did not portray human characters as animals, except in his adult fairy tale *The Enchanted Pig*, he certainly employed a cartoon-like effect to create an Aristophanic world of fantasy. In his play *Turds in Hell* (which he co-wrote with company member Bill Vehr), the main character, Orgone, is described as a baby hunchback, pinhead, sex maniac with an enormous phallus attached to his body. Here, a direct visual correlation can be made with Aristophanes' *Lysistrata*, wherein the men, having been forced to forgo intercourse with their wives due to a sex strike by the females, end up with gigantic phalluses at the end of the play, each one bigger than the last. Both playwrights relied on the visual to accentuate a point.

In his play *Secret Lives of the Sexists*, subtitled *The Farce of Modern Life*, Ludlam actually derived his themes of gender identity, the war between the sexes, and the parody of other dramatic forms directly from the Aristophanic farce *Thesmophoriazusai*. In this play, the theme of sexual identity is dominant throughout and is often used as an excuse for the jokes, slapstick gags and buffoonery. Many of the sexual allusions in the play are homoerotic in nature. Indeed, by the end of the play, all the males are dressed as women. Transvestitism is a tool Ludlam shared. He used drag to some extent, whether male to female or female to male, in almost all of his plays.

Thesmophoriazusai is, on the whole, a parody of Euripides' dramaturgy. Not only are the plots of his plays parodied, but also the scenic devices, the acting style and the language. One of the main actions in the Aristophanic comedy is Euripides' attempt to rescue and free his friend Mnesilochus, who has been discovered dressed as a woman while spying for Euripides at an all-female assembly. Mnesilochus initiates his first escape plan. Aristophanes takes the idea of sending Euripides a message written on oar-blades from *Palamedes*, but uses votive tablets from the temple instead. Nothing happens. Aristophanes then has Euripides try to rescue Mnesilochus by pretending to be Menelaus as in a scene from Euripides' play *Helen*, but it fails. The next rescue plot involves recreating the roles of Echo and Perseus from Euripides' *Andromeda*. Mnesilochus acts as Andromeda, but Euripides, unable to deceive the Sythian guard, leaves. Aristophanes also parodies Euripides' *Alcestis* and *Hippolytus* throughout the play. He used parody in this play to comment on the state of dramatic writing, just as Ludlam used parody to comment on the state of American twentieth century theatre. One need only observe classical Greek pottery depicting comic characters with their padded behinds and grotesque masks, to begin to discover the link with Ludlam's outrageous vision of character and visual comedy.

Another important ancestor of ridiculosity is commedia dell'arte, which emerged in sixteenth century Italy. Of course, this genre can be traced back to Roman comedies, which in turn sprang from Aristophanes. One important trait to link with Ludlam here is the development of a troupe of actors who perform together over an extended period of time in various locations. Because a fundamental characteristic of commedia dell'arte was improvisation, actors worked together over a prolonged period of time in order to develop a trust with one another. They merely worked from an outline that consisted of entrances, exits, characters and lazzis, which were separate comic moments included only to arouse laughter, not to move the story along. The actors would learn the structure of the scenario and from there improvise the story. The generalized plots put the emphasis on the characters and their zany antics and vulgar tricks.

One can see this influence in Ludlam's early works, which were plotless and often improvised in the wee hours of the morning. All the actors knew the basic structure of the play, but were encouraged to add any and all bits, no matter how corny or irrelevant. When rehearsing some of his plays, he would actually write during rehearsal in order for the actors to improvise their skeletal parts using their own comic gifts, and then afterward pen the written dialogue. In fact, Ludlam vigorously studied commedia dell'arte and even taught its techniques at New York University in the early 1980s. Like the commedia troupes, Ludlam's theatrical troupe was a popular theatre, utilizing the personality of the actor in the character as opposed to using the character to mask the actor.

In fact, one of Ludlam's earliest plays, *The Grand Tarot*, was fashioned directly from the commedia concept of improvisation and character. Each actor played a character on a tarot card, all fashioned after the stock commedia characters. He constructed twenty-two interchangeable scenes, each representing a different card of the Tarot. Before each performance an enormous deck would be shuffled and laid out on stage, thus determining the order of the scenes that night in the performance. Although *The Grand*

Tarot was originally performed this way, it eventually evolved into a fixed structure of the twenty-two scenes. In one scene between the Fool and Death, Ludlam's dialogue is reminiscent of a commedia lazzi:

> THE FOOL: Good sir, could you offer some advice?
> DEATH: I'll advise you if I can.
> THE FOOL: I need a life's work. But no profession suits me.
> DEATH: Here's something you can do. Turn around. Bend over.
> *(The Fool does so and Death kicks him in the ass. The Fool falls on his face.)*
> THE FOOL: But this is nothing. And you don't get nothing for nothing.
> DEATH: Take this rose. *(Death gives The Fool a white rose.)* When you smell
>   its sweetness you will desire nothing.
> THE FOOL: *(Smelling the rose.)* I desire nothing.
> DEATH: Shall we have another go at it?
> THE FOOL: Practice makes perfect. *(He turns around and offers his ass to be
>   kicked)*
> DEATH: *(Kicking his ass)* Very good. But don't forget to smell the white rose.
> THE FOOL: *(Smelling the rose)* Oh, thank you, sir.[2]

By its very nature, it is conceivable that this scene was developed and scripted from improvisations. In many ways, Ludlam's persona on stage in each of his shows, veiled under a character, was his stock character. As with the audiences of commedia dell'arte, the public came to a Ludlam play with certain expectations. They knew they were watching a story unfold, but they also waited anxiously for the antics and buffoonery which Ludlam, the actor, would share with them, often completely devoid of the character. Beneath each of Ludlam's character portrayals on stage was the character of Charles Ludlam, which was just as relevant as the character itself as far as the audience was concerned. Although he viewed commedia as valuable to his style, he thought it misleading for artists in today's world to attempt an authentic reconstruction of the commedia style. He was more interested in combining the various techniques of commedia with his own approaches to theatre to better reflect his twentieth century world view.

Finally, an important aspect of Ludlam's work which parallels the style of commedia dell'arte is the fact that in Italian commedia, each actor spent a lifetime mastering one role, either Brighella, Harlequin, Pulcinella, Panatlone, the Doctor, or the Captain. According to author James Fisher, "Typically a commedia actor played one character throughout his career, although he could work extraordinary variations on the emblematic traits of his stock mask, depending on the requirements and opportunities presented by a particular scenario."[3] The same could be said of Ludlam. Although he portrayed many different "characters" of his creation, Ludlam's mask was *himself*, with his commanding presence and dynamic charisma. If one were to have seen every performance of a Ludlam play with Ludlam in the lead, it would be clear that the most magnetic element was Charles Ludlam himself. He had the ability to play a character, yet reveal his charismatic personality at the same time. People came to the Ridiculous Theatrical Company to see Charles Ludlam and his lunatic antics.

Another direct ancestor of Ludlam and ridiculosity is the French seventeenth century playwright-actor-director Jean-Baptiste Poquelin, known to the world as Molière. To many, Ludlam was the modern Molière. In fact, one of Ludlam's most successful plays was his adaptation of Molière's *Le Bourgeois Gentilhomme* (*The Would-Be Gentleman*), titled *Le Bourgeois Avant-Garde*. Both were subtitled *A Comedy Ballet*. Ludlam took Molière's comic play of a man trying to convince everyone that he is of a higher social caste than he really is, and transposed the situation to a middle-class grocer from Long Island, Rufus Foufas, who desperately wants to be known as the premier patron of the avant-garde. Both plays are biting satires — Molière's on the false airs of the upper class, and Ludlam's on the pretentiousness of the avant-garde movement.

Molière wrote two different styles of plays: comedies of character and manner and farces. His farces are direct descendants of the commedia dell'arte, with their simplicity of plots, recurrence of certain roles and characters (as well as of situations and episodes), liveliness and rapidity of action and dialogue, and verbal inventiveness and humor. The heavy influence of commedia on Ludlam's early career is one obvious link to Molière.

But the more important parallel between the two men is their definition of theatre and the role each played to bring that idea to fruition. Each struggled early in his career to keep a company of actors together with little or no money. Molière was actually jailed for a time because of his heavy debts. Ludlam was never jailed, but he occasionally was forced to supplement his meager earnings from the Ridiculous Theatrical Company with various odd jobs and unemployment benefits. He, like Molière, was undaunted by poverty in his quest for a living, vital comic theatre. They both eventually succeeded because they were both unstoppable. Coincidentally, an early death took each of their lives.

Other, more recent links to past performance styles of Ludlam's ridiculosity are the popular entertainment forms of music hall, burlesque and vaudeville. All three developed in the nineteenth century to meet the needs of the masses of working-class people who were migrating rapidly to the burgeoning industrial cities of Great Britain and the United States. Although there still was a "legitimate" theatre where the highbrow genres of neoclassicism, romanticism, realism and naturalism were enjoying their day with the upper-class, bourgeois audience, these three other popular forms of entertainment appealed to a much larger, lower-class audience, who sought to escape the monotony and sweat of the factories and mills through the less sophisticated vehicles of broad comedy, spectacle, parody and satire.

In 1843 the English government officially banned drinking in legitimate theatres with the Theatre Regulation Act. Urban taverns were suddenly transformed from places in which the clientele participated in communal sing-alongs into theatres. The management of these music halls rearranged the tables, added platform stages, and hired comics, singers and actors to entertain the customers. Drinking was relegated to the back of the room, and the performance soon became the focus. Between 1850 and 1870, music halls sprang up all over England and variety shows became the most popular form of entertainment.

At approximately the same time in the United States, a popular form of entertainment was the minstrel show. It arose before and thrived long after the Civil War, and often parodied race and gender through song, dance and comic bits. When the British variety acts began touring America, the minstrel show felt their influence and vice-versa. The Interlocutor, Tambo and Bones of the traditional minstrel's opening were replaced with the kind of big, splashy production number found in the variety show. A handful of minstrel troupes attempted to remain faithful to the original, but the genre disappeared as a popular medium by the end of the nineteenth century, replaced by what would eventually emerge as vaudeville and burlesque.

An element of the minstrel show which was incorporated into the variety show was parody through drag. Usually, the head minstrel comic would play a "wench" role, impersonating a female. In the variety shows, this cross-gender impersonation became a featured, headline act. Harry Le Clair, one of the top female impersonators (or "imps"), became known as the "Sarah Bernhardt of vaudeville." Eventually, both men and women would perform as the opposite gender. Many shows were made up of an entirely cross-gendered cast.

In 1868, Lydia Thomspon and her British Blondes brought their burlesques of classical drama to America. To play the male roles, the women wore tights and short tunics, which created a scandalous intrigue. William Dean Howells, in his summary of the 1869 theatrical season in the *Atlantic Monthly*, was at the same time titilated and nauseated by this theatrical troupe, who not only parodied well-known dramatists, including William Shakespeare, but also raised eyebrows with their display of a hybrid gender. In spite of their guise of masculinity, they made no effort to conceal their femininity in an effort to deceive the audience: "[T]hough they were not like men, [they] were in most things as unlike women, and seemed creatures of a kind of alien sex, parodying both. It was certainly a shocking thing to look at them with their horrible prettiness, their archness in which was no charm, their grace which put to shame."[4]

The burlesque-extravaganza became one of the most popular entertainments in late nineteenth century America, parodying various well-known plays, operas, current performers and current events. The term burlesque originated from the Italian "burla," meaning jest or mockery. John Brougham, perhaps the most prolific writer of burlesque, found a great success in 1855 with his mockery of the American Indian in his play *Original, Aboriginal, Erratic, Operatic, Semi-civilized, and Demi-savaged Extravaganza of "Pocahontas."* Another writer, George L. Fox, became famous for his parodies of Shakespeare, specifically the plays *Macbeth, Richard III,* and *Hamlet.*

Because of the audience that burlesque was cultivating, "[It] flaunted the language of the street, of the uncultured, and of the urban working classes: slang. In doing so, it flouted the right of bourgeois culture to determine the propriety of public discourse. Burlesque reveled in its illegitimacy."[5] Due to its increasing tendency toward bawdy and often sexually titillating shows, burlesque was reshaped in the 1880s by Tony Pastor, a theatre manager, who strove to transform burlesque into an entertainment which the entire family could enjoy. What emerged from this effort was vaudeville, which maintained the structure of strung-together, independent variety acts, but eliminated the morally objectionable element of sexual innuendo, and it began to attract a different audience:

> Vaudeville existed only as a distinctive presentational, environmental and institutional form; in terms of content, vaudeville was nothing and everything. Although certain types of acts became standards on the vaudeville program, virtually every show business attraction that could fit on a stage appeared in vaudeville — with, of course, the important qualification that it had to be morally unobjectionable and satisfy middle-class notions of propriety and taste.[6]

Eventually burlesque became nothing more than the proverbial "girlie show," with the striptease as one of its staples. After the turn of the century, vaudeville dominated as the most popular form of mass entertainment.

All three of these forms — music hall, burlesque and vaudeville — in one way or another redefined the theatrical event, incorporating elements from the popular culture into entertainment through parody. Prior to the moral censorship that vaudeville imposed, female and male impersonation, parodies, satires, and broad comedies with "bits" and "gags," all of which were laced with sexual overtones, were the main fare of entertainment for the populace. These popular diversions were in direct and deliberate opposition to the "high culture" and "high art" of the upper-class, bourgeois audiences, with their polite dramas and comedies. These wider popular entertainments rejected the pompousness and hypocrisy of the bourgeoisie and its penchant for Puritan values by pandering to a vastly lower-common-denominator audience, ultimately unleashing a basically prurient performance style.

It is interesting to note that another influential theatrical movement with links to Ludlam and ridiculosity occurred at virtually the same time as these popular entertainment modes: the avant-garde and experimental explosion that occurred in European theatre and visual arts in the late nineteenth and early twentieth century. The theatre had recently undergone an experimentation with realism and naturalism. As a genre, realism depicted realistic details from daily life, using archeological accuracy in sets and costumes, and psychological motivation for character. Naturalism, brought to the forefront by the French author Emile Zola, considered heredity and environment to be the determining factors of man's providence. Inspired in part by Charles Darwin's *The Origin of Species*, Zola advocated for the dramatist to search for truth, to observe, record and experiment with the same detachment as the scientist. After World War I, a series of revolts against tradition — fauvism, cubism, futurism, constructivism, Dada and surrealism — helped to break the hold of realism and return artists to form. Perhaps the most influential of these styles to Ludlam is Dada, with Alfred Jarry at the helm. Eventually absorbed into surrealism, Dadaists were skeptical about a world that could produce a global war. They replaced logic, structure and harmony with contention and madness in their reflection of the world's insanity. Like Ludlam, each of these movements and their masters produced a manifesto, or doctrine, which they published as a blueprint for their style. Their theatres were not based on life events or situations, but rather employed distortions, dream-like visuals, and disconnected language in their theatrical visions. If the theatre is truly a reflection of life, then these avant-garde movements describe a world starting to unravel. This aesthetic did not reach the United States in a profound way until the late 1950s and early 1960s, when America was undergoing an unraveling process of its own. Widespread dissatisfaction with the status quo created a countercultural movement in the United States which became embodied in theatrical and visual art movements. And it was precisely at this time that Charles Ludlam, then in his early twenties, moved to the core of it all, Greenwich Village, to explore his own personal artistic voice. If the old adage "timing is everything" holds true, then Ludlam's destiny unfolded as it did because he began developing his own aesthetic voice at a time of extreme artistic exploration. Mid-twentieth century America was now ready to explore the intriguing and perplexing possibilities of the nonrepresentational mode of theatre that had long been established in Europe.

During the 1960s, the United States was undergoing a turbulent cultural revolution. There were many sparks that ignited this fire, but the war in Viet Nam became more than any other single thing, the mantel on which the rebels hung their hats. What appeared as the "generation gap," youth in opposition to authority figures, was actually a societal gap, with the countercultural youth in opposition to anything considered status quo. Figures such as John F. Kennedy, Martin Luther King, Jr., Robert Kennedy, Lyndon Johnson, Abbey Hoffman and Angela Davis are still vivid reminders of the strife and conflict of those times. The war in Viet Nam was raging out of control, with U.S. soldiers seeming more and more like foreign invaders rather than angels of aid. America's youth finally found a unified voice and rallied around the Viet Nam issue, manifesting their discontent through riots, blockades of college administration buildings, sit-ins and general civil unrest.

Another attack on the status quo was the civil rights movement, with bold declarations of total equality for African Americans. Led by the Reverend Martin Luther King, Jr., this movement sought merely to uphold the constitutional requirement for equality, but this shakeup of the entrenched status quo resulted in King's assassination. Both John F. and Robert Kennedy were murdered, at least by extension, because of their social and political beliefs. Music had evolved from the rock 'n' roll of Chuck Berry in the 1950s to the hard, frenetic style of Led Zeppelin in the 1960s. Hippies emerged when young people began discarding old ideas of dress and behavior. Loaded on marijuana, LSD or speed and decorated with flowers, many hippies simply "existed" together in communes in pursuit of their desire for peace, love and harmony. They rebelled against their parents, their teachers, their ministers, and any other authority figure who represented the status quo. But, they were also children of the media, who grew up with television as it was growing up, and it became their guidepost for popular culture: "The rock 'n' roll generation, having grown up on popular culture, took images very seriously indeed; beholding itself magnified in the funhouse mirror, it grew addicted to media which had agendas of their own — celebrity making, violence-mongering, sensationalism."[7] This relationship to popular culture via the media remained an important influence for Ludlam, whose own artistic sensibility, as we have seen, was also heavily influenced by the popular media.

Another group of disenfranchised people also began a revolt against the status quo at this time, again in the heart of Greenwich Village. With the riots at Stonewall, what is known today as the gay liberation movement began. In order to analyze the causes of the Stonewall Riots of 1969, which had a profound effect on Charles Ludlam and all other openly gay men, it is important to trace the years leading up to this pivotal moment.

There has been a large gay population in New York, specifically Greenwich Village, since the turn of the century. Because of the vast numbers of immigrants flocking to New York for sanctuary and freedom, a large working class developed in pockets of Manhattan whose primary concern was not "pansies," nor keeping up with the neighbors, but simply paying the rent. According to George Chauncey's extensively documented research, "as the anti-vice crusaders who sought to reform the moral order of turn-of-the-century American cities discovered, gay male society was a highly visible part of the urban sexual underworld and was much more fully and publicly integrated into working-class than middle-class culture."[8] Although more visible, this society of gays still felt oppressed and disenfranchised enough to develop codes and secret signals in order to identify each other in public. They were called not "gay" but "pansies," an identification which evolved because gay men, at that time, were associated with feminine qualities. Gay men did, in fact, lean towards effeminate mannerisms back then "because they were so central to the dominant role model available to them as they formed a gay identity."[9] Of course today, the role model is the exact opposite. The beefy, masculine, muscular jock is the icon today for advertisers attempting to tap into the vast disposable income of the gay population. Gymnasiums are filled with gay men trying to attain the perfect body in order to attract a mate. But in the New York of the early twentieth century, the dominant image of the homosexual, eagerly promoted by the heterosexual community, was of the effeminate male. So they acquiesced and fulfilled the image. This differentiation also provided straight men a standard by which to verify their masculinity, even if only by differentiating themselves from the pansies. Author Barry Adams points out that "Working within a gender discourse that associated maleness with toughness and effectiveness, in opposition to supposedly female weakness and failure, male homosexuality symbolized the betrayal of manhood — the feminine enemy within men."[10]

Such a break with the traditional masculine image began to cause a certain amount of unease in parts of the city. One must be reminded that at this time homosexuality was still in the textbooks as a psychiatric disorder, a mental illness. There was no organized gay community with the political visibility or clout to change this conception, and the popular image was further cemented by certain eccentric members of the homosexual community. "The clubs put the 'pansies on parade' in order to profit from the curiosity provoked by the pansies' own willingness to parade openly throughout the city."[11] A sharp divide was created, forcing the majority of the homosexual community underground in order to maintain their integrity.

And then, during the early thirties, the police again actively attempted to shove the pansies back into the fringes of society. As Chauncey points out, "Prohibition culture had allowed gay visibility to move into the center of New York's most prestigious entertainment district, but in the early thirties, the authorities were determined to return it to the city's periphery."[12] This see-saw pattern of tolerance and oppression would continue until the Stonewall Riots in 1969 broke it for good. And even beyond the turmoil and friction of the early gay and lesbian crusade, the heart of gay New York remained always in Greenwich Village, which in turn reflected on the city as a whole as indicated in Chauncey's research:

> The gay history of Greenwich Village suggests the extent to which the Village in the teens and twenties came to represent to the rest of the city what New York as a whole represented to the rest of the nation: a peculiar social territory in which the normal social constraints on behavior seemed to have been suspended and where men and women built unconventional lives outside the family nexus.[13]

As late as 1960, antagonistic authorities of New York City were continuing to oppress the gay community. The New York State Supreme Court in 1960 upheld a ruling forcing the owner of a bar in Brooklyn to close because he allowed his saloon to "be used as a gathering place for homosexuals and degenerates who conducted themselves in an offensive and indecent manner; because the majority of the patrons were wearing tight fitting trowsers ... 3 male patrons walk[ed] to the rear of the premises with a sway to the hips ... [and two of them spoke] in high pitched effeminate tones ... and gesture[d] with limp wrists."[14]

This activity continued and the chronic hostility escalated until very early one fateful, hot summer morning — June 28, 1969. For the gay community, this day lives as a milestone in the battle for respect and tolerance, the riot at Stonewall Inn. On the previous day, Friday, June 27, the world had laid to rest superstar Judy Garland in the city of New York. Garland had an enormous appeal for gay people, vast numbers of whom had always peopled her audiences. Perhaps it was her troubled life and her loneliness that gays were attracted to. As one mourner at the funeral noted, "Everyone's got sadness and problems, everyone gets lonely. Judy Garland made all of us feel something ties her and us together."[15] The tension and anxiety and grief that filled that evening, and continued into the early morning hours of Saturday, June 28, reached a breaking point. The closeted and ridiculed gay community had been abandoned by their secular saint and sister who had made them feel okay about themselves. Judy brought everyone to a common human denominator. Gays had for years been experiencing an increase in raids on their local watering holes, and they were angry and felt abused and alienated by their own democracy. Many gay men took themselves and their grief that night to a favorite Village saloon, the Stonewall Inn. This small pub, which was run by the Mafia, was considered:

> the most congenial downtown bar. If they passed "Muster" at the Stonewall door, they could buy or cajole drinks, exchange cosmetics and the favored Tabu or Ambush perfume, admire or deplore somebody's latest Kanecalon wig, make fun of six-foot transsexual Lynn's size-12 women's shoes (while admiring her fishnet stockings and miniskirts and giggling over her tales of servicing the firemen around the corner at the 10th Street station), move constantly in and out of the ladies room, and dance in a feverish sweat till closing time at four A.M.[16]

But what occurred that evening, as depicted in the following *Village Voice* article five days later, would change the politics and the nature of the prejudice against homosexuality forever:

> Cops entered the Stonewall for the second time in a week just before midnight on Friday. It began as a small raid.... But as the patrons trapped inside were released one by one on the street, it was initially a festive gathering, composed mostly of Stonewall boys who were waiting around for friends still inside or to see what was going to happen.
> Suddenly the paddywagon arrived and the mood of the crowd changed. Three of the more blatant queens — in full drag — were loaded inside, along with the bartender and doorman.... A cry went up to push the paddywagon over, but it drove away.... The next person to come out was a dyke, and she put up a struggle.... It was at that moment that the scene became explosive. Beer cans and bottles were heaved at the windows, and a rain of coins descended on the cops. ... I heard several cries of "Let's get some gas," but the blaze of flame which soon appeared in the window of the Stonewall was still a shock. As the wood barrier behind the glass was beaten open, the cops inside turned a firehose on the crowd.[17]

All at once, this collective gay rage had exploded violently. But eventually it would unite scores of gays and lesbians to channel their fury into political action. As noted in the *Village Voice* only a month after the riots, "Gay power had surfaced. Sick and tired of police harassment, of prehistoric sodomy laws, of 'pork protection' in Queens (Queens!), and of vicious busts in the underground haunts where public decency had driven them, homosexuals struck back. A mild protest, to be sure, but apparently only the beginning."[18]

It may not be entirely coincidental that the Ridiculous Theatrical Company's first production, *Big Hotel*, under the direction of Ludlam, with Ludlam portraying the fading star Norma Desmond, occurred the very same year that drag queens, fighting with the police, launched the gay rights movement. Although there is no documentation of Ludlam having been present at these events, he was residing in the Village at the time, and they surely must have made some kind of imprint on his psyche. He had moved to New York City to pursue his artistic vision, and this relocation just happened to position him right in the midst of the most open and liberated gay scene in America. These two factors together would open doors for Ludlam in ways he could never have anticipated. Oddly enough, his most popular legacy is as a male actress, although he actually appeared in drag in only five of his twenty-nine produced plays.

Certainly the drag queen had become a much more visible phenomenon in the city during the late sixties. A courageous and outrageous few boldly flaunted their excesses in public, but the great majority of gay men continued to live quietly with their secret. However, Ludlam never attempted to hide his sexuality. Although he did not flit about town wearing a dress and did not adopt a campy woman's name for an alter ego, he was nonetheless openly gay and was absolutely unashamed about it. Indeed, he conspicuously asserted his sexuality in his writing and in his performances.

Ludlam wore his dresses on the stage, where he breathed feminine life into his female characters. For him, wearing female attire and taking on a feminine persona was partly an exploration and partly an embrace of the feminine side of his nature, as it surely was for the drag queens at the Stonewall Inn on June 28, 1969.

But paradoxically, it was the drag queens who had put up the most memorable fight during the Stonewall Riots, while alongside them were other drag queens, dressed as cheerleaders with pom-pons, aggressively taunting the police with their chant:

> We are the Stonewall girls
> We wear our hair in curls
> We wear no underwear
> We show our pubic hair
> We wear our dungarees
> Above our nelly knees![19]

Indeed, the extent of the visibility of the drag queen was responsible, at least in part, for the unleashing of gay power in 1969. David Bergman insightfully points out in his essay "Strategic Camp" that:

> Gay political activity originated in drag performance: The Stonewall Riots of 1969 — the three nights of confrontations between the gay citizens of New York and the city's police, usually regarded as the beginning of the gay liberation movement — were touched off, not by homophile organizations, but by boys in drag, drowning their sorrow over the death of Judy Garland, who had been buried that day.[20]

There is a strange symmetry to this turn of events, that the day of Judy Garland's burial should become the very birthday of the modern gay movement. But out of the compounded effects of grief and frustration, this burgeoning movement had suddenly succeeded in bringing to the forefront of national and world attention the struggle for tolerance that gays and lesbians had so long desired. Suddenly, a new awareness of political potential arose, which fueled the enabling feelings of power and equality that were emerging in gay and lesbian sensibility. Ludlam brought this sensibility to the theatre, which was itself experiencing a revolution in style. Not only was the decade of the sixties characterized by sweeping changes in political activism, it also witnessed a radical transformation in artistic expression in the visual arts, experimental music, underground films and the rise of Off Off Broadway theatre.

Since the 1950s, artists in various specific media began crossing over and including other media in their work. The electronic and film media began seeping into traditional theatre to create a new style of performance. The traditional linear storyline with a progression of cause and effect began disappearing, as did the conventional concept of character. As noted by theatre critic Gerald Rabkin in the *Performing Arts Journal*,

> The Ridiculous "movement" did not emerge as an aesthetic challenge, bristling with manifestos and polemics. It grew out of a common sensibility which coalesced in New York City in the early to mid-sixties; a sensibility that sprang less from theatre than from the other arts: underground film, happenings, experimental music and, most of all, pop art with its iconography of mass culture.[21]

Probably the most famous artist of pop culture during that time was Andy Warhol, who had an indirect yet powerful influence on Charles Ludlam. Warhol is famous for his theory that everyone gets fifteen minutes of fame in life. He also had what was known as the Factory, Warhol's workshop where he created his art, filmed most of his movies, and entertained scores of the famous and not-so famous who wanted desperately to feel attached to this new guru. Warhol himself was a rather shy and meek man, demonstrative only in his visuals. Warhol took common, everyday images and objects from popular culture and transformed them into art through ingenious ways of self-promotion and public relations. It mattered not so much what or whom Warhol used in his art, but how he used them:

> Warhol's sensibility is one that discovers worthiness in someone, some place or object that seemingly is without any profound value. Warhol appreciates flops, and the fragility that just holds someone or something together. He takes a fresh look at something taken for granted. He includes outakes. Warhol collects — reclaims — "beauty" in the bizarre or the strange or the ridiculous or the absurd.[22]

From Andy Warhol, Ludlam gleaned the sensibility of "recycling" culture in order to present it anew. Actually, the ridiculous movement, as a distinct aesthetic, began with a falling out between playwright Ron Tavel and some of the actors at Warhol's Factory.

Ronald Tavel wound up in the theatre via the underground film movement that was exploding in New York City in the mid-sixties. Asked by Warhol to write a short screenplay based simply on the concept of a screen test, Tavel produced his first Warhol script — *Screen Test One*, a 70-minute close-up of a man's face answering questions from Tavel, who was just off camera. He showed the completed film to Warhol, who did not like it or understand it but, being intrigued by the concept, invited Tavel to become a scenarist at the Factory. A short period of collaboration resulted with Tavel writing, producing and often directing his film scripts for Warhol. Included among these were the *Screen Test* series, *The Life of Juanita Castro*, *Horse*, *Kitchen*, and *Vinyl*, all filmed in 1965. During rehearsals for *Kitchen*, Edie Sedgwick and Roger Trudeau, the stars of the film, were going over dialogue for their scene, which entailed having sex in a shower. Tavel became inspired by this concept and dashed off a play in two days titled *Shower*, about two people stripping naked under a running faucet. As Tavel remembered it:

> In the country, I kept thinking about *Shower*. It was something new for me. It had come quickly, directly from an underconscious level, without the banality of choice or plan, without the error inherent in arrangement. It was dirty like the Mae West I had loved for so many years, it was action packed and streamlined for movement yet totally devoid of character or identity, direction, plot, or subject matter. Each personage parried the others with lightning speed to his own content, but no one ever answered the question posed to him, everyone argued and fought and killed around non-existent objects and indecipherable goals, syllogistic logic reared its weak head only every third

dramatic beat, and word and emotive association held the day. A quotidian nothingness had been built over a foundation of subliminal cement. I was in no way sure what *Shower* was, except that it was where I was at, and that my excitement was the emblem of it.[23]

Tavel took the finished script to Warhol, who again did not like it or understand it. Furthermore, his leading superstar, Edie Sedgewick, became incensed and refused to have any part of what she called "Tavel's perversity."[24] It is odd, if not outright hypocritical, that she would find this particular script offensive, given some of the other outlandish scripts in which she had already participated. More than likely there were underlying personality problems between Tavel and Sedgwick which simply erupted, with the script as a convenient excuse. Tavel, undaunted, marched off with script in hand, abruptly ending his tenure at the Factory.

Tavel then took the script to Jerry Benjamin, who had directed Leroi Jones' *The Toilet*, but he was busy and suggested Tavel contact John Vaccaro, a prominent Off Off Broadway director and nightclub owner, who agreed to direct *Shower* as a play, along with a curtain-raiser, which Tavel agreed to supply. Tavel knew Vaccaro only slightly from his work as an actor in Jack Smith's film *Normal Love*, but Tavel acknowledged that Vaccaro had given the best performance. Smith was at the forefront of the underground film movement, and in his films *Flaming Creatures* and *Normal Love*, "he struck the primary notes of Ridiculous style: travesty, homage to tackiness and celebration of 'bad' taste, sexual ambiguity, eroticism, 'operatic' flamboyance."[25] He had a penchant for presenting his outrageous films at midnight and, in fact, throughout late 1967 and early 1968, "Jack Smith was screening a program called 'Horror and Fantasy at Midnight'— 'Reefers of Technicolor Island! Scrubwoman of Atlantis! Ratdroppings of Uranus! Marshgas of Flatulandia'— at the New Cinema Playhouse."[26] This affinity for midnight performances would transfer from the film to the stage where Ludlam's first endeavors also began at midnight, often not ending until early the next morning.

Tavel took his new "package" to the Coda Galleries, a new showcase for psychedelic art and performance pieces on East 10th Street, where he boldly announced himself as Warhol's scenarist. While there, he watched a play being performed and declared to the management: "'Call that a show? I'll give you material that will really draw the crowds!' 'Fine, you open on July 29th,' Isaac Abrams, the proprietor, responded. That took me aback."[27] Quickly Vaccaro and Tavel assembled a cast and began rehearsing *Shower* and *The Life of Juanita Castro*, a parody of a Hollywood spy movie which Tavel had written earlier that year as a Warhol movie. During rehearsals a friend of Vaccaro's, Yvette Hawkins came to help out, and while watching the wild antics going on, she kept repeating, "But this is just ridiculous."[28] By the time Tavel and Vaccaro opened their plays, they had named their venture Play-House of the Ridiculous.

The Coda Galleries sent out circulars announcing that "New York's *Underground* was moving to the stage,"[29] and thus the ridiculous theatre movement was born. On Thursday, July 29, 1965, both shows opened to packed houses and were received with unanimous praise. "Both plays," a critic recalled, "had most of the stigmata of the early ridiculous style — incomprehensible plot, dialogue rich in non sequiturs, and an all-out bawdiness that came across at times, perhaps because it held nothing back, as childish exuberance."[30]

Vaccaro, Tavel, and Tavel's brother Harvey, along with their lighting designer Bill Waters, decided to pool their talent and resources and officially begin their own theatre company under their new banner — Play-House of the Ridiculous. They began begging friends and relatives for money, and before long secured $800 from a woman who was believed to be a Hungarian countess and who lived in the Dakota.[31] They rented a loft in Greenwich Village and in the spring of 1966 produced Tavel's new script, *The Life of Lady Godiva*. With this production, Tavel also issued a manifesto, in keeping with traditional avant-garde philosophical practice. "We have passed beyond the absurd" it proclaimed. "Our position is absolutely preposterous."[32] For a time, they bandied about the word preposterous to define their work, but eventually settled on ridiculous, because it was easier to say, and also because they thought that preposterous was too close to absurd. As Tavel announced, what they wanted was the "flat and uncagey irrevocability of ridiculous."[33] Critic and theatre historian Bonnie Marranca, who delved into the world of ridiculosity when no one else gave it much credence, illuminates the difference between the absurd and ridiculous in her book *American Playwrights*: "Unlike the theatre of the absurd, in which dramatic metaphors embody a moral vision, Tavel's ridiculous world is a valueless, anarchic place which refuses to take life more seriously than as imitation of art. It is metaphysical burlesque."[34]

When casting *The Life of Lady Godiva*, Vaccaro hired a young actor, Charles Ludlam, then fresh out of Hofstra University. Ludlam, who had been on the fringes of the underground film movement himself for a time, was on a path which was destined to intertwine with Tavel and Vaccaro's new Ridiculous Play-House. Ludlam was cast as Peeping Tom in *Lady Godiva* and his acting was so broad, so flamboyant, and so hysterical that he nearly stole the show every night. Seeds somehow were planted in the minds of the Tavel brothers and Vaccaro that Ludlam wanted to take over the company. He certainly had formed many allies within the group.

Although they could not deny that Ludlam was good for business, and that he was gifted with a voracious wit and supreme comic timing, they were uneasy about the amount of attention and adulation he was getting. Although there was tension between Ludlam and Vaccaro/Tavel, the experience would prove to nudge Ludlam in his fated direction — not only as an actor, but as a playwright. In Tavel's script are all the kernels of ridiculosity that are later found in Ludlam's plays. As critic Bonnie Marranca points out in the *Performing Arts Journal*, "In the structure of the play, which parodies medieval and Elizabethan literary conventions and movie westerns, Tavel manages to blend medieval lore with references to television, the *New York Post*, the Rockettes, Franz Liszt, and art in one camp, anachronistic whole."[35] In the same journal she also states that "Tavel is a master punster and spinner of the multiple entendre; he also revels in sexual word play (most often generating homosexual imagery), spoonerism, obscenities, literary conceit, distorted references to Shakespeare, allusions to grade-B movies, popular songs and advertising slogans."[36] For Ludlam, as we shall see, immersion in this kind of theatrical experience sealed his artistic fate and paved the way for his emergence onto the theatrical scene. Ludlam had found his voice and now was determined to nurture it to fruition. He saw the possibilities of writing plays to suit his own creative sensibility, which had been so harshly criticized in his college days.

In the fall of 1966, the Play-House of the Ridiculous opened its third production, consisting of *Indira Ghandi's Daring Device* and a curtain-raiser, *Screen Test*, one of the scripts Tavel had written at Warhol's Factory. The only notoriety *Indira Ghandi* ever garnered was a protest by the Indian Students Union at a university where Vaccaro and troupe were invited to perform. The administration naïvely thought that any play with Ghandi's name in the title must surely be a paean to the great individual herself, as well as to the nation of India. When the play was actually performed, in all its irreverence, the student uproar that ensued threatened to close down the Play-House altogether with a lawsuit. Even though it caused this brief explosion, the play was generally not well received. *Screen Test*, however, took off and began developing a life of its own.

Screen Test began as a 30-minute teaser in which a woman would stand on stage while the director (Vaccaro) would shout directions at her from the back of the house. Because it was totally improvised, the specific events and the storyline were never the same from one night to the next. Starring as the "female" was renowned transvestite Mario Montez, who had become notorious through his work in Jack Smith's hit cult film *Flaming Creatures*. This film was nothing more than a gathering of drag queens who assemble early one morning to gossip and share makeup secrets. *Flaming Creatures* manifested what Smith found "implicated in Maria Montez and von Stern-berg's films, and without the interference of a plot. What he brings to the fore is what has been latent in those films — visual texture, androgynous sexual presence, exotic locations."[37] It seemed only natural that Vaccaro would cast Mario Montez in the female role of *Screen Test*, as both he and Smith were obsessed with the many movies of the 1940s Queen of Technicolor, Maria Montez. Indeed, they felt that Mario was Maria reincarnated. Smith is quoted as saying, "[Maria Montez] believed and thereby made the people who went to see her movies believe. Those who could believe, did. Those who saw the world's worst actress couldn't and they missed the magic."[38] For these two gay men, working with Mario was an indulgence in a vicarious fantasy. He had risen to become the star of many underground films and his characterization of Maria Montez was as sensuous, erotic and "bad" as the original.

Because of the initial success of *Screen Test*, Vaccaro, Tavel and Montez slowly began changing and lengthening the performance, and put Vaccaro as the director on stage. Vaccaro's antics of humiliation, however, began to wear thin with Mario at the level of degradation to which Vaccaro would plummet in the name of ridiculosity. Eventually Montez asked Ludlam, whom he felt to be a kindred spirit, if he would come on stage in drag and try to liven things up a bit. Although Ludlam had been in drag once, only briefly, in a small film, he had never ventured on stage in such costume. Many friends and colleagues advised him that if he appeared in drag he was liable to ruin any type of career he may have hoped for. Fearlessly, Ludlam took on the challenge, though he felt he needed a "hook." He couldn't just put on a dress and parade around as himself; he was an actor. He somehow inherited an old wig once tossed aside by Salvador Dalí, and when he put it on, the character of Norma Desmond from *Sunset Boulevard* emerged in full bloom. "Looking like Joan Crawford on a bad night, Charles Ludlam created a melodramatic star who over-acted everything, even herself. And it wasn't long before she had taken over the whole stage, as Norma Desmond, the fading screen star trying to make a comeback."[39] Ludlam began to acquire the same esteemed reputation that Mario Montez had earned in the underground film and theatre worlds. It became increasingly clear that Vaccaro and Tavel could no longer ignore the talent and vision of Ludlam, who instantly became the star of the Play-House of the Ridiculous. What started as a 30-minute "teaser," simply using a rehearsal process as a performance piece, evolved into a two-hour improvisation, and Charles Ludlam carried the weight of the entire play.

Screen Test became an important theatre piece of the new American avant-garde, according to Marranca:

> The notion of the dramatic situation alone is devastating — an improvisational performance which carries performance to its limit — a competition not only aesthetically, but sexually as well, with the audience the immediate arbiter of taste.... The sexual dialectic — the simultaneous gesturing of transvestite and actress — dares the audience into the idea of the play, which goes beyond emphasizing the lie, the artificiality of acting. It explores the mask behind the mask, as real personalities compete with each other in the contest of posturing. A socio-cultural treatment of "performance," *Screen Test* was a radical theatre piece for its day.[40]

Not only was *Screen Test* Ludlam's drag debut on stage, but it also provided him with an enormously gratifying glimpse of the extent of his comic possibilities. Through this play Ludlam solidified his deft ability to improvise, and this important element would prove crucial when he began creating his own scripts.

The next project for the Play-House of the Ridiculous was another play written by Tavel, titled *Gorilla Queen*. Vaccaro, Ludlam and the remainder of the company were looking forward to this piece, envisioning "jungle movies, Montez films, the camp idea of a monster gorilla that's gay, that's a queen."[41] What they received, however, was an intellectual and didactic three-hour play. Vaccaro began ripping pages out right and left, incensing the Tavel brothers. They feared that Vaccaro and Ludlam were attempting to depose Tavel as resident playwright. Another Off Off Broadway theatre at that time, the Judson Poets' Theatre, offered to mount a production of *Gorilla Queen* uncut, so the Tavels yanked it away from Vaccaro and ran full-steam for this new offer. This left the Play-House of the Ridiculous without a project. Ludlam informed Vaccaro, though, that he had been working on a play called *Big Hotel*, which was loosely based on the classic *Grand Hotel* with Greta Garbo, and would also be a vehicle in which his successful alter ego, Norma Desmond, could appear. Despite the Tavel brothers' resentment at the treatment *Gorilla Queen* had received, and the fact that they thought *Big Hotel* an obscene and vulgar play, they gave Vaccaro and the company $1,000, the lease on the theatre, and the name Play-House of the Ridiculous upon their departure.[42]

Vaccaro opened *Big Hotel* in February of 1967 and closed it almost immediately. The lawsuit over *Indira Ghadni's Daring Device*, brought by the Indian consul-general through the demands of irate students at Rutgers and Columbia, had materialized by this time. Anticipating a lengthy court battle and expensive legal fees, Vaccaro closed *Big Hotel* and relinquished the lease on the theatre in order to save money.

Ludlam, however, had been working on another play, *Conquest of the Universe*, which he submitted to Vaccaro for production. Drawn from Marlowe's *Tamburlaine the Great* and H.G. Wells' *The War of the Worlds*, as well as scores of snippets from other classical dramas, old movies and popular culture as a whole, *Conquest of the Universe* revolved around an intergalactic battle for power, using sexual intercourse on the planet Mars as a metaphor for "affairs of state."[43] During rehearsals, however, the relationship between Ludlam and Vaccaro began deteriorating when Ludlam objected to Vaccaro's artistic choices as director. Ludlam felt that Vaccaro was too tame and didn't take enough risks. Vaccaro was reluctant to present homosexuality and nudity on the stage for fear of being arrested. The arguments intensified until finally Vaccaro fired Ludlam from his own play. He, like the Tavel brothers, also felt threatened by Ludlam's talent and ambition. Clearly, the director in Ludlam was beginning to emerge, as his arguments with Vaccaro were strictly over the artistic choices being made. Although Ludlam recognized that Vaccaro could be mean and intimidating, he credited him with "[giving] my whole theatrical life back to me." He stated further that "He let me do anything I wanted. In companies I had always stood out — not as a good actor, but as a sore thumb."[44] Regardless, Ludlam was kicked out of the Play-House of the Ridiculous and abruptly left, taking seven other company members with him. Leaving not only in protest over Vaccaro's treatment of Ludlam, but also probably recognizing the true genius of the two, the group (consisting of Mario Montez, Bill Vehr, John D. Brockmeyer, Black-Eyed Susan, Lola Pashalinski, Jeanne Phillips, a young man who called himself Eleven and Ludlam) met the following afternoon at Montez's apartment and decided to remain together and form a new company. Jack Smith, who attended this gathering but decided not to commit to a new company, suggested they call themselves the Ridiculous Theatrical Company. According to Ludlam, "we felt that Vaccaro could be the Playhouse, but we are the company. We decided to do my play [*Conquest of the Universe*] the way we wanted to do it."[45] Ludlam soon learned, however, that he had signed away the rights to the script and Vaccaro had hired a slew of actors from Warhol's Factory to perform in his production of *Conquest of the Universe*. Ludlam and his newly formed Ridiculous Theatrical Company decided to remount *Big Hotel* which, luckily, he still held the rights to, and a new version of *Conquest* titled *When Queens Collide*. It seems curious that this new version and title came directly after Ludlam's bitter fight with Vaccaro. Perhaps Ludlam was subtly commenting on the ordeal that had just occurred. Truly two queens did collide — artistically. Fortunately for Ludlam, this feud, in hindsight, launched his entire career, putting him in a position to see his dreams materialize.

The Ridiculous Theatrical Company was launched at the Tambellini Gate movie theatre, which specialized in underground art films. They struck

a deal with the owner, Aldo Tambellini, and agreed to perform their repertory — *Big Hotel* and *When Queens Collide* — after the last movie, usually
around midnight. They were responsible for taking down the screen and
setting up and tearing down their set at every performance. They paid a
minimum of $35 rent each night, which was a hardship seeing that the
largest total box office receipts for any one performance hardly ever
exceeded $70.[46] For a short time, Ludlam changed the name of his com-
pany to the Trockaderro Gloximia Magic Midnight Mind Theatre of Thrills
and Spills in an effort to distance himself from the Play-House of the Ridiculous, but it soon reverted back to the original name, the Ridiculous Theatrical Company. Ludlam believed that anyone could be an actor, and often
these performances were all-night, drug-induced affairs. People regularly
wandered in off the street, only to find themselves in a role in one of the
plays. Company member John D. Brockmeyer recalled in an interview
that

> Charles abided by the theory that all the world's a stage, and it worked very
> well back then. Anybody who showed up could be in the theater. Charles
> picked up a trick who ended up doing endless Al Jolson imitations onstage.
> It was always very crazy when we were doing the first shows — these people
> would come from nowhere, everywhere. The woman who came backstage
> to sell bras and G-strings would end up being in the show. The Hell's
> Angels would show up because of somebody's trick, and they would be in the
> show.[47]

After producing, directing and starring in the first four productions,
Ludlam decided to pare his group down to five members — John D. Brockmeyer, Bill Vehr, Black-Eyed Susan, Lola Pashalinski and himself — and
this committed ensemble decided to venture forth and create an American
Comic Theatre. This core company would remain with Ludlam until the
early 1980s, giving witness to Ludlam's tenacity, charisma, power and talent. Ludlam finally had achieved his goal of forming a theatrical company
to produce his works — ones that he could star in. Ridiculosity as a genre
emerged and began charting a path with Charles Ludlam as its guiding
force, which continued for nearly 20 years until his death from AIDS in 1987.
Ronald Tavel and John Vaccaro remained in the arts, but both eventually
veered off in other directions. It was Ludlam who actually championed a
style and developed it into an established comic tradition. Although his
artistic strategies and choices changed and evolved throughout the years as
he matured and grew, there were always elements of his origins in evidence.
As Ludlam once recalled, "I wanted to find ways of getting beyond my own
personal taste and avoiding aesthetic decisions. I wanted to get rid of that

no, and to say yes to everything."[48] Ridiculous theatre is firmly associated today with the late Charles Ludlam, who developed the concept of ridiculosity and pushed it to a great height as the trademark of his work and his company.

— 3 —
Ridiculosity in Theory

Ridiculosity, as we have seen in the previous chapter, did not exactly emerge in a vacuum. Although glimpses of it could be seen in various theatrical forms in the 1960s, it finally found its proper outlet in Charles Ludlam. He had the courage to follow through, dauntlessly, with his vision and unleash ridiculosity upon the masses, freeing something that had heretofore been somewhat underground and clandestine. Ludlam had a passionate, life-long love affair with the theatre, and theatre was therefore the natural vehicle for his expression of ridiculosity.

The elements that constitute ridiculosity are many, both in theory and in practice. Before delving into the practical aspects of Ludlam's work in the Ridiculous Theatrical Company, including the evident artifices in acting, design and playwrighting throughout Ludlam's ridiculous canon, this chapter will explore the major theoretical components of ridiculosity, independent of their actual physical theatrical expression: homosexuality, 1940s "B" movies and their stars, drag and irreverent gender-bending, camp as a social and cultural strategy, and opera. Although each of these is its own distinct category and will be explored independently, it should be noted that there are many overlaps between them as well as common ideas crossing through them, making it difficult sometimes to pinpoint where one stops and the other begins.

So just what exactly is ridiculosity? Is it simply bad art? Is it parody? Is it satire? Can it be defined at all? Several critics and theatre historians who took a special interest in Ridiculous Theatre have tried over the years. One of these, Bonnie Marranca, in her survey of American playwrights, states,

> The Ridiculous reflects the modernist — particularly Dadaist — preoccupation with pop culture. It is consciously "bad" art raised to the level of an aesthetic category. (It's so bad, it's good!) The Ridiculous is an exaggerated politics of consciousness whose narcissistic stance could only have been taken by artists

who felt themselves manipulated by, yet at the same time outside and critical of, the American cultural mainstream.[1]

Another critic, Ronald Argelander, has written about Ridiculous Theatre and its players since the early 1970s. In his *Drama Review* article titled "Ridiculous Theatrical Company," he writes,

> An intimate way of working has emerged based on a shared creative sensibility most like the activity of play—the kind of play children share in creating backyard fantasy drama. It is a sensibility that takes plots, dialogue, and characters from movies, comics, and other familiar or personal sources; that considers as everything except "playing oneself"—it is disguises, sexual role switching, artifice, caricature, stereotype; in which acting is broad and expressive but not "good" or "bad."[2]

Stefan Brecht, son of Bertold Brecht, worked intimately with Charles Ludlam and others in the Ridiculous Theatre. In fact, his wife Mary is credited with designing some of the costumes for Ludlam's early productions. In his book *Queer Theatre*, he writes,

> The [Ridiculous] Theatre leaves us with an image of social life in its most basic and most salient aspects: the relations between the sexes, of political life or organized state power. It presents both of these as the playing of roles. And after showing us the arbitrariness of all role-playing, it points out that the actual roles played are both evil and ridiculous. The theatre of the ridiculous is radical social satire and protest-anarchist ... possibly nihilist.[3]

Finally, Charles Ludlam himself, in a 1978 interview for *Performing Arts Journal*, states,

> [Ridiculous Theatre] has to do with humor and unhinging the pretensions of serious art. It comes out of the dichotomy between academic and expressive art, and the idea of a theatre that re-values things. It takes what is considered worthless and transforms it into high art. It draws its authority from popular art, an art that doesn't need any justification beyond its power to provide pleasure.[4]

A common thread which weaves its way through each of these perspectives is the recycling or revaluing of established, popular, mass-cultural art forms, usually ones which have been discarded as irrelevant or naïve. However, homosexuality, the underlying catalyst at the nucleus of this aesthetic, is not fully developed in any of these scholarly positions. When studying the various ridiculous artists, it is readily apparent that homosexuality is a common bond between them, something that exists at the core of their personal perspective. Most, if not all, artists of the ridiculous mode are open, unabashed homosexuals; it is clear that homosexuality plays a dominant role in this sensibility. According to Frank Browning in his book *Culture of Desire,*

> To live in the gay demi-monde has been to snatch up the fragments of other people's artifacts and transform them into a living aesthetic, an aesthetic that assembles the disintegrating garments of the old order into a new, high-style wardrobe of ironic kitsch and brings Camp into the practice of daily life (and, indeed, claims that all contemporary life is a prolonged exercise in Camp.[5]

The homosexual, forever outside of the American cultural mainstream, and without the apparent historical chronicle of the mainstream, has been forced to exist within a sub-culture which has been invented practically in a vacuum, without the advantages of a linear, historical perspective. The concept of a gay identity has emerged only recently, thanks to a few diligent scholars and historians who have attempted to chronicle the gay experience throughout history. Up until this time, gays and lesbians have felt generally disenfranchised from the American consciousness, having suffered discrimination based merely on their sexual orientation. They have had no *apparent* voice in shaping the American culture, though it cannot be denied that homosexuals have had, and continue to have, what could best be called an *unconscious* impact on American trends. At the end of the twentieth century, it is safe to say that today's society is shaped to a significant degree by mass media, of which homosexuals have been an active, dynamic part from the beginning. Television, films, stage, dance, radio, journalism and art have long been peopled by homosexuals needing to conceal their "secret" for fear of being ostracized by the public at large. This heterosexual mask has caused the gay sensibility and identity to be defined in deliberate contrast to the straight, patriarchal community, which in turn reinforces the attributes of the subculture. It has also caused the gay community to establish its own set of rules and standards by which it exists as a community, separate from the mainstream.

At the core of this subculture is the issue of sex, specifically homoeroticism, which is, after all, its defining element. This issue of sex has historically been the weapon which the puritanical elements of society have used to suppress homosexuality and the homosexual community. Sexuality is one of the most obsessively debated issues in our society today. Many feel threatened by the proposition of sex for pure physical pleasure rather than strictly for procreation, a position which is loudly proclaimed as sinful by many religious leaders. As Michael Bronski points out in *Culture Clash,* "Western civilization has been characterized from its beginning by deep-seated erotophobia. This fear and hatred of sexuality informs and poisons our basic ideas about sex, gender and race upon which we base our assumptions about power, politics and equality."[6] These assumptions are foisted upon the masses by the few who claim to represent the moral position of the majority of society, thus portraying a biased and constricted American identity heavily influenced by our puritanical background. As a matter of fact, the terms homosexual and heterosexual did not exist until the end of the nineteenth century. These words suddenly categorized the individual rather than the behavior, which had been the practice up until then. These new classifications gave rise to the concept of an individual's sexual identity, a reconceptualizing of human sexual practices and a blueprint from which conservative authorities could interpret and then dictate and judge moral conduct. Again, as Michael Bronski points out,

> By refusing to conform to the gender and sexual arrangements that define and reinforce the patriarchal heterosexual cultural norms, homosexuality — the sexuality itself and any of its cultural manifestations — becomes both a threat and a political issue.[7]

This unacceptable threat to the status quo forced the homosexual community to dive underground in order simply to survive and exist. Because they had no collective historical tradition of their own to fall back on, and no accepted role within mainstream America, homosexuals had nothing around them in their everyday lives with which to identify, so they simply looked to the past, staking claim to certain cultural landmarks and certain guideposts. They were at the same time attempting to define and create both a present and a past identity.

Most gays and lesbians begin feeling estranged at a very early age. This usually happens as soon as they become aware that they do not fit in with the images produced by the media. Such abundant images of heterosexual wholesomeness, coupled with pervasive adolescent peer pressure, compel young homosexuals either to disguise themselves as heterosexuals or to disengage completely from the usual kind of sexual exploration and experimentation their peers are undertaking. Regardless of which of these two paths is taken, the underlying reason for choosing either one is to hide a terrible secret — that they are different. The consequences of being found out are simply too frightening to risk. Thus, either path leads directly into the infamous "closet."

The closet is based upon intimidation and maintained by duplicity. Naturally, this only further confuses an already confusing situation by forcing perfectly honest people to live, in essence, a life of deceit. This heaps more guilt upon young homosexuals, already burdened with the guilt and shame of being different, of being sexually attracted to members of their own sex. Further, this wound is constantly irritated by the persistent, conflicting urgings of the heart that there really is nothing wrong with them whatsoever, that they truly are blameless and innocent. These years of turmoil, along with the compromises demanded by life in the closet, result in a deep anguish which is shared throughout the gay community. Social critic Mark Thompson points out that

> Gay people have had to live on the edge of the global village or to work within its mainstream in denial or disguise. As a result, emotional wounds run deep and are long remembered. It is here, at this wounded place, that our lives find shared ground, our spirits a common tongue. This myth about our sexuality had been devised by those who could not possibly understand us yet who knew enough to benefit from our oppression.[8]

It is at this place — the wounded and ostracized soul — where the point of emotional commonality exists among homosexuals, and this is particularly evidenced by homosexual artists, thanks to their passionate need to express themselves. Again, by existing outside of the cultural mainstream, gays and lesbians have had to create their own culture with its own rules and traditions. Many looked to past cultural deadwood which had been tossed aside and appropriated the elements of it they liked as their own to validate and affirm their community identity. If homosexuals were to be left out of American society, unable to draw upon their surroundings for inspiration, then they would plagiarize previously existing structures which had been unavailable to the homosexual in their time, and create new meaning for them. So the homosexual population began incorporating discarded elements of culture, revamping them in line with their sensibility as an excluded caste, and cultivating an entirely new vocabulary of cryptic images and language, thus providing themselves with a basis for an identity, not only for the community at large, but also for its constituent individuals.

They realized it was necessary to challenge history, to point out that many commonly held perspectives are not always completely accurate or unquestionably valid. If historians could simply ignore the existence or the contributions of homosexuals in the canon of western civilization, then gays and lesbians felt entitled to take that same history and put a different "spin" on it, revealing that assumed objectivity can sometimes be merely a subjective exercise in editing. By looking back they can attempt to retell the history of our society in their own manner, and from their own perspective, usually by exposing and explaining the roles we all play, regardless of our sexual orientation, in order to survive.

Charles Ludlam was always outside of the mainstream as a result of both his sexual orientation and his vivid imagination. In the majority of his plays, Ludlam searched the archives and the trash heaps of culture, seized what he thought had value and truth, and then recombined and recycled them through his own, unique voice. As New York theatre critic Mel Gussow observed, "Mr. Ludlam sees culture stretched out before him, pleading to be transvestied. He is, by his own estimate, an environmentalist. He recycles old movies, myths and legendary tales of dead civilizations such as ours and labels it all ridiculous."[9] Another critic who reviewed many of Ludlam's works over the years, Michael Feingold of the *Village Voice*, also remarked that, "like objects rescued from an antique shop and given new value by restoration, [Ludlam's] ventures into old modes, texts and structures are tributes paid to the present by the past, signs that tell us not where we're going but where we came from."[10] So at the very core of ridiculosity is the concept of a gay identity, the dynamics of which allowed certain artists, including Ludlam, to express the extent of their frustration and outrage at their exclusion from society. It also allowed them to use the elements of their personality that had been camouflaged, usually their homosexuality, to create an aesthetic which they could call their own. Ridiculosity is, therefore, one of the wellsprings from which a gay identity has emerged, and Charles Ludlam is the icon that is enshrined at its heart.

With homosexuality as its trunk, many other components branch off to incorporate the gamut of ridiculosity. One of the most crucial of these branches is film, specifically the "B" movies of the 1940s and their stars. As noted in Chapter II, the underground film movement of the 1960s played a significant role in the development and expression of ridiculosity. Jack Smith and his colleagues used film to display erotic and esoteric images which could not be found in commercial movie houses. Their use of the camera as audience and the bold, sensual images they presented directly influenced the theatrical aesthetic that evolved.

Many gays and lesbians were particularly drawn to the medium of film because of their history and experience of watching movies as youths. It was in the movie theatre where a young, guarded homosexual male could allow himself to feel emotions which were at the time confusing or condemned. In many of the films of the 1940s and 1950s, women were the vehicles of emotion and sexual passion, so it seems clear that gay men, unallowed to express their innermost fantasies, would identify strongly with these heroines in the socially anonymous environment of the movie house.

Charles Ludlam, as a young boy, lived across the street from a movie house and spent countless hours watching Garbo, Davis and Crawford wield their celluloid magic. These were strong women playing passionate and committed characters — and usually in love with handsome, sexy leading men. What young gay man would not immediately transpose himself onto the screen, indulging pent-up, hidden emotions and fantasies of falling in love with a handsome, brawny man? Actresses such as Greta Garbo and Bette Davis exuded passion of such intensity that it seemed to transcend gender. Although many of these heroines were presented as innocent and noble, in the context of the film they represented the deviant and were often left either dead or alone. In Garbo's legendary *Camille*, for example, which Ludlam parodied in the early 1970s, her character tragically dies of an unrequited love, although her demise only reinforces how powerfully and brightly that passion burned. Garbo's forbidden love is analogous to the situation that every young gay man experiences. The identification is not only with the freely expressed passion, but also with the anguish of forbidden love. Many homosexuals, unable to experience fully and express heartfelt emotions, finally discovered a private comfort in that "the movies provided an emotionally safe place where the imagination could flourish. In the movies, it was possible to go 'over the rainbow'."[11]

Ridiculosity drew heavily from many of the so-called "B" pictures that Hollywood was churning out in the 1940s and 1950s for source material and aesthetic trappings. The aesthetic for many of these films was often excessively ornate, the acting usually terrible and the plots routinely inane. The genres that attracted a gay audience were usually science fiction and flying saucers, jungle epics, "road" pictures, and horror films. Many of these films allowed the imagination to run wild with their often opulent, always tacky, and usually silly stories. As noted earlier, Maria Montez was dubbed the "Queen of Technicolor" and was considered the reigning star of "B" films. Although Maria Montez was a huge star, her films were not very artful, critically speaking. In one of her most famous films, *Cobra Woman*, which is a gay cult classic, she portrays the timeless story of a benevolent person in combat with her evil twin. The film takes place, for the most part, on a lone island, Cobra Island. The costumes appear to have been swiped from the Mardi Gras in New Orleans. Each maiden waiting upon the evil Queen is dressed in various shades of orange and purple pastels, resembling a chorus of Easter Eggs. Their headpieces look as though someone has cut off the top of a plastic Clorox bottle and then spray-painted it. Their terrifying spears look less like metal than like cardboard. It is clear that these were not big-budget films, but the stories usually revolved around some fantastical element whereby one could escape into another reality. In one of his plays, *Utopia, Inc.*, Ludlam borrowed and then parodied lines, settings and business from such icons as *Curse of the Mummy's Tomb, Forbidden Planet, Lost Horizon*, and of course *Cobra Woman*. As one critic noted, "This play very often feels remarkably like a Maria Montez jungle epic, even going so far as to borrow names (Martok) and lines ("I have spoken") from *Cobra Woman*, one of her most famous films."[12]

It is easier to comprehend the homosexual's desire to enter the world of celluloid fantasy when you put his position in society in its realistic context. Homosexuals are laughed at and scorned. They are denigrated by portrayals of stereotypical behavior and mannerisms, used to provide cheap and easy laughs for the unenlightened. They are denied basic rights and liberties that are taken for granted by most tax-paying Americans. But most important, until they "come out of the closet," they alone must live with their secret, petrified that somehow the world will discover their grotesqueness and damn them to a life of misery. Because most young, closeted homosexuals cannot express any of their deep, intimate feelings and urges, they are forced to exist within their fantasies. Since it is nothing new for gays and lesbians to dwell inside a secret life of imagination, when they entered the movie house, they simply transferred those intimate feelings onto the characters in the films. In a sense, these characters (usually women) often were acting out, if only symbolically, the young homosexual's innermost passions. Because many of these gay men identified so exclusively with the females in the movies, they began to cultivate their feminine nature. This cultivation led many to outwardly establish their feminine possibilities by creating a female persona, fully attired in the appropriate chiffon, satin, or gold lamé.

This leads to another very important ingredient in ridiculosity, one that is evident in almost all Ridiculous works — drag, that is, dressing up in the clothes and appearing as a member of the opposite sex. "The term 'drag' itself, the brake on a coach, had filtered from the cant of thieves and fences into homosexual slang, to connote the drag of a gown with a train. To *go on the drag* or *flash the drag*, i.e., to use female attire to solicit men, is dated by Eric Partridge to around 1850."[13] Drag, or female impersonation, was an active part of the gay community long before the riots at Stonewall, where it was the drag queens who spirited the revolt. In early New York City, the underground gay society would put on enormous parties called drag balls. Because of the unlawful nature of their orientation, gays and lesbians were forced to throw themselves huge underground parties in order to strengthen and rejoice in any kind of community social life. "In a world that disparaged their culture, it was at the drag balls, more than any place else, that the gay world saw itself, celebrated itself, and affirmed itself."[14]

So the cultural purpose of transvestism is two-fold: first, it provides a way for gay men and women to explore their inner feelings of identification with the opposite sex; and second, it publicly challenges the viability of any standard societal binary categorization such as male/female, masculine/feminine and gay/straight. In recent years there has been an abundance of critical writing on the issue of drag and gender. Social critic Esther Newton points out that "Gay people know that sex-typed behavior can be achieved, contrary to what is popularly believed. They know that the possession of one type of genital equipment by no means guarantees the 'naturally appropriate' behavior."[15] Throughout history, behavioral sex roles have been determined by genital equipment, which consigns the homosexual to a cultural limbo.

Drag forces the observer, whether consciously or unconsciously, to reevaluate certain ideas pertaining to sex and the sex roles. Since genital equipment does not necessarily determine sexual appetite, as in the case of the homosexual, then it obviously follows that sexual orientation cannot be determined by genital identity alone. The difference between male and female is rather obvious, but when a man dresses as a woman, or vice versa, suddenly the roles thought to be naturally prescribed take on new meaning. Femininity and masculinity are blatantly demonstrated to be socially constructed roles, cultivated by the individual in the process of socialization and cultural rearing. Is a woman feminine because she applies makeup and wears jewelry and high heels? Is a man masculine because he works out at the gym and has big muscles? These are categories that human beings automatically subscribe to without question or hesitation. However, when a man dresses up as a woman, he is applying femininity in the exact manner a woman does; it is just that the dimensions of his body usually belie his appearance. Feminist writer Judith Butler points out in her book *Gender Trouble* that "When the constructed status of gender is theorized as radically independent of sex, gender itself becomes a free-floating artifice, with the consequence that *man* and *masculine* might just as easily signify a female body as a male one, and *woman* and *feminine* a male body as easily as a female one." [16]

As far as male homosexuals are concerned, having already challenged stereotypical gender assumptions, the natural next step is to attempt to reverse the outward expression of their gender. As long as society discriminates against them because of their distasteful sexual orientation, they claim the freedom not to subscribe to society's restrictive concepts of gender and sexuality. Drag as a political weapon on the one hand liberates the homosexual from the fear of displaying a false identity, and on the other hand outrageously points out the performative nature of customary gender roles. As Esther Newton points out in her book, drag "is a double inversion that says 'appearance is an illusion.' Drag says 'my outside appearance is feminine, but my essence "inside" [the body] is masculine.' At the same time it symbolizes the opposite inversions; 'my appearance "outside" [my body, my gender] is masculine but my essence inside [myself] is feminine.'"[17]

Because gender is perceived by many in the homosexual community as merely a role that is performed, it is natural that so many gay and lesbian performers embrace the subject so wholeheartedly. In fact, as Laurence Senelick points out, "Gender exists *only in so far as it is perceived*; and the very components of perceived gender — gait, stance, gesture, deportment, vocal pitch and intonation, costume, coiffure — indicate the performative nature of the construct" (italics added).[18] These men drawn to ridiculosity saw the opportunity to use their abilities and desires to perform as an added voice in the ongoing debate regarding gender and transvestism.

As Polish theater critic Jan Kott so eloquently describes in his treatise, *The Theater of Essence*, "When an actress is asked to act like a woman, walk like a woman, sit like a woman, sip tea like a woman, she will at first be surprised and ask: 'But what woman?' ... femininity can only be acted by a man."[19] Kott is asserting the need for objectivity in order to perform femininity. Because a man can objectively observe and study the trappings of femininity, he can therefore act them with greater precision. The gay performer in drag adds an entirely new dimension to the notion of performing and illustrates the duality of roles the actor encompasses; one is the character and the other is the actor himself.

Drag also breaks down the theatrical concepts of realism and naturalism. As Ludlam said once in an interview,

> I think my theatre is the most real, the most natural, but it isn't realism, it isn't naturalism. It's evoking reality by showing us what isn't real. If a man can put on make-up, false eyelashes and mascara, all the artifices of being woman, then obviously all those things are not part of being a woman. So something is created in that negative space, and that's where the mystery of reality is evoked.[20]

Charles Ludlam firmly believed that it was his right as an actor to perform any role he thought sufficiently challenging or enticing. His homosexuality and his curiosity about his feminine nature permitted him sometimes to act in drag. Although he is usually publicly remembered for his work in drag, it is ironic that he appeared in female roles in only five of his twenty-nine published plays. And only in *Camille*, *Galas*, and *Salammbo* did Ludlam portray one female character throughout the entire play. In *The Mystery of Irma Vep* and *Big Hotel*, he played various characters, some female and some male. However, often when a talented male actor can convincingly portray a female character, it is for this and this alone that he is immortalized. This attitude mirrors society's fascination with and abhorrence of transvestism. It wants to see it and laugh at and with it, but it doesn't want to discuss it or analyze it. It marvels at the actor's ability to transform, but does not condone, let alone embrace, the underlying meaning in the performance.

According to Ludlam, aside from actively negating any of their own emotions which are generally ascribed to the opposite sex, the very bias that people have towards drag enforces the already established prejudice against women in our society:

> Drag is something people today are prejudiced against, because women are considered inferior beings. A woman putting on pants, on the other hand, has moved up. So to defiantly do that and say women are worthwhile creatures, and that I'll put my whole soul and being into creating this woman and give her everything I have, including my emotions (and the most taboo thing is to experience feminine emotions), and to take myself seriously in the face of ridicule, that's it. That is the highest turn of the statement. It's different than wanting to make women more like men. It allows audiences to experience the universality of emotion, rather than believe that women are one species and men another, and what one feels the other never does.[21]

Of course there are feminist writers who vehemently oppose this outlook. Jill Dolan, in her article "Gender Impersonation Onstage," states that, "Women are non-existent in drag performance, but woman-as-myth, as a cultural, ideological object, is constructed in an agreed upon exchange between the male performer and the usually male spectator. Male drag mirrors women's socially constructed roles."[22] Although she admits to the socially constructed roles played out by men and women, she feels that drag only adds to the objectifying of women, already pervasive in our society. Although her ideas may seem valid when viewed from such a limited perspective, they fail when viewed in terms of the big picture of human development because they deny the social relevance of gender role-playing and the cultural implications of drag to debunk preconceived assumptions. Ludlam strengthens his argument by stating that "People are troubled that a man would play a woman or that a woman would play a man, and these are the same people who want to break down the idea that men's work is for men and women's work is for women, and they cannot see that this crossover is a stunning manifestation of that."[23]

Ludlam saw the political ramifications of drag in a much broader way than most others. He is correct in warning the very political machinery that has opened up the workplace to include females in jobs traditionally thought of as men's work not to be surprised when they see that equation taken to such an extreme where the crossover becomes complete, even down to the very appearance. Therefore the political impact of drag, according to Ludlam, is that "You get levels of reality and unreality, depending on the point you're trying to make, and what ultimately happens is that the rigidity in how we look at sexual roles and reversals and who we are breaks down."[24] A paradox is encountered in contemplating the very idea of behaving or appearing opposite to one's prescribed genital assignment. We have seen that stereotypical gender roles, just like drag, are cultivated, relying on the essence of role-playing; hence the male actor in drag not only defies his ostensibly innate male personality, but also his actual male physical characteristics — the ultimate paradox. As Ludlam described it, "When his dream of the part calls for playing the opposite sex, the actor must reconcile his sense of truth with his sense of the theatrical. The drag embodies the paradox of acting."[25]

It was important to Ludlam to see the world through the eyes of a complete human being, rather than to limit his scope to his homosexual sensibilities. He was not making any specific overt statement by performing in drag. Rather, he respected the audience enough to allow them to postulate their own theories and come to their own conclusions on the subject. In those moments onstage as Maria Callas or Salammbo or Marguerite Gautier, he was acting, and that is all he was doing. As Clive Barnes of the *New York Times* reveals in his review of *Galas*, "When Ludlam acts a woman he doesn't become a woman — he is far too grotesque, even too androgynous for that — but he captures the spirit of women."[26] This was evidenced by the fact that when Ludlam performed the role of Marguerite Gautier in his version of Dumas *fils*'s *Camille*, he wore a ringlet-curled wig, long eyelashes, and low-cut dress exposing his hairy chest. His intention was not to fool the audience into believing he was a woman, but rather, as he says, to "invite the audience to laugh at me from the first moment by showing my chest hairs. I'm not tricking them like those female impersonators who take off the wig at the end of the act. Yes, I want the audience to laugh, but they should also get the impact of forbidden love — it is really tragic and shocking."[27]

When feminist critic Kate Davy wrote about his performance in *Camille*, she observed that, "in the process of enacting the passionate and doomed love affair between Marguerite and Armand that dominates the Camille narrative, Ludlam and [Bill] Vehr made manifest the desire of two men for each other."[28] This perspective seems skewed perhaps by some kind of sexual or political bias. In truth, Ludlam was acting a role like any other role, with the only difference being that this character was a woman. As he himself admits, "We were out there on that stage the same as everyone else — hoping to give an honest, bona fide account of ourselves as characters in a play."[29] Although Ludlam acknowledged the political and social influence of drag on the consciousness of society, his immediate job was to create a character that people would enjoy watching. This, to Ludlam, was the ultimate political statement. He had no desire to dictate any theories or politics through his work, but rather trusted the power of the visual to make its own impact. Because of his respect for them, Ludlam put a lot of faith and trust in his audiences. He was aware that he was ridiculous, or as Clive Barnes noted, "grotesque," but he knew that his portrayal of ridiculosity was deliberate, and it was comprised of various contradictions and juxtapositions. Perhaps the very core of these contradictions, drawn upon by the tactics of drag, the old Hollywood "B" films, homosexual culture, and certainly by the artists practicing ridiculosity, is the deliberate exploitation of camp, making it a visible style and an inspirational basis for design.

Camp is defined in the *American Heritage Dictionary* as "(1) An affectation or appreciation of manners and tastes commonly thought to be artificial, vulgar, or banal. (2) Banality, vulgarity, or artificiality when deliberately affected or when appreciated for its humor."[30] To say the least, this is a very narrow, clinical, and uninteresting definition. Although the manifestations of camp behavior have been around for years, only recently has there been any detailed critical analysis of camp as a social and cultural strategy. As George Chauncey reveals about gay life in New York in the early 1900s, "Camp was at once a cultural style and a cultural strategy, for it helped gay men make sense of, respond to, and undermine the social categories of gender and sexuality that served to marginalize them." He goes on further to state that "the social order denounced gay men as 'unnatural'; through camp banter gay men highlighted the unnaturalness of the social order itself."[31] From the onset, the use of camp became a survival technique, an invented language and style, by which gay men could covertly communicate with each other with sly winks and nods and certain cryptic phrases and codes, without the threat of social or legal retaliation. As Scott Long writes, "[Camp] is a private language for some who intuit that public language has gone wrong."[32] Camp means different things to different people — it is elusive and practically defies definition. By its very nature, camp has developed covertly within the secretive and dark confines of prejudice, fear, and confusion, and its manifestations are as varied as the many persons within the gay community. The one common thread in the expression of camp is homosexuality, which permits and encourages this style of communication. The gay sensibility is at the very heart of camp, according to Michael Bronski's *Culture Clash:*

> Gays have hidden themselves from oppressive straight society through circumlocution — Camp — and defended themselves through wit. In gay life nothing is what it seems to be. By pulling the rug out from under the usual gender expectations — is it a boy or a girl? — or sexual arrangements — what

do they do in bed?— homosexual life and culture undermine patriarchal and heterosexist social assumptions.[33]

Not only does Charles Ludlam "pull the rug out from under the usual gender expectations," he takes the position that camp enables him to define himself as ridiculous, thus thwarting any critic's effort to label him as such. As he says,

> One of the greatest weapons that people use on you to get you to conform is ridicule. So you don't dare to do anything that people will laugh at. It's a way that society exerts pressure on you. However, if you take the position that you are already going to be ridiculous, they are powerless. They ridicule you? They are doing what you want them to do.[34]

Camp allows the homosexual to parody the things mainstream society worships as normal by exaggerating and stylizing, thus commenting on the original, while at the same time presenting no real threat to its existence.

And, as we have seen previously in this chapter, the basis of the fear of homosexuality for many heterosexuals is a socialized, puritanical fear and guilt connected with sex and eroticism. Camp not only allows homosexuals to communicate with each other, most often incognito, but also to rejoice in and celebrate their shared sexuality and to ridicule the mainstream's restrictive views of sex and gender with humor. According to David Bergman in his article "Strategic Camp," camp's "sacred parodies are a strategy to reinvoke a divinity that has fled; it seeks entrance to the Dionysian mysteries through its bawdy revelries."[35] Because homosexuals are free from the legacy of procreation, they have a perspective on sex not shared by the majority. They can view sex purely as a means of pleasure and fun. Because camp was born and bred within the gay community, it evolved into a form of group reinforcement, a social bonding. Not only was camp a strategy for political communication, but also it strove to create a kind of link, or connection identifiable within the community itself. It became a way of not only defining their differences from society's sexual expectations, but also of celebrating them. And more often than not, the filter through which camp is funneled, by its unabashedly low nature, is comedy, often ridiculous farce.

In attempting to synthesize the many views on camp, it should be noted that Susan Sontag, in her 1966 essay "Notes on Camp," boldly pioneered a critical examination of camp at a time when others merely scoffed at the very notion of camp as a legitimate artistic style. According to Sontag, "Camp is the consistently aesthetic experience of the world. It incarnates a victory of 'style' over 'content,' 'aesthetics' over 'morality,' of irony over tragedy."[36] She goes on to say, "Camp is a vision of the world in terms of style — but a particular kind of style. It is the love of the exaggerated, the 'off' of things-being-what-they-are-not."[37] Although Sontag is correct in pointing out that the underpinning of camp is style over content, as she develops her idea she begins identifying certain things as having inherently camp qualities, thereby contradicting herself along the way. On one hand she admits that camp is a sensibility rather than an idea — a vision or taste that is elusive, rather than a plan or system. But then she goes on and proclaims such items as Tiffany lamps, or feather boas, or fringed and beaded dresses as being inherently campy, somehow defined by some order or method. According to Sontag, anyone who looks at a Tiffany lamp or a flapper dress will see it as campy. Although she acknowledges the homosexual influence in camp, she does not subscribe to the notion that camp is inherently gay.[38]

Another principle within Sontag's delineation of camp is that "Homosexuals have pinned their integration into society on promoting the aesthetic sense. Camp is a solvent of morality. It neutralizes moral indignation, sponsors playfulness."[39] Here, Sontag touches on homosexuality as the thrust behind camp, but again she does not thoroughly explore the issue. Of course, it should be pointed out that in 1966 when her book was published, homosexuality and gay rights were not nearly as prevalent in society as they are today. After all, this was three years before the Stonewall Riots which launched the modern gay rights movement. Nevertheless, she does credit the homosexual influence in camp. She theorizes that homosexuals were using camp as a strategy for assimilation into society. This begs the question, however, of whether a gay man, dressed to the nines as Gloria Swanson, is really using this or any other strategy to assimilate himself into society. Rather than a strategy for assimilation, as Sontag suggests, it seems more logical that camp was and is used by gays to bolster solidarity among themselves, a way to relish their difference. Sontag is on the mark, however, in her observation that camp "neutralizes moral indignation" by "sponsoring playfulness" and appearing ridiculous, thereby deflating the opposition's hatred and bias.

Camp was and is used by homosexuals as a social strategy, relying on the particular weapons of humor and buffoonery. This style of humor is based on a feeling of detachment from mainstream society, of having been in a subcultural ghetto and facing the need to redefine and revalue everything familiar. In response to Sontag's essay, Rosalyn Regelson, in 1968, wrote in the *New York Times:*

> Real homosexual Camp is in fact the opposite of this "style" without content. Like authentic Jewish humor, it is an ironical response to a hopeless situation

in which the world is structured against one's existence. Courage for survival is gained through humorous criticism via irony and parody of the unjust and phony aspects of the structure.[40]

Irony is one of four elements intrinsic to camp, according to Jack Babuscio in his article "Camp and the Gay Sensibility." The others are aestheticism, theatricality and humor. Babuscio sees camp as a strategy which he illuminates thoroughly on these four precepts. He sees the development of camp as a reaction to homophobia and ostracization. Every underpinning of camp, according to Babuscio, lies within the homosexual experience:

I define the gay sensibility as a creative energy reflecting a consciousness that is different from the mainstream: a heightened awareness of certain human complications that spring from the fact of social oppression; in short, a perception of the world which is coloured, shaped, directed and defined by the fact of one's gayness.[41]
When the world is a rejecting place, the need grows correspondingly strong to project one's being — to explore the limits to which one's personality might attain — as a way of shielding the inner self from those on the outside who are too insensitive to understand.[42]

Babuscio also points out that gays who believe they must pass as heterosexual develop an increased understanding of disguise and impersonation and the need to assert one's personality in a society that, more or less, dictates normalcy. This insight describes gay experiences and reactions to the challenges of survival in an antagonistic environment. However, Babuscio goes on to delineate the particular elements which define the parameters of camp as a definitive genre. He states that "Camp is never a thing or person per se, but, rather, a relationship between activities, individuals, situations and gayness."[43] And it is this emphasis on the correlation which makes camp so elusive. It is not always easy to identify camp using this philosophy because it lies somewhere between the object itself and the viewer's perception.

Irony is a literary tool in which an artificial intention is imposed upon an object or a concept, which is in sharp contrast to its literal meaning, and its success depends on a knowing audience's recognition of the intended meaning. Often, irony betrays a sense of the author's detachment from or impartiality toward certain events and times, objectively commenting on a certain attitude or situation. According to Babuscio, "Irony is the subject matter of camp, and refers here to any highly incongruous contrast between an individual or thing and its context or association."[44] Within the context of homosexuality, one of the principal ironies used in camp is drag, the contrast between the masculine and feminine identities. Feeling excluded from culture and needing to project an identity, the homosexual in drag undermines the status quo, challenging preconceived ideas about gender identity. Utilizing the incongruity of gender allows homosexuals on the one hand to express their personality and innate feelings, and on the other, to comment upon the bias against them. The irony lies in the incongruity between the known or assumed sex of the individual (male) and the imposed trappings of the opposite gender (female), which compels an audience to contemplate not only the identity of the person perceived, but the very nature of gender itself. By placing a masculine persona within a feminine context points out the very irony of gender identity itself.

The next factor in Babuscio's ideas on camp is aestheticism, or how an object or event is perceived. Babuscio writes that with an "outrageous" aesthetic, "the emphasis shifts from what a thing or a person is to what it looks like; from what is being done to how it is being done."[45] For example, in his play *Der Ring Gott Farblonjet*, Ludlam used plastic bottles of laundry bleach, cut in half and dyed and bejeweled, as helmets for the gods. We, as audience, immediately recognize the thinly disguised source of these regal helmets, but the arrangement and decoration of their parts have transformed them into something else. Here, the emphasis placed on what the object looks like versus what it really is creates the incongruous nature through which the campy quality emerges. The aesthetic component of camp is one of the main tools gays use in order to show that the perception of an object or person does not always correspond to its true nature, reinforcing the notion of revaluing culture and, perhaps, reassigning new meaning to something of low value in an effort to ridicule society's preconceived beliefs. By rearranging something's inherent qualities to signify something else, one makes the artificial and theatrical nature of that thing apparent.

As Babuscio writes regarding theatricality, "Camp, by focusing on the outward appearances of role, implies that roles, and in particular, sex roles, are superficial—a matter of style. Indeed, life itself is role and theatre, appearance and impersonation."[46] Here it is easy to understand why Babuscio defines camp within the homosexual context, as gay men know only too well that sexual identity does not always coincide with gender identity, and through the homosexual perspective, it is easier to understand that masculinity and femininity are roles we impose upon ourselves. By mixing up the perceived gender and demonstrating the superficial and artificial nature of roles, performers like Ludlam allow the theatrical nature of camp to explode in the form of excessive and outrageous drag and grand, artificial behavior. Theatricality, as opposed to the realistic or natural, denotes a showy and artificial style, exposing the need to both establish an identity and also comment upon society's very perception of identity.

Finally, Babuscio places humor at the very apex of camp, humor being the strategy through which each of the previous elements functions. He writes that the strategy of humor in camp is "a means of dealing with a hostile environment and, in the process, of defining a positive identify. Laughter, rather than tears, is its chosen means of dealing with the painfully incongruous situation of gays in society."[47] One reason why camp is so joyous is that gays, more often than not, feel the need to look at the world through comic lenses, not only in order to deal with the pain of feeling ostracized, but also as a means of deflating the hatred and condemnation they face. With humor, or comedy, gays can laugh at themselves before anyone else does, thereby challenging the status quo to come up with a different tactic with which to carry out their biased agenda. Comedy has been used for thousands of years as a neutralizing and corrective agent within a society. Aristophanes used it in Classical Greece to point out the foibles of certain individuals, hoping to influence public opinion. Molière used the comedy of satire to criticize the behavior and manners of the upper class. Gays use humor in the form of camp to criticize the prejudice and narrow-mindedness of mainstream society and also as a tool for solidarity. According to Babuscio then, it is through humor that the ironic perception of outrageous and excessive theatricality becomes camp, and the artificial nature of role-playing becomes a language which the homosexual community can use as a weapon and as a comfort.

Social critic Esther Newton, in her book *Mother Camp*, spent years on the streets of American cities living among the transvestite subculture and documenting their existence. She witnessed both the pain and the joy in the lives of homosexuals forced to live on the fringe. Her perspective is less from the performer's use of camp and centered more on the individual struggle with a conflicted identity, using camp behavior as a mode of survival. She also limits her definition of camp within the context of gay sensibility and, like Babuscio, believes that "incongruity is the subject matter of camp, theatricality its style, and humor its strategy."[48] As opposed to a political tool, Newton sees camp as a means for the homosexual to create a positive identity, both individually and as a people. By acknowledging the incongruous nature of homosexuality within the framework of a predominantly heterosexual society, camp allows gays to laugh at themselves instead of crying. According to Newton, "[camp] humor does not cover up, it transforms."[49] Facing so much hatred and intolerance, homosexuals use camp humor to battle feelings of insecurity and insignificance; it gives them the power to recast their plight by creating new, more positive roles and, hence, provides a tool for edification and support within the homosexual community. Many mainstream heterosexuals probably view camp as strictly a way for homosexuals to cover up their pain and suffering, but Newton's perspective places the emphasis on camp as a transforming power, giving gays the ability to survive within a subculture that is continually belittled and chided. In contrast to other minority subcultures in our society, which use the very same tools of violence and hatred that the majority uses against them in order to combat prejudice and exclusion, gays use camp as a peaceful and humorous way to bolster their insecurities and redefine their perspectives. The homosexual community, according to Newton, uses camp in order to better understand themselves and their culture, and also to reinforce their significance as individuals and as a community. She writes admiringly of the courage of young gay men, struggling with their sexual identity, usually living their day-to-day existence as transvestites, with camp being their only available way to reconstruct an identity.

According to Charles Ludlam, "Camp is a way of looking at things, never what's looked at." He vehemently disagrees with Sontag's assessment that specific things are camp — a Tiffany lampshade, or a Hollywood movie with a Busby Berkeley number in it. "What's wrong with that is camp ceases to be an attitude toward something and loses all of its relativity. It nails it to the wall and makes it very literal."[50] He agrees with Babuscio and Newton in their view that camp resides within the homosexual sensibility: "Camp became a sly or secret sense of humor that could only exist to a group that had been through something together; in this case, the gay world."[51]

However, Ludlam objects to the heterosexual appropriation of the term camp and the attempt to tie it down to mean something specific. It loses its elasticity and serious intent and evolves into silly, inane farce. Ludlam views camp as a seriously funny method of recycling and revaluing everything. Camp is at the very heart of his ridiculous vision; it speaks through every element of his creative genius. For Ludlam, camp was a very sophisticated style of communication within his gay community. Without coming out and proclaiming himself homosexual, he garnered a gay cult following in his first few years simply by virtue of the campy nature of his productions. With the recycling of culture as an integral part of ridiculosity, camp allows the homosexual to admire things people hold in contempt, and to hold in contempt other things that people think are valuable.[52] By using camp in his ridiculous theatre, Ludlam provided a world where gays could embrace, celebrate and acknowledge their uniqueness, in a safe and unthreatening environment. In the same manner that Ludlam picked through abandoned genres like a cultural scavenger, his ridiculosity

embraced camp with complete awareness of the critical bias against it in
the mainstream press:

> The more people have told me that I had to get away from the word "Camp,"
> that it's terrible that people would call my work "Camp," the more I decided
> to embrace it. If nobody wants it, come to me! Bring me your poor, your
> tired, your yearning to be free! Let my theatre be the repository of all for-
> bidden theatrical conventions![53]

One of the major theatrical conventions which Ludlam and other gay
artists of the ridiculous drew upon to promote their aesthetic was opera,
because of its often garish and extravagant excess. In Ludlam's canon of
plays, he parodied two operas and based one of his most legendary characters on a famous opera diva. His play *Camille* was inspired by Verdi's *La
Traviata* as much as by the original novel and the Garbo movie. The
grandeur of the music and the brazen emotional display by the characters
were in direct communion with his own creative sensibility. He also condensed Wagner's epic *Der Ring des Nibelungen*, comprising 15 hours of
music in four full-length operas, into a three-hour parody called *Der Ring
Gott Farblonjet*, with the Valkyries portrayed as lesbians on motorcycles.
And finally, his play *Galas* was a loving and hysterical tribute to the famed
and controversial opera diva Maria Callas. Although only these three works
were directly influenced by opera, one can easily see that each of his productions included the operatic elements of excess and artifice. He loved
opera because of "its shameless theatricality,"[54] which was the very foundation of everything that he did.

From its inception, gay men have intuitively been drawn to opera.
According to Wayne Koestenbaum,

> Opera's apparent distance from contemporary life made it a refuge for gays,
> who were creations of modern sexual systems, and yet whom society could
> not acknowledge or accommodate. Opera is not very real. But gayness has
> never been admitted into the precincts of reality. And so gays may seek out
> art that does not respect the genuine.[55]

As we have seen with other aspects of ridiculosity, such as old movies, opera
became yet another vehicle through which gay men could feel and express
emotions that were otherwise covered. Because the image of the heterosexual man is the predominant one in our society, gay men have grown up
feeling not only disenfranchised, but disqualified to represent the male sex.
If the straight man is what is thought of as a real man, then the gay man
must be some kind of imitation or fabrication. At an age when he begins
to comprehend some of these ideas, the young gay man looks for outlets

where he can attempt to synthesize and cope with his raging hormones, the uncomfortable stares, the illicit rendezvous, the hateful prejudice, and his own rage. Opera became, for some gay men, a safe place where they could vicariously live through fantasy and imagination. Because the emotional life of most gay men has developed in a whirlpool of confusion, guilt and anxiety, it is often buried beneath piles of psychological rubbish from years of inapplicable socialization. As Michael Bronski points out, "Opera plays on our emotions through the deliberate manipulation of a predictable form. This predictability can allow the safe experience of emotions which we may have been taught to ignore or repress."[56] Because the actual form of opera usually remains constant, the content being the only variant, the gay man attending can emotionally prepare himself, knowing generally what type of experience to expect. The gay man with a penchant for opera goes equipped for an emotional experience, usually having already seen the opera previously, memorized the music and story, and experienced the emotions. There are rarely any surprises in the world of opera, outside of a magnificent voice or an arresting set.

Most gay men who people the opera world seem to have a unique affinity for a particular opera singer, whom they often refer to as the diva. What they relate to, actually, are the roles that these singers have performed and also the quality of their impassioned singing. Usually the diva role in an opera is that of a love-torn, victimized heroine, willing to risk personal safety by freely expressing her individual sentiment. Homosexuals, having been persecuted for the majority of their lives, and often love-torn themselves, can connect on a very personal level with these roles and, hence, the singers performing them. And if the diva sings with the virtuosity and ardor of a Maria Callas, a Joan Sutherland, or a Beverly Sills, the gay man transfers that communion from the character portrayed to the actual singer herself.

The heroines in opera, however, don't bury their feelings, but instead display them with vocal grandeur, passion and theatricality. This is what the gay man yearns for — the ability and courage to express that passion and vocalize their feelings of victimization. At the same time, opera also expresses to listeners that they have, in fact, swallowed their emotions and buried their passions:

> Opera has the power to warn you that you have wasted your life. You haven't acted on your desires. You've suffered a stunted, vicarious existence. You've silenced your passions. The volume, height, depth, lushness, and excess of operatic utterance reveal, by contrast, how small your gestures have been until now, how impoverished your physicality; you have only used a fraction of your bodily endowment, and your throat is closed.[57]

It is easy to see why gay men can become so intense in their passion for opera and why opera is so actively supported by many in the gay community. It is an individual and cathartic affair. Many gay men wear their proclivity for opera as a badge of honor and are adamant about their likes and dislikes of particular singers and scores. In the gay community, these individuals are frequently referred to as "opera queens": "Opera Queen is like a beauty-prize title (Miss Cucumber); it subtly mocks the girl riding on the float, the girl rewarded with the crown, but it thrills her too, and seems a ticket to a future, and places her in a social configuration, a lineage."[58]

Being an Opera Queen permits the gay man to acknowledge his position and wink at himself and his love of theatricality and indulgence, while at the same time allowing him to feel an enormous sense of belonging and purpose.

Although Charles Ludlam was not necessarily an opera queen, he did appreciate the grand style that this artform provides. He seemed to have a love/hate relationship with opera. He loved the grand, sweeping music and theatricality, and usually imitated it in his productions, but he hated the lack of invention and creativity that most operas succumb to. Within that lack of invention and creativity, however, he did revel in the absurdities of opera:

> When I saw Tebaldi sing *Tosca* at the old Met, she and Scarpia were gigantically fat. He was chasing her around the room, and when she went to throw herself off the parapet, she stepped behind a flat and screamed, and you could see her hand coming out, pulling her gown after her. It's so delicious. Or *Lucia* with Sutherland. She comes down to the wedding guests covered in blood, carrying a dagger — and the guests don't bat an eye. They are perfectly polite, eating.[59]

Perhaps this is the reason why Ludlam could not completely give himself over to the emotional extravagance of opera; he always viewed any theatrical endeavor through the lens of ridiculosity. He could appropriate the style and indulgence of opera, but not its serious, dramatic nature. Ludlam's comic sense turned everything on its head, exploring the silliness and parodying even the most tragic of stories. His play *Galas* offers, on the one hand, a very loving and sympathetic portrait of the famed opera diva Maria Callas, and on the other hand, a hysterical parody of her unrestrained and often outrageous lifestyle. He was always fascinated with incongruity and his work usually incorporated these themes in some ridiculous manner. Opera's influence afforded Ludlam the ability to explore passionate emotions and tell compelling stories in a theatrical world of artifice and exaggeration.

Attempting to clarify the critical theories underneath ridiculosity is akin to debating the existence of God. It is elusive and it attracts a particular group of people. Ridiculosity is a sensibility or taste, rather than a belief or concept. The components of ridiculosity which we have explored here are merely the most prominent ones, although at its innermost core exists the gay sensibility which informs all of ridiculosity. Although there may be other minor elements, these main ingredients, the "B" movies of the 1940s and 1950s, questions of gender identity as perceived through drag, the strategies of camp, and the inordinate world of opera, all communicate through the mouthpiece of the homosexual.

Ridiculosity is a sensibility that was born out of the oppression of prejudice and intolerance. Gay men were not only providing themselves a sense of solidarity with ridiculosity, but also were expressing their willingness and need to be seen as something other than mainstream. In a sense, ridiculosity provided an outlet for the gay community to acknowledge and demonstrate their uniqueness by publicly declaring, "We're not like them," the *them* being the heterosexual majority. This gentle dissent, unlike the hatred continually thrown at them, gave gays a chance to laugh at themselves and their situation, while at the same time constructing an identity and a way to communicate. Many in the straight world have attempted to appropriate ridiculosity, but they generally fail because they do not have that unique experience of being an outsider. They do not sense the absurdity of the gender-prescribed roles that society promotes. And they have not had to suppress taboo emotions, resulting in enormous guilt and fear. Ridiculosity could be considered the very embodiment of a gay sensibility, with Charles Ludlam one of its most acknowledged and influential innovators. He took ridiculosity and fashioned an entire theatrical style around it, incorporating everything from the sets and costumes to the acting and writing. And the entire aesthetic underpinning of ridiculosity is the deliberately transparent perception of artifice.

— 4 —

Ridiculosity in Practice

Ridiculosity in theatrical form, as Ludlam defined it, was based on the concept of recycling dramatic traditions and popular culture using artifice, parody and exaggeration, with a notion of truth. As *New York Post* critic Clive Barnes once observed, "Ludlam is a caricaturist who exaggerates to tell the truth, but the underlying line is bold and clear, and the final effect unforgettable."[1] With his ridiculous theatre, Ludlam was trying to get away from, in his terms, the pretentiousness of art. Art which takes itself too seriously. Art which neither informs nor entertains, but merely confuses. Ludlam thought that playwrights like Brecht, with his didactic theatre, and Beckett, who had advanced the world of minimalism in his plays to the point of nearly nonexistent drama, and realists such as Ibsen and Chekhov were not the hooks on which modern drama should hang their hats.

He also felt that the commercial Broadway houses were similar to factories, shoveling out products in mass proportion, with hundreds of people involved in the creative process. Ludlam felt strongly that if he stayed in his small 150-seat theatre in Greenwich Village, he would be able to realize his artistic goals more completely. Numerous times he was given the chance to join the ranks of Broadway, but each time he declined because of his fear of diluting the creative process, which he nurtured, with too many chefs. Ludlam was a born leader and functioned best when in complete control.

This need and desire for ultimate control over all aspects of his productions led Ludlam to function in all capacities of his productions. He designed many of the sets and costumes, wrote the plays, directed the plays and starred in the plays. And in every aspect of this self-collaboration, the element of artifice played a significant role; it is the cornerstone of Ludlam's ridiculosity. By the very nature of artifice, it is clear that Ludlam's aim was not to hold a mirror up to nature and reflect, accurately, the state of the world. But then again, as Louis Montros states in the journal *Helios*,

"If the world is a theatre and the theatre is an image of the world, then by reflecting upon its own artifice, the drama is holding the mirror up to nature."[2] The question seems to boil down to what is real and what is artificial. Are these absolute rather than relative terms? When asked these questions, Ludlam responded, "I think my theatre is the most real, the most natural, but it isn't realism, it isn't naturalism. It's evoking reality by showing us what isn't real."[3] He goes on to illustrate his point using the artifice of femininity, make-up, wigs and false eyelashes. If it is possible for a man to wear these artificial applications of being a woman, then they are obviously not some integral part of being a woman. By truly holding the mirror up to nature, Ludlam elicited reality by demonstrating the artificial nature of "applied" femininity. In this culture we take for granted that women wear makeup and we actually judge them on their beauty by the manner of their artwork. Artifice liberated Ludlam from having to subscribe to any specific theatrical model or cultural convention. "Ludlam urge[d] people to free themselves from society's preconceived notions of what makes happiness, what determines morality and what is proper."[4] And it was theatrical artifice that liberated Ludlam as an actor, playwright and designer.

Ludlam's set designs were usually begun at the very outset of the creative project. In fact, it seems that often Ludlam developed his play and his designs simultaneously, with one feeding off the other. He often carried the idea of recycling right onto the stage in his designs, converting rubbish, trinkets and household objects into wonderfully inventive set designs, costumes and props. Most likely this grew out of a need to economize, as early on in the history of the Ridiculous Theatrical Company Ludlam and his troupe were forced to set up and tear down after each performance.

When Ludlam's first play, *Big Hotel*, was first performed, the Tamellini's Gate Theater in 1967 was a rundown, seedy movie house which attracted the experimental film crowd. Each weekend night after the final film, Ludlam and his gang would take down the movie screen and convert the space into an old hotel. This required them to rely on imagination and use anything they could find that wasn't nailed on some floor or wall. They also were just barely making the rent on the theatre with the box office, so they had no money to put toward a set. As Richard Schechner recalls, "Everyone was at the hotel — a rundown place represented scenically by whatever the directors and actors found or made out of the stuff in the theatre — half-painted flats, an open second story, plastic plants and toy telephones. This was not an artistically designed half-set, but an undesigned hodgepodge."[5] Although the Ridiculous Theatrical Company eventually became more financially solvent (as financially solvent as any theatrical company can be), Ludlam continued to utilize the same scenic concepts in his plays. But because of an increased budget and a track record of success in his later career, Ludlam could now cultivate and organize this aesthetic instead of just hoping for the best. In his final play, *The Artificial Jungle*, Ludlam designed a pet shop which resembled an explosion from the deep, with every wall and the ceiling covered with bright painted starfish, seashells, seaweed, etc. He also had an aquarium on stage filled with water, and there were three piranhas swimming happily around in it — each one obviously plastic and being controlled by a very apparent stick and, it seemed, watching the action on stage. Eileen Blumenthal noted in her *Village Voice* review of the play that, "[While the] set — including walls painted with starfish and seaweed in magenta, chartreuse, and orange — is more facile than some earlier Ridiculous sets, it is full of wonderful kitschy touches."[6] Although Ludlam's budgets increased, his sense of theatrical artifice in his sets was always apparent. In his early days, his production of *Bluebeard* was performed across several planks laid across the bar at Christopher's End in the Village with only minimal props and set pieces. By 1975 he opened *Bluebeard* at the Evergreen Theatre in Manhattan complete with cardboard icicles of blood dripping off the stage, bats and cobwebs covering the furniture and a leopard skin draped over the piano.

In *Galas*, Ludlam begins the play at a Verona train station with a small table and chairs to the side for coffee. On a very small stage, we first see puffs of smoke and then a grand, long two-dimensional cardboard train, detailed with ringing bells and flashing lights, enters, trailing smoke, and off steps Maria Magdalena Galas, a famous diva. Here he begins the very theatrical event with a bold stroke of theatre artifice. In *Der Ring Gott Farblonjet*, Ludlam's parody of Wagner, Valhalla was depicted in slides; a combination of Lincoln Center and the Cathedral of Saint John the Divine. He also created a forge out of glued-together egg crates, and in order to create the flaming finale, instead of trying to invent some sort of fake fire, Ludlam projected a 16mm film of a fire in a fireplace on the back scrim. As Michael Feingold of the *Village Voice* characterized Ludlam's design aesthetic, the sets were "the work of an artist with a vision such as one rarely sees on stage; they made me think of David Hockney's Grimm illustrations, which use contemporary modes and junk objects the same way, for epic effects."[7]

Ludlam's costumes for his plays were also designed with theatrical artifice in mind. In its early period, partially as a result of the rather haphazard way in which the shows were mounted and performed, the Ridiculous Theatrical Company was not terribly particular about costumes. In keeping with the aesthetic concept of recycling, company member John Brockmeyer remembered that "we were able to walk down the street in an evening and costume the show out of things that had been thrown away."[8] Local transvestite star and Ridiculous colleague Mario Montez, according to Ludlam, had a "gift for scavenging Lower East Side and SoHo trash heaps. Once, he came in with a bale of sequin material.... It was the stuff out of which sequins had been punched — he'd found it discarded outside a sequin factory — and we used it to make a headdress, which fell apart during a dance, scattering the stage with glitter. It created a set of incredible splendor."[9]

Mary Brecht, wife of Stefan Brecht and daughter-in-law of the famous German playwright and director, designed the costumes for Ludlam's 1971 revival of *The Grand Tarot*. As Mel Gussow noted in his *New York Times* review, "As the crazy Fool, Mr. Ludlam is an exploded pack of Tarot cards, a one-man harlequinade — with his feet firmly rooted in silly red sneakers. The Lady Moon, with funnels for breasts, ... Marriage is personified by a hermaphrodite, a startling costume by Mary Brecht, which splits the actor Sebastian Swann completely in half. On one side he is a tuxedo bridegroom, on the other, a virginal bride."[10] These costumes were so well received critically that New York theatre critic Martin Gottfried wrote a feature article in *Vogue* based on the costumes for *The Grand Tarot*.

In *Der Ring Gott Farblonjet*, which garnered him an Obie award for design, the Rhine Maidens wore blue lamé cocktail gowns and the Nihilumpen army were dressed in plastic black and brown garbage bags with plastic bleach bottles, cut in half, on their heads as helmets. In his salute to Molière, *Le Bourgeois Avant-Garde*, perhaps the most outrageous costume was worn by Rufus Foufas, a Long Island green grocer who wants desperately to be considered the premiere patron of the avant-garde. He enters in Act Two in a suit made entirely from artificial turf, and in attempting to prove his devout patronage, he takes a nutrient enema. While the enema is being given, his grass suit begins to expand, growing to an enormous size, when a blackout occurs and a loud blast is heard. We are made to believe that this enema has filled him to the point of explosion and, in fact, he enters again in distressed underwear. Actually the costumer, Everett Quinton, installed an inflatable innertube within the costume which caused the suit to expand on cue.

In his famous *Camille*, Ludlam wore a low-cut, sleeveless mauve gown, obviously showing his chest and armpit hair. At one point in the play, Ludlam calls attention to the costume when Marguerite and Olympe De Taverne meet at a party, both wearing the same gown, although Ludlam's is a bit more lavish.

Ludlam often utilized nudity on stage as a costume. "When he appears nude in his plays, it's nudity as artifice, as revelation through theatrical illusion."[11] Ludlam did not view nudity as pornographic but rather as one of the elements of theatrical artifice. Whenever he had actors or actresses appear nude on the stage, he always made sure that they wore some element of clothing, however subtle, even if only a hat or a scarf. In one scene in *Stage Blood*, for example, Ludlam disrobes in order to go to the bathroom, but leaves his shoes on. For Ludlam, complete nudity on stage was too clinical. It was a chance for the person, as well as the character, to reveal himself to the audience, thus further layering the theatrical event. As he stated once in an interview, "In the theatre, even when you're a character, you've always exposing *yourself* to the audience. An actor is one who dares to stand up before an audience in person."[12]

Aside from the necessity of an inexpensive design approach, Ludlam and company were intent on exploring the recycling nature of ridiculosity in every aspect of the theatre, including the sets and costumes. As he says, "Since we're parodists, we adopt the style of what we're doing. But there is a theatricality and a decorative richness in which we specialize. We concentrate on countering '70s minimalism with comic maximalism: richness, variety, complexity."[13] By the design choices that Ludlam and cohorts made, he created a Ridiculous event that was all-inclusive — from the moment you set foot into whatever space they were performing in, you were entering Ludlam's ridiculous world, where boundaries were blurred and theatrical artifice was in full bloom. He raised "tackiness" to new heights with his visual contrasts and clashes. For Ludlam, however, ridiculosity in theatrical design was the veneer which served to balance and support his dramatic intent as a playwright.

The seeds of Ludlam's ridiculosity germinate in each of the plays he wrote, 29 of which were fully produced under his guidance. His philosophy was, "Life provides an inexhaustible source of the ridiculous, so I never have to worry about running out of material."[14] The material he used, however, was usually taken from earlier genres, even dialogue lifted verbatim from older scripts. He gleefully stole stories and dialogue with the intent of reinventing them for a modern audience, who were, in his opinion, being lulled to sleep with boring, didactic theatre. Sometimes he reworked entire plays or novels such as *Camille*, *Le Bourgeois Avant-Garde*, and *Salammbo*, or he would use an old movie as his canvas, as with *Utopia Inc.* and *Bluebeard*, or a number of movies, as for *Big Hotel*, and occasionally he would write an entirely original work, such as *Galas* and *How To Write a Play*. Usually in his plays he makes reference to various genres and authors, such as in *The Artificial Jungle*, where he appropriates and combines the *film noir* style and genre of the movie *The Postman Always Rings Twice* with plot elements and character similarities from Zola's naturalistic novel *Therese Racquin*. His intent was never merely to poke fun at the original source material; his deep respect and regard for the theatre and its history would never allow that. He saw value in these old works and felt that with his sensibility, he could create something new from something old and, in doing so, comment on the often ridiculous and painful nature of human existence. As theatre critic, scholar and director Richard Schechner observed:

> The greatest playwrights of the western tradition (and, it would seem, of every civilization) were not inventors of plots. They stole their situations and often great chunks of dialogue. They stole from each other, from the public domain, from the existing work, from other cultures, from history. They worked as craftsmen, not "poets."[15]

Ludlam the playwright was a craftsman by his own admission: "I do a play like a shoemaker makes a pair of shoes. I really have a laborer's attitude to work ... I'm an expert at making plays because I approach them as a craftsman."[16]

As a craftsman, he worked in the realm of comedy and farce, keeping alive the tradition of ridiculing the injustices of human nature in order to comment upon them and hopefully remedy them. Prior to Aristophanes in Classical Greece, comedy developed as a corrective tool for society, a way to maintain order and control, and this system remained in place for hundreds of years. Today it seems that comedy has taken a turn toward the banal. Many plays seem to be aggressively working toward emulating television's situation comedies, with their reputed goal of three jokes a page. With the abundance of cheap entertainment, as in mass-media films and television, comedic play scripts are tending more and more to play to a lowest-common-denominator concept of humor, eliciting shallow laughs that ring hollow.

Ludlam attempted a corrective step to this trend with ridiculosity, however, by placing the ridicule on the orthodox and "normal" rather than the depraved. Most good comedy punishes eccentricity and creates humor by making the eccentric or the deviant the funny one. Ridiculosity treats the normal as ridiculous. It turns the normal, the conventional, the standard, into the figure of fun, and the deviant, the eccentric, the minority, triumphs over the norm. Ludlam is indeed using comedy as a corrective tool, but he inverts the intent and ridicules the status quo by creating wildly bizarre characters which, when juxtaposed against the norm, serve up a bold challenge to that standard.

There is a fine line between comedy and tragedy for Ludlam. As Ludlam stated, "Othello is the same plot as a French bedroom farce — husband mistakenly thinks wife is committing adultery. One ends in disaster, the other in laughing at people's foibles. The basic human situation is the same. Both are deeply tragic in their way."[17] For this very reason, he recycled old plays and styles in order to glean new meaning, to offer a different perspective. Given the underpinning of homosexuality in ridiculosity that was explored in the previous chapter, it makes sense that Ludlam would take existing forms and offer a new viewpoint. This is precisely how he felt as a gay man in a predominantly heterosexual society, with its prescribed notions of masculinity and femininity. He and many others did not fall within these specific parameters of manhood, so he was compelled to find and present a different perspective, a different twist to the traditionally accepted story. Through his life as a gay man, and from observing the gay community as a whole, Ludlam clearly saw the fine line between comedy and tragedy and explored it fully as a playwright. As he shared once during an interview, "All I'm doing down here is working within a comic tradition using character types that have been around for centuries. I'm just trying to make them live again in a way that's funny and thought-provoking."[18] In all of his plays, though, he never lost sight of the element crucial to any dramatic event — conflict.

Above all else, Ludlam sought to present conflict in his plays, no matter how absurdly wrought. He recognized the distinction between drama and theatre, in that drama performs the storytelling functions and theatre provides the aesthetic experience of the event. Because he majored in dramatic literature in college, he was aware of the importance of form and structure and the dynamics of their influence on the story being told. Early on in his career, Ludlam experimented with a more open, epic-type structure in *Big Hotel, Conquest of the Universe, Turds in Hell*, and *The Grand Tarot*. Ludlam used the term "collage" to describe these plays, because he would cut-and-paste quotations, scenes, poems, one-liners and cartoons and combine them into what usually turned out to be all-night affairs. As he himself admitted, "We knew what the plot was, but I don't know if the audience did."[19] This was an important time for Ludlam, though, because he began establishing parameters for his ridiculous sensibility. He was developing the outrageous nature of performance under the Ridiculous banner, rather than furthering dramatic literature. However, in 1970, after achieving moderate success and a modest but loyal cult following, Ludlam as a playwright had a major breakthrough upon deciding what his next project would be, and hence, the future course of his company:

> Before writing *Bluebeard*, [Ludlam] had reread the works of Ibsen and Scribe. "I was afraid of plot," he explain[ed]. "I'd felt it was something I couldn't do."

But in *Bluebeard* he had come up with a highly serviceable plot, and audiences had been captured by it. Ludlam's theatrical goals changed as a result. Instead of loose, unstructured epics that presented the "real actor" giving free rein to his fantasies, Ludlam embraced the older dramatic verities. "Drama is the playing out of combat and conflict," he says, "and I realized I didn't want to give that up." He also came to the conclusion that art was finite, after all — no more wandering in the Cagean fields of random non-decision. "Art means finding your way through a tangle of possibilities," he said. "It's a closed world, a microcosm."[20]

Indeed, after having wallowed in the muck of psychedelic, free-love theater for a couple of years, Ludlam wrote *Bluebeard*. It had the structure of a well-made play, and it was a resounding hit. This critical turning point for Ludlam gave him the confidence that he could write plays with structured plots without compromising the exploration of the artificial and theatrical style of performance with which he had become associated. He came to believe firmly that drama occurs in a fixed space and time and the story should be told with a definite beginning, middle and end. Instead of running from the confines of plot and structure, he embraced them yet still managed to incorporate the outrages of ridiculosity within this design.

Although his later works contained many more standard plot elements, many of his plays were developed out of the improvisatory work of his company. Because he worked with the same core of actors throughout the majority of his career, he had the advantage of writing characters specifically for the actors who would perform them. Often his actors' suggestions and ideas found their way into his plays. Also, there were many times he would bandy about titles for plays and then write a play to fit a title. His was an unorthodox approach, but it was entirely in keeping with his highly unconventional theatrical vision. As he once stated in an interview, "The actors are constantly giving me ideas and wanting parts. They *want* those parts, and that's why I write the plays. If there was no company wanting parts, I would never write a play. I've never written a play where I didn't know who was going to be in it beforehand and that it was definitely going to be done."[21]

Although his plays were designed to fit the members of his company, the magic in Ludlam's gift as a playwright ensured that the plays also work apart from the original casts, and the reason for this was his discovery that he could still advance his concept of ridiculosity and write compelling, tightly structured plays at the same time. Even when there were moments of improvisation on a given night, if Ludlam happened to think it inspired, he would, with total recall, return home and write it down word-for-word, and hand it back to the actor at the next night's performance. This made his plays very organic and personal.[22]

Although the tone of almost every Ludlam play is a parody of one or another specific genre, style, novel, play or movie, he worked diligently at making his version as truthful as possible. Ridiculosity merely added to the parody. According to Ludlam, "In order to do parody right, you have to do it as well as the original. That gives you the authority to make fun of it. Basically, I'm using these materials not to make fun of them, but because I think they are valuable."[23] He thoroughly researched and studied the original material to be parodied and strove to maintain the basic truth of the initial version. For example, in his production of *Camille*, Ludlam sought, on one hand, merely to tell the story of this love-torn, deviant woman as straightforwardly and faithfully as possible. Then on the other hand, he branded his production with his own sense of fun and outrageousness, especially in taking on the lead role himself in perfect Marguerite drag, except for the chest and underarm hairs. Because of the nature of parody, there was a double edge to everything that Ludlam did, and rarely was either edge subtle.

One of the most important ways in which Ludlam incorporated parody into his playwrighting was his deft use of language as a tool in promoting his sense of ridiculosity. When he was not inventing a new language like that of *Der Ring Gott Farblonjet*, he was using jokes, puns, double-entendres, epigrams and malapropisms, harkening back to the days of vaudeville and burlesque. He was, according to Bonnie Marranca, "A master punster and spinner of the multiple entendre ... he also revels in sexual word play ... spoonerisms, obscenities, literary conceit, distorted references to Shakespeare, allusions to grade-B movies, popular songs, and advertising slogans."[24] In *Reverse Psychology*, he includes the following exchange between Dr. Leonard Silver, a psychiatrist, and Freddie, his patient:

> FREDDIE: Doctor, Doctor, my wife thinks she's a Volkswagen.
> LEONARD: Well, why don't you tell her she's not a Volkswagen?
> FREDDIE: And walk to work?
> LEONARD: Lie on the couch and I'll sit over here. Are you a bed wetter?
> FREDDIE: Yes.
> LEONARD: In that case you sit here and I'll lie on the couch.
> FREDDIE: Doctor, I've had three wives and all of them died.
> LEONARD: What did your first wife die of?
> FREDDIE: Poisoned mushrooms.
> LEONARD: What did your second wife die of?
> FREDDIE: Poisoned mushrooms.
> LEONARD: What did your third wife die of?
> FREDDIE: Fractured skull.
> LEONARD: Fractured skull?
> FREDDIE: She wouldn't eat the poisoned mushrooms.[25]

In *How to Write a Play*, the character of Charles, a playwright, receives a bouquet of flowers which his companion Everett brings to him:

> CHARLES: Who are they from?
> EVERETT: I don't know. Look at the card.
> CHARLES: "With sincere admiration, Ima Pussy."
> *[Mr. Poussy at the front door]*
> CHARLES: Come right in Mr. Pussy.
> POUSSY: How do you do? I know that you didn't care for my ...
> CHARLES: Care for it? I found it fascinating! Sit down, Mr. Pussy.
> POUSSY: Poussy. Ima Poussy.
> CHARLES: Oh don't say that. I'm sure you're wonderful once you get to know you.[26]

In *Bluebeard*, Ludlam not only played with the language, but recycled a characteristic from the Richard Sheridan play *The Rivals*, of the character Mrs. Malaprop, who is constantly misusing words in an attempt to seem erudite. The following passage from *Bluebeard* demonstrates Ludlam's ingenious thievery:

> BLUEBEARD: That is because of a little surprise I have for you. There will be a little entertainment tonight while we are taking our evening meal, a little play I wrote myself.
> MISS CUBBIDGE: Wrote it yourself? You've a touch of erosion, I see, Baron. And yet you studied medicine?
> BLUEBEARD: I write for amusement only.
> MISS CUBBIDGE: Were you indoctrinated? I mean, did you receive the doctorate? On what theme did you write your dissipation? Which degree did you receive?[27]

In two of his plays, Ludlam created an entirely new language, used both for comic effect and to further the parody of the original. In his loving tribute to Molière, Ludlam's *Le Bourgeois Avant-Garde* introduces the character of Moderna, the premiere artist of the avant-garde. Everyone in the play is attempting to make a fool out of Rufus Foufas, a grocer, and his inane desire to be the premiere patron of the avant-garde. Not only does the audience know that Moderna's language is artificial and invented, but we watch as Foufas is duped into believing that this new language is actually something being used by the avant-garde:

> HACK: This is the celebrated graffiti artist, Moderna 83.
> MR. FOUFAS: How do you do?
> MODERNA: Doy de doy.
> MR. FOUFAS: I beg your pardon?
> HACK: He says, "How do you do?"

MR. FOUFAS: He did?

HACK: Moderna expresses himself in Newspeak.

MR. FOUFAS: Newspeak?

HACK: Yes, it's the latest thing. Newspeak is composed entirely of monosyllables which, while having no lexical meaning, convey inner emotional states.

MR. FOUFAS: You mean this speech is pure emotion?

HACK: Not quite. This speech is actually a substitute for emotion.[28]

Here is Ludlam using language not only as a comic tool, but also to make a critical statement about the state of the arts, especially experimental and avant-garde theatre which had abandoned language in the quest for esoteric and symbolic significance. All that was needed was to speak gibberish to classify oneself as avant-garde.

In his parody of Wagner's epic four operas *Der Ring des Nibelungen*, Ludlam invents an entirely new language, beyond everyday speech, which functions within the logic of the story he tells. All the characters, except the gods, use it at one time or another. It is actually derived from the English pronunciation of German and Yiddish words:

SIEGFRIED: Der birds ist gesinging! Und der spring ist geschpringing! Und der animalisch creetures all got another creeture to be animalische with. But Siegfrieds aint got nobody. Er ist ein loneliscshe knabe.

NINNY: Yous got mich, Siegfried.

SIEGFRIED: Eeeeeecht. Du bist eine uglische Dwarf!

NINNY: Ich bin dein vater.

SIEGFRIED: Mein vater? Den who ist mein mutter?

NINNY: Ich ben yer mutter, too.

SIEGFRIED: Das ist unnaturalisch! Ich know dat ich got a mutter and a vater too. Like dem animalische creetures! You bin nix mein farter! Mein vater vin pretty like ich ben. Du bist uglische, yechtilche dwarf!

NINNY: Ich bin ein vater und mutter in one.[29]

These examples help to demonstrate how Ludlam used language to expand the dimensions of parody and artifice in ridiculosity. Either he invented a new language which worked within the logic of the world he had created, or he used puns, jokes and double-entendres to obtain the ridiculous and artificial comic effect. As he himself said, "The theatre is the last repository of the spoken word, a place where the language, unhindered by mundane pragmatic usage, soars to a higher purpose."[30] And Ludlam's higher purpose was to heighten the sense of theatrical artifice in an effort to create a world which functioned completely within its own set of rules; rules which lassoed the representation of ordinary, everyday life on the stage and hurled it toward the grand.

An important inspiration for Ludlam as playwright in his effort to put more grandeur in theatre was, oddly enough, Pablo Picasso. He stated in an interview in 1981 that "I would say, although I've studied Ibsen and Feydeau more, that the great influence on my playwrighting has been Picasso."[31] Perhaps the most important aspect of Picasso which stimulated Ludlam was that, for Picasso, the meaning of art was to be derived from other works of art, not directly from nature itself. Picasso experimented with both form and content throughout his entire career, which led him in various directions, each one building on his previous mode of expression. Ludlam, like Picasso, also viewed art as an articulation of previous forms, evidenced by the fact that he borrowed heavily from past genres. Each experimented a great deal with his personal aesthetic, and each was able to assimilate and work in a variety of styles.

Picasso's influence on Ludlam is also a clue as to how Ludlam conceived of the theatrical event. In addition to Ibsen and Feydeau, he had studied many other playwrights in college and was quite familiar with how each of them structured the theatrical event, but Ludlam insisted on a broader focus, more on the complete aesthetic experience than simply the written story. Picasso's inspiration for Ludlam was not only the need for exploring every aspect of his personal vision, but also the concept that the form of art was just as important in telling a story as the substantive content of the words spoken. In other words, Ludlam created a complete theatrical event, just as Picasso had created a complete work of art, not solely dependent on the characters and dialogue.

Rather, when taken as a whole, Ludlam's work burst through the boundaries of conventional theatrical techniques. Another crucial element for Ludlam in his ridiculous theatrical equation was the acting, which ranged from good to awful, but, under Ludlam's leadership, was always provocative and excessive, and sometimes outright offensive. Ludlam placed a great deal of trust and respect in his actors as participants in the creative process. As we have seen, he was only too willing to incorporate an actor's improvisatory addition to the dialogue if he thought it had merit. Often the play would develop in rehearsals, with actors placing their unique stamp on the characters during the developmental process. He constantly preached to his company that the actor should be self-reliant rather than dependent solely on the playwright and director for creative inspiration. According to Ron Argelander in an article in *The Drama Review*, Ludlam did not "dictate the psychology of the character or block movements."[32] He allowed the actor the freedom to explore a variety of choices during the rehearsal process, with himself acting as editor rather than dictator.

Ludlam worked with mostly untrained actors, but he turned their unpolished acting into an asset; he cultivated their individual styles and helped them lace it with artifice in voice and gesture, and somehow was able to merge them all into a cohesive production. One of the most important things he learned from Vaccaro and the Play-House of the Ridiculous was the importance of the actor's personality in conjunction with the character he was playing. According to Ludlam in a 1981 interview, "I threw out the idea of professionalism and cultivated something much worse than amateurism. I used actors for their personalities, almost like 'found' objects. The character fell somewhere between the intention of the script and the personality of the actor."[33]

Due to his academic stint at Hofstra University, he was familiar with many styles of acting: Elizabethan, melodramatic, commedia dell'arte, classical, etc. Instead of adhering to a slice-of-life realism which he felt was the equivalent of trickery and lies, he approached acting as he approached playwrighting: he recycled past styles and synthesized them all into a unified and unique style intrinsic to ridiculosity. As Stefan Brecht observed during the early years, "Though burlesque and melodrama predominate, a great variety of acting styles brings out the acting and stylization, the variety emphasizes that the performers are developing their own styles according to personal relevance."[34] With Ludlam, everything was possible and almost anything should be tried.

Of course, the argument could also be made that Ludlam surrounded himself with untrained, novice actors in order to highlight his own gifts as an actor and to stand out. This contention not only fits in perfectly with his objective of infusing as much artifice as possible into the concept of ridiculosity, but also it reveals the level of control and authority he had within his company. It would not be unfair to say that Ludlam had an ego; in fact, it was a huge ego. He wrote the majority of his lead roles not for others, but for himself. To anyone who has had the pleasure of seeing Ludlam perform in one of his plays, either live or on videotape, it is instantly clear who is the star and who remains on the audience's mind long after they leave the theatre. As critic James Magruder once remarked, "Ludlam sets himself off from the tone of the stage picture with an attitude or an aside that italicizes himself and punctures either pretensions in the other characters or the pretensions of his own script."[35] Ludlam was usually the only one on the stage with complete mastery of the skills of manipulating the audience and creating an aura of grandeur and focus around himself. For example, in his production of *Salammbo*, he cast a ferociously handsome bodybuilder, Philip Campanaro, who had no previous acting experience, as his love interest Matho, the barbarian. Reviewer Howard Kissel reflected that this Brooklyn-born adonis "apparently studied diction with Yogi Berra and acting with no one...."[36] Of course, Ludlam as Salammbo shone brilliantly against this Greek barbarian who sounded and acted more like Sylvester Stallone. The level of artifice was thereby boosted astronomically, and at the same time, it was clear who was to receive most of the attention.

One cannot fault Ludlam for placing himself in this spotlight; the entire company was fashioned, developed and maintained by him. Since he wrote and directed all the plays, surely it was his right to feature himself. Above all else, Ludlam was a performer and he functioned with a performer's ego. He not only wrote the parts for the other actors, but also fashioned the other lead roles around his own particular comic strengths. He always remained true, however, to his overall objective of defying the conventional modes of realism to attain a level of theatrical artifice which called attention to itself. He just happened to be the most accomplished actor on his stage and the one who, by far, best understood the delicate balance between good and bad acting within the broad scope of ridiculosity.

While in college, Ludlam read a book entitled *Art and the Actor* by the French actor Constant Coquelin, first published in 1880, which left a strong impression on him and was instrumental in the development of his approach to the craft of role creation. Coquelin's main thesis in his book is the discussion and proof, in his opinion, of acting as a creative art. There was ongoing argument in France at that time over the validity of acting as a creative artform because it is not actually creating something from nothing. According to the detractors, who believed acting to be an interpretive craft rather than a purely creative art, the actor works with existing words and characters which have been created by the playwright. Coquelin had a firm belief in acting as a creative art form. He, like Ludlam, believed in the autonomous, creative nature of the actor, and felt that actors should be elevated to repose alongside other esteemed arts, such as painting, composing and sculpting, in the artistic pantheon. Coquelin states in his book,

> I hold that acting is an art; analogous to that of the portrait-painter, for instance. The type which the actor must reproduce (and this is a difficulty unknown to the painter) is not always set before him; he must begin, as we may say, by conjuring it out of empty air like the magician. The author, if he have talent and genius, holds up a perfect image before the mirror of his mind; in other cases — most frequently, as I said before — the actor has but a sketch, a rough model to work from; yet again, he is forced to borrow from the common fund, — that is, human nature, — and to paint in imagination, by dint of observation and reflection, the figure to be realized later on.[37]

Coquelin seems to be emphasizing the actor's act of interpreting a role based freely on his or her own experience, as opposed to by some prescribed method. It is clear to see why Ludlam gravitated to this book, as his ideas concerning the work and the role of the actor fall directly in line with Coquelin's. This may help to illuminate why Ludlam gave his actors total freedom in creating a role, and relied upon and used their often undeveloped talents. He believed that the actor's personality plays as important a role in the process of creating a character as does the written word. This attitude also gave Ludlam permission to incorporate many styles of acting within his aesthetic instead of attempting to present some kind of unified approach, since each actor, in reality, brings only what he or she knows to the creative process.

Not surprisingly, Coquelin also elaborates greatly on the artist's need to look back to forgotten genres in order to develop something new, which by now we know was Ludlam's *modus operandi*:

> There are certain masterpieces — somewhat antiquated, it is true — which are greatly admired when read, but which all agree in pronouncing impossible of representation — let us be bold; which all would call stupid if performed, and which would be so if intrusted to ordinary actors. But let a man of talent come forward; let him take possession of the work buried beneath the dust of indifference — or respect, which sometimes produces the same results as indifference; let this man step in, lavish his powers and his genius upon it, and behold the mummy bursts its cerements, is once more fresh and blooming, and the mob rushes to gaze and goes wild with enthusiasm, and the forgotten masterpiece draws crowded houses! In this case, art is not content with creating, it brings the dead to life![38]

It is conceivable that Ludlam read this passage and took it as his personal call to arms. Luckily, Ludlam had the powers and the genius to create the mummy that "bursts its cerements," and it surely must have been deeply gratifying for Ludlam when the mobs rushed forth, "wild with enthusiasm," and when he brought the "forgotten masterpiece" back from the dead to packed houses.

Although Ludlam may have initially received his inspiration for theatrical artifice from Vaccaro and the early Play-House of the Ridiculous, he took it to new heights unimagined by the early ridiculous visionaries. In his determination to create and develop a new approach to theatre, Ludlam assimilated theatre artifice into every aspect of his production: sets, costumes, playwrighting, acting. His goal was to point out that artifice was a part of our daily lives, whether apparent or not, and that the assumptions we make about ourselves and others are based on biased and, all too often, incorrect information. The Ridiculous Theatrical Company was a performer's theatre with myriad aspects of theatre artifice in place to spotlight the performer. This was the forum from which Ludlam could speak most convincingly about the artifice of human nature. The disguise and impersonation associated with acting reveal its inherent deceptive quality, and for Ludlam, this was the essence, "this business of role play — that the roles are interchangeable, that personality is an artifice in life, and that it can be changed or interchanged."[39]

Ludlam was able to take the theoretical underpinnings of ridiculosity, which we have seen are in direct correlation with a gay sensibility, and combine them with his personal theatrical vision to create a style of theatre which grew out of the depths of cult status into a thriving and energetic expression of theatre. He willingly broke nearly every rule of conventional theatre, imposing his insights onto the theatricality of human existence. And he made people laugh along the way.

Although his style was unique to him, Ludlam's use of theatrical artifice had substantial roots in Brecht and Pirandello and reverberations in British playwrights Tom Stoppard and Joe Orton, who were contemporaries of Ludlam. Brecht's philosophy of alienation dictated that the audience should always be aware that they were watching acting on the stage and not be fooled into believing that a proverbial "slice of life" was being represented. Ludlam, too, was intent on presenting acting that was real by creating a world of pretense through the use of an eclectic, exclamatory style. From Pirandello came the sense that nothing is what it appears to be, that we all wear mask upon mask upon mask, thereby rendering a true and definitive identity utterly elusive. Both Stoppard and Orton used the artifice inherent in melodrama to tell their stories. Stoppard recycled Shakespeare's *Hamlet*, fusing Elizabethan speech with modern language in his play *Rosencrantz and Guildenstern Are Dead*, which interestingly echoes Ludlam's *Stage Blood*. Both playwrights turn the plot of *Hamlet* inside out and rearrange the language and characters in order to gain a new perspective, using parody and artifice. Ludlam and Stoppard also employed the identical tactic of deconstructing text in their respective plays *Le Bourgeois Avant-Garde* and *Travesties*, by starting with a piece of paper that has a line of text written on it, having a character rip the paper up into pieces, each piece containing one word from the line, placing the pieces in a hat, and then connecting the words in whatever order they happened to come out. Obviously, Ludlam and Stoppard shared the view that much of postmodern poetry was the literary equivalent of pulling a rabbit out of a hat. Stoppard is more Shavian and perhaps a bit more didactic in his approach than Ludlam, but the levels of artifice and parody soar in both. Joe Orton shares the expression of homosexuality and defined sexual categories in his plays with Ludlam, while successfully utilizing the same transparent artifice of melodrama. They both also collaged the language of popular culture by assimilating advertising jargon, tabloid journalism and the artificial sensibility of "B" movies, fusing them into a distinctive and satiric dialect. In addition, they each toyed continuously with the fourth wall, sometimes acknowledging it but often ignoring it, thereby heightening the sense of comic theatricality.

"To be or seem to be," which is the basic tenet of Ludlam's play *Stage Blood*, could easily be extrapolated as a motto for his entire theatrical endeavor, illuminating the concept that theatre is inherently not a slice of life, and the attempt to manipulate an audience into believing it is is inherently dishonest. All five of these playwrights — Ludlam, Brecht, Pirandello, Stoppard and Orton — were adamant in the belief that theatricality must be celebrated in the theatre, by definition its natural home, and that a linear cause-and-effect sensibility in dramatic structure and the reflection of everyday life on stage was not necessarily the form which best illuminated profound ideas. All five shared the view that to strongly establish the completely artificial nature of theatre itself was the most effective way to engage an audience into active thought, rather than to attempt to lull them into some sort of a mental stupor and then "brainwash" them.

Ludlam established himself as a theatrical entrepreneur of artifice and pretense in the plays he produced, directed, designed and starred in at his small, rather dungeon-like theatre in Greenwich Village. In order fully to understand Ludlam's vision and the concept of ridiculosity, it is necessary to look more closely at his plays, especially those which were pivotal in both his career and in his artistic growth.

— 5 —
The Ridiculous Plays,
Part One: 1967–1979

Charles Ludlam wrote 29 complete, published plays and numerous unfinished plays throughout his abbreviated life. He produced and directed all of them, designed the majority, and starred in all but one, *Der Ring Gott Farblonjet*. The Ridiculous Theatrical Company, after the schism with Vaccaro, comprised a small group of dedicated actors who were committed to Ludlam and the new company above all else. There were some who came and went over the years, but the devoted few consisted of Ludlam, Bill Vehr, John D. Brockmeyer, Lola Pashalinski, and Black-Eyed Susan. In the mid–1970s Ludlam met Everett Quinton, who became his lover and a faithful follower of the ridiculous as a regular member of the company.

Only Ludlam and Black-Eyed Susan were trained actors, so Ludlam was able to mold this eclectic group according to his own vision. Ludlam's theatre was a performer's theatre. The texts of the plays, which were published posthumously in 1989, offer only part of the story of Ludlam's theatrical vision. An analysis of the plays is meaningless without analyzing the performances as well, when possible, for it was the combination of these two elements that created the Ridiculous Theatrical Company.

Indeed, it is difficult to reconstruct an analysis of the plays in performance without having seen them live on stage. Unfortunately, Ludlam did not discover the value of videotape until the early 1980s, so only a handful are memorialized this way. And viewing these videos does give one invaluable insight into the general nature of ridiculosity in Ludlam's canon. Although Ludlam may have appeared more sophisticated in his later theatrical work with the appearance of more elaborate sets and costumes, the underlying force which drove this aesthetic, theatre artifice, remained constant. And with the publication of his plays, we have the essential resource of the texts to aid in a more thorough analysis of Ludlam's work.

Without the firsthand experience of being in the audience at a Ludlam performance, it becomes necessary to turn to the critics who reviewed the plays to attempt to fill in as many blanks as possible in attempting a more complete assessment of a ridiculous performance. Of course, one must look beyond the personal biases of each critic in order to construct something at least approaching an objective view, as reviewers' opinions are generally more a reflection of their individual tastes than a critical analysis of the work per se. Luckily, Ludlam gave many interviews over the years, and they become a valuable supplemental tool in conjunction with the published reviews.

This section will explore how Ludlam developed his style through the development of the plays and their performances from 1967 to 1979, including, among other things, his use of artifice, drag, design, deliberately bad acting, and the original sources which Ludlam recycled. We will examine the plays, starting with his first play in 1967, *Big Hotel*, up to *A Christmas Carol* in 1979, when the structure and focus of the company underwent some drastic changes, and observe the unfolding of Ludlam's vision, stopping along the way to look more closely at his dramaturgical and theatrical devices and skills in specific plays.

BIG HOTEL

The first play to be examined, indeed Ludlam's first produced play, *Big Hotel*, is classified together with *When Queens Collide, Turds in Hell*, and *The Grand Tarot* under the stylistic banner of collage because in this early period, Ludlam was experimenting with an open, epic-like structure of playwriting and performance. Actually, it was not playwrighting in the traditional sense because Ludlam would take various tidbits from a variety of sources and paste them together, thus creating a collage impression without regard to a logical flow of cause and effect. He was fascinated with the language found in cinema and literature, and his reverence for it was such that he felt he could not contribute a single word of his own for fear of degrading the original. Hence, the approach to these early plays was a veritable "everything but the kitchen sink." As former company manager Steven Samuels noted, "These were chaotic, nonconformist, often all-night affairs."[1]

Big Hotel was first done under the direction of John Vaccaro, prior to the rift that split the ridiculous camps. It was originally just a notebook filled with various lines, quotes, etc., that Ludlam carried around with him, never intending to create a play out of them. It was Vaccaro, however, who persuaded Ludlam to fashion them into a play inasmuch as Ronald Tavel, resident playwright at the time, had left Vaccaro's company. At this point Ludlam and Vaccaro still enjoyed a harmonious working relationship. After the split with Vaccaro, as noted earlier, Ludlam and his faithful followers decided to re-mount *Big Hotel* under the banner of the newly formed Ridiculous Theatrical Company.

Obviously, the very title, *Big Hotel*, is a parody of the 1932 MGM movie *Grand Hotel*, directed by Edmund Goulding and starring Greta Garbo, John Barrymore, Wallace Beery and Joan Crawford. The substitution of "Big" for "Grand" suggests from the top a certain lack of elegance and grace. *Big Hotel*, like *Grand Hotel*, takes place entirely within the confines of a hotel, with many subplots weaving their way around each other. Ludlam's *Big Hotel* includes many familiar names of American films of yesteryear — Norma Desmond, Trilby, Svengali, Lupe Valdez and Maria Montez — but its plot all but defies synopsis because of its many detours in logic and sequence. This was the perfect vehicle for Ludlam to apply his collage technique to because of the many different plots unfolding simultaneously within the hotel.

One of the main plots of *Big Hotel* involves aging film star Norma Desmond, on the run after a string of bad luck and being chased by her manager/agent, Elwynn Chamberpot, who is demanding strict adherence to her contract. Another main plot involves a mystical man from the East called Magic Mandarin, who has come to impart the secrets of yoga to a West that has lost its spiritual way. At the hotel, he meets Birdshitskaya, a famous Russian ballerina, who attempts to commit suicide three times by throwing herself off the roof (actually, in full sight, she throws a dummy off the roof, and then descends to retrieve it). When Mandarin and Birdshitskaya first meet, they dance slowly and rhythmically, pulsating to the tune of *Sophisticated Love*. Although *Big Hotel* is not a musical, it does include a number of musical moments, none of which is intended to further the plots in any explicit way. In between these two plots are various subplots involving the desk clerk and bellhop, two mysterious gangsters, Mr. X and Chocha Caliente, Svengali and Trilby, and even Santa Claus, who makes a brief appearance when the elevator doors open and he falls forward, dead, with a knife stuck in his back. At the end, all the participants in the play/hotel gather in the hotel restaurant, the Firepit, and indulge in the Cobra Cunt Ceremony. Again, this is Ludlam's first attempt at playwrighting, and this play was, in many ways, a manifesto of his denunciation of conventional drama.

Although *Grand Hotel* was the overall inspiration for *Big Hotel*, the direct references to the film are few. The obvious one is, of course, the hotel as a thoroughfare through which an odd assortment of people travel, bringing with them danger, murder, intrigue and glamour. The Greta Garbo role, Grusinskaya, a Russian dancer, is usurped into Birdshitskaya, also a Russian dancer, played in a ridiculous way by Black-Eyed Susan. This is the movie where Garbo utters her famous "I vant to be alone!" In *Big Hotel*, Ludlam takes this famous movie image and burlesques it with Birdshitskaya, who speaks in an ultra-thick Russian accent:

> BIRDSHITSKAYA: Tell to effrevan Ayam not to be disturbed for.
> CRAMWELL: How's that?
> BIRDSHITSKAYA: No von understandse me!
> CRAMWELL: I beg your....
> BIRDSHITSKAYA: Leef me alone! Leef me Lone! Ven vill dey see Ayam just a vomon for? Vat is the use of beingt the great artist for? No von sees me for vat Ayam! *(She rushes out desperately)*
> CRAMWELL: My Russian is rusty!²

The other inspirations and material for this play were many, starting with the obvious, *Sunset Boulevard,* and the character of Norma Desmond. Ludlam also layered his play further by giving Norma Desmond lines from the Dietrich film *Shanghai Express.*

The Cobra Cunt Ceremony is a parody of the Maria Montez classic *Cobra Woman,* and the characters of Mr. X and Chocha Caliente were taken from the Marx Brothers film *Coconuts,* while the Svengali scene is a spoof of the movie *Trilby.* The Blondine Blondell character is taken from a Marilyn Monroe film, *Niagara,* and there are direct passages from Joyce's *Ulysses* and Ben Jonson's *Epicoene* throughout. Bela Bartók's "The Miraculous Mandarin" was the inspiration for the character Magic Mandarin, and other brief moments and bits throughout *Big Hotel* are lifted from comic books (French, Spanish and English), commercials and print advertising, a first-year French grammar, and lines from various Shakespearean plays.

Ludlam ridicules conventional drama and the idea of the well-made play at various points throughout *Big Hotel.* At one point he "reads a passage from *The Poetics* off a paper tissue, and when he comes to the section having to do with the spectacular effects that depend more on the art of the stage machinist than of the poet, [Ludlam] blows his nose in the text."³ At another frantic moment in the play, the bellhop enters screaming that he has lost the thread of the narrative.

Of course, there was intentionally very little thread of the narrative to lose. As Ludlam recalled later in an interview, "What was important for us was to break down that rote quality that you get in most theater — the conventions, the blocking, the techniques used over and over to get points across."[4] One of the methods Ludlam used in *Big Hotel* to break down those conventions he felt produced vapid theatre was to pull people in off the street and shove them up onto the stage. Once an old vaudeville actress came backstage during a performance to hock makeup and Ludlam, admiring her eccentricities, invited her to go on stage and relive some of her vaudeville days, which she did with aplomb. Also, during a scene with a rather riotous chorus line of drag queens, Ludlam opened the door to every drag queen in New York City who wished to participate, and many did. They would show up on any given performance night in their feminine apparel and would instantly become part of the cast, making up the play just like everyone else.

Aside from the parts of the play which were open to the actors' imagination and improvisatory skills, many of the scripted moments included some outrageously corny lines and sight gags, all of which became seeds for Ludlam's garden of theatre artifice. An example of this occurs when Mr. X and Chocha Caliente sneak in after the commotion caused by Birdshitskaya tossing a look-alike dummy of herself off the roof:

> MR. X: It was a lucky thing for us we were able to slip in here during the confusion caused by Birdshitskaya's plunge.
> CHOCHA: She wore a plunging neckline.
> MR. X: One more line like that and I'll wring your neck.[5]

One can almost hear the groans in the audience after this exchange.

A good illustration of how Ludlam took old vaudeville routines and incorporated them into his plays occurs in *Big Hotel* in a scene between Drago Rubles, a drunken gambler, the desk-clerk and the bellhop:

> DRAGO: Hi! My horse just came in first and I won a trillion dollars.
> BELLHOP: A trillion dollars! Why, Drago Rubles, a few hours ago you were a broken-down gambler, and now you're a trillionaire. Wow!
> DRAGO: Not exactly. Then I bet a trillion dollars on a horse and it came in last.
> CRAMWELL: So now you're a completely penniless bum.
> DRAGO: Not exactly. Then I found two dollars in a urinal and bet it on a horse who came in first.
> CRAMWELL: How much did you win?
> DRAGO: A buck and a half.
> CRAMWELL: That's not enough for a room.
> DRAGO: I know. Anyway, I spent it on a cab coming up here.
> CRAMWELL: You can't stay here with no money.
> DRAGO: Coming up the front steps, I slipped and broke my back.
> CRAMWELL: But …
> DRAGO: Let me finish. So I sued the hotel and won.
> CRAMWELL: Then you own the hotel, sir …

DRAGO: Not exactly. I bet the bellhop he couldn't spell the words "portnoy trusses" backward *(Turns to BELLHOP, who spells "Portnoy trusses" backward)* ... and he won the hotel.

CRAMWELL: Then he's my boss.

DRAGO: Not exactly. While the hotel was mine, I fired you, and the position is still open.

CRAMWELL: *(To BELLHOP)* Hire me! Hire me! Please!

BELLHOP: I choose ... *(Spins in circle blindfolded)* him! *(Points to DRAGO who immediately goes behind desk. CRAMWELL starts out)*

DRAGO: Where are you off to, Cramwell?

CRAMWELL: The races! *(exits)*[6]

This particular scene has nothing whatsoever to do with furthering any plot; it is added only to emphasize the artificiality of the theatrical event.

Another example of this is found where Ludlam combines sight gags with the recycling of movie dialogue. Here, it happens with the characters of Norma Desmond and her agent Elwynn. The image of Gloria Swanson in *Sunset Boulevard* descending the stairs and requesting her "close-up" is enshrined in the annals of film culture which Ludlam appropriates for his play, but with an added twist:

NORMA: Tell Mr. deMille I'm ready for my close-up.

(Agent throws a pie in NORMA's face. Blackout.)[7]

From television commercials and print advertising comes a scene between Drago and the Marilyn Monroe-like Blondine Blondell as they enter the Firepit Restaurant for the Cobra Cunt Ceremony:

(Enter BELLHOP as in old Philip Morris ad.)

BELLHOP: Call for Blondine Blondell! Call for Blondine Blondell!

(Enter BLONDINE on the arm of DRAGO RUBLES.)

DRAGO: We're going to go to Marshall Field. I'm gonna buy you the sleaziest sexiest gownless evening strap you ever saw. *(To Waiter)* Table for two.

BLONDINE: Oh Drago, that sounds just elegant and kind of dreamy, if I may say so ... *(Looking at menu)* How about some orange juice, Joey? *(Aside to audience)* I ate Limburger cheese with bagels for breakfast. I ate mofongo with garlic dressing at lunch. I ate steak and onions at dinner. But he'll never know, 'cause I always stay kissing sweet the new Dazzle-Dent way.[8]

In the original script, Ludlam has Norma and Blondine audition for a radio commercial:

NORMA: Be proud of your bathroom bowl tonight after you use poop-off bowl cleanser. Because poop-off cleanser is 100% poopoo-proof, get your bowl bold-white tonight. Insist on poop-proof cleanser, the cadillac of toilet bowl cleansers. Feel fully secured the next time you sit down to take a load off your feet.[9]

Here Ludlam is snatching elements from popular culture to bolster the sense of artifice and camp by alluding to advertising, one of the icons of a free-market, capitalistic society. By taking these kinds of moments out of context and putting them on stage, he points out the very artificial nature of mass-market advertising, as well as the ridiculously arbitrary method in which consumers decide what and what not to purchase. These moments are not intended to function solely as disembodied snippets of satire. Their sheer absurdity adds to the overall comedy in the play.

Ludlam begins *Big Hotel* with a scene taken directly from the "Prologue in Heaven" from Goethe's *Faust* with the characters of God and the Devil, only this God gooses the Devil and pinches his cheek. He follows this with a prologue, spoken by Elwynn Chamberpot, the agent, taken verbatim from Ben Jonson's *Epicoene*. Of course, what may have attracted Ludlam to this play in the first place was Jonson's own habit of "borrowing" from other sources, such as the mock combat between La Foole and Sir John Daw in *Epicoene*, which is recycled from Shakespeare's *Twelfth Night*, from the counterfeit duel between Sir Andrew Aguecheek and Viola. Jonson, in the overall plot of a melancholy protagonist (in *Epicoene*, even the character's name is Morose) who is tricked into marrying a verbose wife, is taken from a number of old and familiar sources: the Greek sophist Libanius, Ovid's love poetry, and the Roman comic dramatists Plautus and Terence. Although Ludlam was a maverick in his approach, he was by no means the original.

After the wildly frantic Cobra Cunt Ceremony, Mofonga, as King Cobra, "dances wildly, sensuously, pointing to each member of the cast in turn. When selected, the actor screams, 'No, I don't want to be a dishwasher,' and is thrown into the flames of the Firepit Restaurant by perfumed slaves with oiled bodies. Finally, all are sacrificed and the slaves too throw themselves into the flame,"[10] and *Big Hotel* comes to a screeching halt.

The two characters in the play featured in drag were Ludlam as Norma Desmond, wearing the traditional Desmond turban and using his eyes and hands as if they were being manipulated by some outside power, and Mario Montez, cult film drag queen, in wildly exotic drag as Lupe Valdez. From the original production photographs, he looked like a cross between Rita Moreno and Joan Rivers. Ludlam sets the stage here for his ideas of role-playing and gender identity in plays to come. Since each actor played numerous roles in *Big Hotel*, the emphasis was not on drag, but instead on the chaotic tendencies toward surrealism in Ludlam's experimentation.

Because of the transitory nature of the performances, the sets were little more than moldy flats scattered with garage-sale junk, creating an overall aesthetic which could best be described as tacky-elegant. For example, as hotel furniture there was a chair with steer-horns on stage.

Overall, this play has no meaning behind it and was not intended as a political or social statement; it must be taken at face value. It laid the groundwork for the other plays to come and started the pursuit of ridiculosity off with a bang. When *Big Hotel* first opened under Ludlam's Ridiculous Theatrical Company, however, it was not well received by the critics. Truthfully, Ludlam was lucky to have even had one critic in attendance at all since he was on the fringe of the fringe of Off Off Broadway. The *Village Voice* noted that "a vast and numberless cast of characters flops around uselessly for several hours, striking few sparks and starting no fires." The reviewer went on to add, "Ludlam permits his cast to stretch every scene well past its breaking point, each collapsing like a deflated balloon."[11]

Undaunted, Ludlam continued experimenting with this lack of dramatic structure, which was popular in the avant-garde experimental theatre of the 1960s, and continued his "collage" approach with the three plays that followed: *Conquest of the Universe or When Queens Collide, Turds in Hell* (co-written with company member Bill Vehr), and *The Grand Tarot*. Critical response continued to be mixed, but more and more reviewers began to take notice of Ludlam's gifts and were willing to give a second look at what they had originally thought was just bad theatre. For *Conquest of the Universe*, the *Soho Weekly News* observed, "*Conquest* takes Marlowe's *Tamberlaine the Great*, the great *maker* of dramatic literature, and introduces him to Flash Gordon. On the way, they rip off Shakespeare, Alexander the Great, the borscht belt, *Faust*, The House of Atreus and Leonardo da Vinci."[12] Martin Washburn of the *Village Voice* called *Turds in Hell* "very ingeniously staged, with unrelated scenes — simultaneously presented, focus shifting form one to the next, somewhat in the manner of a complex baroque painting."[13] And Martin Gottfried of *Vogue* magazine, in his review of *The Grand Tarot*, wrote that Ludlam had created a "deliriously ridiculous and tacky baroque, combining the broad performances of silent movies with the extravagant plotting of melodrama."[14] Throughout the development of these plays and the working dynamics of the ensemble, Ludlam experimented and explored the terrain of his versatile imagination, lifting dialogue and scenes from a variety of sources and fashioning them into an often incoherent, but nonetheless theatrical whole. But even the raves Ludlam received from various critics did not translate into money at the box office. He struggled to pay rent, to buy a minuscule amount of advertising, and to build a following larger than the mere smattering of cult-attenders in the audience. Ludlam also began to realize that infinite drama and plot were actually negations of themselves.

So, as the sixties closed, so too did Ludlam's version of epic and collage theatre, where the loosely structured to nonexistent plots gave free rein to the actors' fantasies. He began to rethink his priorities and goals and to develop a different kind of play, one that more closely resembled the structure of the well-made play, with a linear beginning, middle and end, and a more logical (if that word can ever be applied to Ludlam) sequence of events. The collage period was important in that it launched Ludlam's aesthetic tendencies, but it was not bringing him closer to his ultimate goal — a thriving American comic repertory theatre. His next play, *Bluebeard*, was the product of this period of rethinking and the first one to attract any major press. As Calvin Tomkins of *The New Yorker* noted, "In *Bluebeard*, [Ludlam] had come up with a serviceable plot, and audiences had been captured by it."[15] It was to be a decisive turning point in Ludlam's career.

BLUEBEARD

Although the main source for *Bluebeard* was H.G. Wells' novel *The Island of Dr. Moreau*, later turned into a movie, *The Island of Lost Souls*, starring Charles Laughton and Bela Lugosi, Ludlam also borrowed from Marlowe's *Dr. Faustus*, Bela Bartók's one-act opera *Bluebeard's Castle*, Sheridan's *The Rivals*, and every Gothic melodrama and "B" horror movie and villain ever created. Determined to change the course of his company, Ludlam toiled over the structure of this new play, struggling to write a drama that was actually confined by time and space but was still permitted the excesses of ridiculosity. Although there were still some elements of collage in *Bluebeard*, this time they were added expressly to further the plot, as opposed to his previous plays where various unrelated elements were tossed together deliberately to create an unstructured, chaotic effect.

The primary source, *The Island of Lost Souls*, centers on Dr. Moreau, a recluse and medical school dropout who has exiled himself onto a deserted island in order to create a new race of beings. Dr. Moreau is experimenting in his laboratory, dubbed the "House of Pain," with the creation of a half-man, half-animal he called a "Manster." Although he has not been completely successful thus far in these experiments, he has formed several laboratory rejects, looking like hairy men with big ears, who huddle together in a cave under the terror of Moreau and are forced to live by "The Law," a set of rules devised by the doctor in order to maintain some semblance of order. Dr. Moreau is a classic evil man, a mad scientist out of touch with society, whose intention is to deflate Darwin's theories of natural selection and evolution and to prove that the continuing development of science can systematically change the course of evolution, and thus of mankind, forever. He is visited by a young man, washed ashore from a shipwreck, who becomes the subject of Moreau's next experiment. Moreau's efforts fail and he is ultimately destroyed at the end of the film.

A secondary source, Bartók's *Duke Bluebeard's Castle*, with a libretto by Béla Balasz, is based on Perrault's well-known fairy tale. In that tale, Bluebeard's last wife is given the keys of his household and told that she may open every door save one. Naturally, she opens the forbidden door only to find hanging there the severed heads of his former wives. Balasz and Bartók's version internalizes the horror; the figures take on universality, becoming Everyman and Everywoman; the wives' heads are not actually severed, but they suffer a severance still more terrible. When Judith, Duke Bluebeard's new wife, opens the doors she finds a torture chamber behind the first, an arsenal room behind the second, jewels and crowns (spotted with blood) behind the third, a field of white roses (spotted with blood) behind the fourth, a panorama of meadows, forests, and mountains behind the fifth, a vast lake of tears behind the sixth, and behind the seventh the former wives, each bedecked in jewels and riches and entombed for eternity. Bluebeard fetches a crown and places it on Judith's head, despite her avid protests. However, the weight of the crown is too much, and she takes her place among the other wives, slowly retreating behind the door, leaving Bluebeard alone with his memories.

Ludlam, in his version, created the main character of Baron von Khanazar (pronounced with a long gargling and stuttering "kh"), a medical school dropout from Denmark (he studied with I. Kutchakokoff!), whose experiments seek to create a third type of genitalia. As in both the movie and the opera, he lives on a deserted island, banished from the rest of the world. The play opens with Sheemish, the butler, and Mrs. Maggot, the housekeeper, who are both products of Khanazar's failed experiments, preparing for the arrival of the Baron's niece, Sybil, who is sailing in on the *Lady Vain*. While dusting and cleaning, Mrs. Maggot tips over a vial with liquid and it smashes to the floor. Sheemish, in an attempt to gain the upper hand in this relationship, threatens to tell Khanazar, who will undoubtedly send Mrs. Maggot to the "House of Pain." In an effort to replace the sticky liquid of the vial, Mrs. Maggot puts the test tube under her dress and urinates in it.

The Baron sees his niece, Sybil, as the perfect specimen for his experiment, and he begins preparations for the operation. Unknown to Khanazar,

Sybil brought with her to the island her fiance, Rodney Parker, and her governess, Miss Flora Cubbidge. At first Khanazar is incensed at the presence of the uninvited guests, but he soon realizes that he now has two specimens — Sybil *and* Miss Cubbidge — which only adds to his diabolical pleasure. With his mystical powers of persuasion, he manages to convince both of them that he loves them and gives each a key to his laboratory, forbidding them ever to use it. Meanwhile Lamia the Leopard Woman, another failed experiment, is found spying around Bluebeard's castle, seeking revenge on the malevolent Baron. Eventually Sybil unlocks the laboratory door and, under Khanazar's spell, becomes his next victim. Listening from outside the locked door, Rodney, Lamia and Miss Cubbidge hear blood-curdling screams as the operation gets under way. The Baron makes it a point never to use anesthesia. When the door is opened we behold Sybil, wrapped in gauze from head to toe, wearing only high-heeled shoes. As the gauze is slowly unraveled we see the results of the experiment: a nude Sybil with a new sexual organ which looks terribly like the claw of a chicken with the nails painted red, coming out of her crotch and moving as if it has a life of its own. We then learn that Mrs. Maggot is really Sybil's mother, and they all, including the servants, are relieved of their fear of Khanazar and immediately leave the island, promising to tell no one of what has happened. As the play ends we find Baron von Khanazar alone, screaming that he is a failure, while Sheemish, the only servant left, tries to console him by telling him that he has a heart and talent as our Bluebeard exits yelling, "Heart! Talent! These are nothing, my boy. Mediocrity is the true gift of the gods."[16]

Ludlam has taken the basic tenet of the movie, the attempt by man to manipulate the biological evolution of humans, and has translated it into a ridiculous attempt to create a new sexual being. Of course, Ludlam's ridiculosity is always laced with elements of candor, this play notwithstanding. Thematically, this play works on a number of levels. First, the very need to create a third sexual being indicates Ludlam's frustration with the level of bigotry against homosexuality. A gay man is not sexually attracted to women, and if society makes it difficult, if not torturous and impossible, to be true to one's homosexual desires, then that society has forced the logical, if not absurd, solution of a third type of genital organ onto the homosexual community. As ludicrous as this may sound, it must have seemed equally ludicrous to Ludlam, and to many other gay men as well, to feel so maligned by the straight world for merely being sexually attracted to other men. Indeed, how difficult it is to develop and maintain a "normal" relationship in a society that constantly tells you how abnormal you are. Also, this is perhaps an insight into Ludlam's fears of his own fate as a homosexual. All throughout his early diaries and notes, Ludlam constantly bemoans his fate and wonders if he will ever meet a nice man and fall in love. It is apparent that his love life, prior to meeting his life partner Everett Quinton, was not always pleasant or fruitful. In *Bluebeard*, Khanazar, in a quandary, articulates his feelings, which Ludlam based on a famous speech from *Dr. Faustus*:

> KHANAZAR: Is to end desire desire's chiefest end? Does sex afford no greater miracles? Have all my perversions and monstrosities, my fuckings and suckings, led me to this? This little death at the climax followed by slumber? Yet chastity ravishes me. And yet the cunt gapes like the jaws of hell, an unfathomable abyss; or the boy-ass used to buggery spread wide to swallow me up its bung; or the mouth sucking out my life! Aaaagh! If only there were some new and gentle genital that would combine with me and, mutually interpenetrated, steer me through this storm in paradise![17]

On another level, and perhaps one that could raise a few eyebrows, Ludlam chose a female in *Bluebeard* to be the bearer of the third genital. Was he making some sort of statement about how he felt about women? Just because he was not attracted sexually to females, did he feel they were dispensable? If the experiment with Sybil is any indication, what he has created is a female body with a phallic protrusion. However, given the fact that Ludlam and company chose different objects at different times to serve as the new genital, it is clear that he was not using the chicken claw to symbolize, or comment on, anything specific. According to Black-Eyed Susan, "We used different genitals sometimes. At one college we used two parsnips and an eggplant. Charles Ludlam thought the genital should be organic. When we were in Brussels, they thought the lufa was too phallic; so we used a cabbage — purple with sparklers in it."[18] It wasn't the actual physical appearance of the new genital that was important, but instead the destruction of the dualistic yin and yang philosophy. Ludlam was particularly drawn to Aristophanes in Plato's *Symposium*, and to the description of people as spheres who were divided into male and female by an angry god and spent their lives searching for their other half. According to Ludlam, "To me, the third genital means the synthesis of the sexes."[19] For Ludlam, who obviously experienced both feminine and masculine tendencies, this idea seems particularly appropriate. However, the fact remains that this new creation was for all intents and purposes a woman, alluding, possibly, to some bisexual tendencies in Ludlam.

Ludlam even throws in some of Christopher Marlowe's *The Tragedy of Doctor Faustus* in the first act of *Bluebeard*. Of course, the obvious correlation between these two tragic characters — Faustus and Bluebeard — is mortal man attempting to acquire powers beyond human understanding and limits. As in the Marlowe play when a Good and a Bad Angel appear to Faustus, symbolizing the internal struggle, each tempting Faustus toward its side, Ludlam does the same in *Bluebeard*:

> GOOD ANGEL:
>   Bluebeard, lay these thoughts aside,
>   And think not on them lest it tempt thy soul
>   And heap God's heavy wrath, upon thee.
>   Take half — one sex, that's all — for that is nature's way.
> BAD ANGEL:
>   Go forward, Bluebeard, in that famous art
>   Wherein all nature's treasure is contained:
>   Be thou on earth as God is in the sky.
>   Master and possessor of both sexes.[20]

Ludlam even has Bluebeard draw a circle of blood on the ground, which was borrowed from Marlowe's account of Faust conjuring Mephistopheles.

As for the elements of artifice in *Bluebeard* that contribute to Ludlam's furtherance of ridiculosity, there are many. Given the transitory nature of the early company, the set for the original production was necessarily minimal. A gay bar in Greenwich Village, Christopher's End, set up a couple of planks between the bars for the stage, and the company worked with only props and a few inventive set pieces. For example, the laboratory, or "House of Pain," was merely a tiny chair which looked like an explosion of box springs, providing ample opportunity for shtick. A bit later, though, Ludlam and company were renting customary theatres and the sets became more detailed and involved.

By the time *Bluebeard* appeared at the Evergreen Theatre at 53 East 11th Street, Ludlam had created an entire horror chamber complete with bats and cobwebs. Dangling from the proscenium arch dripped cardboard icicles of blood, and an exotic leopard skin covered the piano. At the rear of the stage, through a small, high window, the audience could see a gigantic hearing aid, which Khanazar used as a spying device, eavesdropping on everyone and everything.

Ludlam's beard (and pubic hair, for that matter) were the color of a bright blue Brillo pad, and the red Shriner's fez he wore on his bald head was a perfect complement to his bright red pantaloons, creating a Turkish whirling dervish effect. According to critic Martin Gottfried, "[Ludlam's] Bluebeard is nothing short of a comic masterpiece, complete with a blue beard, a crackling horror-movie laugh and endless details (like a pinky ring on rubber gloves)."[21] By this time, Ludlam had perfected the art of declamatory acting. "Flamboyant gestures and mincing speech combine in an extravagantly grotesque performance,"[22] wrote Sylviane Gold of the *New York Post*. "His eyes roll; his body quivers with anxiety; and, truth to tell, the spittle flies, in a passionate demonstration of the art of possession. Ludlam's creation is unforgettably maniacal,"[23] wrote David Sears of the local New York paper, *Villager*. Ludlam was trying to bring back to the theatre a grand tradition of theatrical acting, where the artifice of style, so totally infused with the text, appears to be the only logical choice.

John Brockmeyer, who played the Karloffian servant Sheemish, had a hump on his back so big that it "totally obscure[d] his head when he turn[ed] his back."[24] To some, it appeared as if this hump had a mind of its own. Although Brockmeyer's imposing stature gave him the appearance of invincibility, whenever his Sheemish was threatened with detention by Khanazar, he would grab his groin and scream, "No, no, not the House of Pain!"

Lola Pashalinski, who played the governess, Miss Flora Cubbidge, was continually described in the press as "Rubenesque" because of her voluptuous figure. Perhaps the most memorable scene in the entire play occurs when Khanazar, in an attempt to steer Miss Cubbidge toward the laboratory, seduces her using every inch of the stage. According to the stage directions, "They begin to breathe heavily as they undress slowly. They move toward each other, wearing only their shoes, socks, stockings, and her merry widow. They clinch and roll about on the floor making animal noises. There follows a scene of unprecedented eroticism in which MISS CUBBIDGE gives herself voluptuously to BARON VON BLUEBEARD."[25] In a review of a faithful 1991 revival of *Bluebeard* by Everett Quinton, we get a glimpse of Ludlam's original staging of this spoof on every pornographic movie ever made:

> [Bluebeard] slowly removes each article of his clothing, patent-leather zippered jock strap and all, folding them meticulously till Miss Cubbidge is driven into a state alternating between frenzy and complete boredom. He sniffs her armpits, wedges her open with painstaking effort and then dives into her head first, disappearing, poof, right before our eyes. Bluebeard re-emerges after a time, slightly dazed, pulling out after him a turban which he had neglected to remove.[26]

In every production of *Bluebeard*, just when the audience thought the seduction scene could not possibly get more absurd and hysterical, Ludlam always pushed the limits, drawing out the laughter to an uproarious pitch. At one performance, Lotte Lenya (the chanteuse and wife of Kurt Weill) was in the audience, and backstage after the show in the dressing room said, "I've never seen anything like it. It was very pure. After this who could go to shitty Broadway."[27]

Although much of the success of *Bluebeard* was a result of Ludlam's inspired comic staging, his ingenious use of language contributed greatly to the overall effect of artifice. For example, when Sybil's intended, Rodney, asks Sheemish about the strange Baron, Sheemish answers with:

> SHEEMISH: I have been his servant on this island nineteen years and I will say this — just between us — that in my master, Baron Khanazar, the Bluebeard, you see the vilest scoundrel that ever cumbered the earth, a madman, a cur, a devil, a Turk, a heretic, who believes in neither Heaven, Hell, nor werewolf: he lives like an animal, like a swinish gourmet, a veritable vermin infesting his environs and shuttering his ears to every Christian remonstrance, and turning to ridicule everything we believe in.[28]

Later in the play the Baron's niece Sybil, staring at her uncle while in a trance, asks Khanazar if he is really as bad as everyone says; the Baron replies, "When I am good, I am very, very good; but when I'm bad, I'm not bad. I'm good at being bad ... I do it well."[29] And Ludlam kept the audience constantly aware that they were in the theatre watching a play:

> MISS CUBBIDGE: What about dinner?
> BLUEBEARD: I've lost my appetite.
> MISS CUBBIDGE: What about the play?
> BLUEBEARD: I detest avant-garde theater.[30]

Perhaps the most resourceful use of language was Ludlam's gentle reminder in the character of Miss Cubbidge (who, as noted in the previous chapter, harkens back to Mrs. Malaprop in Sheridan's *The Rivals*) that what he was attempting to accomplish was not entirely novel. Both characters tend to select words that sound similar to what they intend to say but have different meanings, creating a level of humor which rises directly out of the text, rather than from physical gags.

For Ludlam, *Bluebeard* began a journey into a theatre oriented toward the classics — reinvented and parodied — and performed in a style that many saw as harkening back to the Elizabethan and Restoration styles, with a smattering of modern soap opera layered in for good measure. As theatre critic Tish Dace observed, "All this not only imbues the plays with theatrical values of former ages, but it makes the burlesques of the classics grounded in thorough mastery of the original."[31]

Following the success of *Bluebeard*, Ludlam and troupe managed to secure a tour to Europe, where they performed *The Grand Tarot*, *Bluebeard*, and a new play they had been developing called *Eunuchs of the Forbidden City*, set in prerevolutionary China. They performed to enthusiastic audiences in avant-garde theatre festivals in Belgrade, Zagreb, Vienna, Berlin,

Frankfurt, Copenhagen and London before various booking fiascos and miscommunications forced them to return to the United States, broke and exhausted. Upon return, though, Ludlam discovered that the Ridiculous Theatrical Company had received a grant of $10,000 from the National Endowment for the Arts, and he suddenly felt that his dream of a national comic repertory theatre was closer to reality than he ever imagined. He immediately wrote a country & western musical, *Corn*, with music and lyrics by Virgil Young. It starred Lola Pashalinski, who in the course of the play, ends up resolving the ancient Hatfield and McCoy feud. It was Ludlam's next play, though, that brought him the most praise and critical bravos to date. In fact, his performance cast such an indelible impression that it would remain his "signature role" throughout his entire career. He had always fantasized about playing Marguerite Gautier, the Lady of the Camellias, and now he proceeded to write his own version which he called *Camille: A Tearjerker.*

CAMILLE

Ludlam's rendering of this famous romantic story is a mixture of the original Dumas *fils* play, the Verdi opera *La Traviata*, and the classic film with Greta Garbo as the ailing courtesan. The story of the Lady of the Camellias began as a very successful novel by Alexandre Dumas *fils*, the son of an already successful writer, in the mid–1800s. The narrative begins at an auction of the property of the debt-ridden Marguerite, who has just died from consumption at the tender age of 23. This worked beautifully in the novel, but Dumas knew that the story transposed to dramatic form could not begin at the ending. He was acutely aware that the play must end with her death.

The original play begins at the theatre where Armand Duval first meets Marguerite, although he has been amorously aware of her for over a year. Armand emphatically proclaims his undying love for this creature of the night and vows to take her away from all this depravity. Although she is nagged by a constant cough, she insists on maintaining the only life she knows — the night-life. She "employs" various gentlemen who, in turn, keep her well supplied with lace, jewelry, flowers, carriages and apartments. Armand cannot hide his jealousy. After doctors order Marguerite to rest, she and Armand go away to the country for a summer and Marguerite is at once filled with memories of her humble and simple childhood. She is happy and in love, perhaps for the first time in her life. However, Duval père arrives and asks Marguerite to abandon his son because she is not a respectable woman and is squandering his son's fortunes. Marguerite informs him that she, in fact, has been selling her jewels and belongings to pay off her debts, that she has not taken a single penny from Armand. Duval ceases his indignant insults but persists with his request that she leave Armand and forget him forever. She returns to Paris, which crushes Armand's heart. They do not reunite until the very end of the play, when Marguerite is on her deathbed. Armand rushes in, knowing the truth now about why she left. She sees him and they hold each other passionately. Now she can die in peace, and she does, in the arms of Armand.

Ludlam's attraction to this character was, no doubt, steeped in his homosexuality. Like most other gay men, Ludlam was made his entire life to feel like an outcast and a deviant. He felt an identification with and a compassion for Marguerite, who found herself marginalized because of who she was. No matter how hard she tried, society would always think of her as inferior. In a sense, she was forced to her lonely death by an arrogant and hypocritical society. This kind of discrimination was something that Ludlam understood very well: an outcast longing for and dreaming about a perfect love, forbidden to them by society's rigid and self-serving moral dictates.

Ludlam was determined to maintain the integrity of the original story, but from a ridiculous angle, naturally: For example, in the original story the Baron de Varville brings roses and white lilacs to Marguerite. Marguerite defiantly asks the Baron what she is known as — the Lady of the Camellias — and why. She asks her maid to put them in the other room. In Ludlam's version, Varville brings birds of paradise and aspidistra, and instead of asking the maid to dispose of them, she throws them on the stage from offstage while screaming, "Now take your birds of paradise and get your aspidistra out of here,"[32] a not-so-subtle comic twist on the action and the words.

Ludlam basically followed the plot of the original play. Dumas ends the first act on a fairly melodramatic note:

> MARGUERITE: Armand, do not deceive me — remember that any sudden shock can kill me; Armand, remember who I am, and remember what I am.
> ARMAND: You are an angel, and I love you!
> NANINE: Madame —
> MARGUERITE: What is it?
> NANINE: I have a letter for you, Madame!
> MARGUERITE: A letter! It seems to be the night for them. From who?
> NANINE: The Count
> MARGUERITE: Are they waiting for an answer?
> NANINE: Yes, Madame

MARGUERITE: (clasping her arms around ARMAND) You tell them — you tell them there is none — CURTAIN[33]

In the first act ending of Ludlam's parody, he concocted a ritualistic sadomasochistic dance between Marguerite and the Baron, heightening the melodrama and the ridiculous simultaneously:

MARGUERITE: You play beautifully.
VARVILLE: You lie beautifully.
MARGUERITE: (Masking Varville) Thank you, that's more than I deserve.
VARVILLE: On no, it's not half as much as you deserve. (They laugh. Doorbell. The clock begins striking twelve) I wonder who it could be at this hour.
MARGUERITE: (Handcuffing Varville to the piano) If I told you, you wouldn't believe me.
VARVILLE: Try me.
MARGUERITE: (Whipping him) I could say that someone has found the wrong door. (Laughs).
VARVILLE: The great romance of your life! (Laughs)
MARGUERITE: That might have been! (Starts to whip the piano)
(They both laugh — she ironically, he bitterly — as the curtain falls.)[34]

At the end of Ludlam's *Camille*, a dying Marguerite lies in bed, coughing and wheezing, when she calls across the room to her maid:

MARGUERITE: I'm cold. Nanine, throw another faggot on the fire!
NANINE: There are no more faggots in the house.
MARGUERITE: No faggots in the house? Open the window, Nanine. See if there are any in the street.[35]

Knowing that on any given night, a large gay contingent filled his audience, Ludlam was pulling off a gigantic "wink" at the audience with such lines, a wink that would become a mark of his artistry. As New York critic Clive Barnes explains, "It is the art of the melodramatic comic aside seen in terms of the movie camera."[36]

Ludlam's *Camille*, although faithful to the events of this sentimental story, is filled with sight gags and "bits" intended to keep the audience emotionally involved with the story, but at a safe comic distance. For example, in Act Two when Marguerite and Armand escape to the country, at one point she pours herself a cup of tea and proceeds carefully to place twelve sugar cubes in her cup, one by one, and then hesitates with the thirteenth, deciding against it. Later in the very same scene Ludlam's Marguerite exclaims, "'Marriage is nothing but legalized prostitution' (Salutes with a fist. Throws a strawberry up and catches it in her mouth)."[37] But in the final act of Ludlam's play, the gags and bits subside somewhat and a sincere dedication to the melodramatic death scene prevails. It was always Ludlam's intent to infuse this tragic love story with ridiculous lunacy, to tread the fine line between the sublime and the grotesque. As Calvin Tomkins remarked, "The first act of *Camille* was played for laughs, but in the second act matters grew increasingly serious, and the third act death scene almost invariably reduced some in the audience to tears."[38] Of course, this was Ludlam's design all along as evidenced by his admission, "When I finished writing my adaptation, the comic and the tragic converged perfectly."[39]

When Ludlam appeared on stage in drag as the ill-fated courtesan, what the audience saw was a faithful rendering of a nineteenth century melodramatic heroine with hair in black ringlets, gloves, a fan, and a low-cut, sleeveless mauve gown — which openly displayed Ludlam's abundant chest hair. According to Ludlam, "I invite the audience to laugh at me from the first moment by showing my chest. I'm not tricking them like those female impersonators who take off the wig at the end of the act. Yes, I want the audience to laugh, but they should also get the impact of forbidden love — it is really tragic and shocking."[40] Ludlam was making the point that he was an actor playing a role, just like every other actor in the play. Of course, the tradition of cross-gender casting is as old as the drama itself, but in today's homophobic society where men fear their feminine side, Ludlam used the tragic story, combined with his versatility as an actor to "lure them gradually into forgetting, to make it more amazing later on."[41] He was also providing graphic demonstration concerning the very nature of femininity, showing that many of its aspects which are assumed to be innate are actually applied and cultivated.

By keeping artifice at the surface, Ludlam was able to tell the story of the Lady of the Camellias faithfully, and also simultaneously to comment on it by juxtaposing the comic with the tragic. As one critic noted, "Ludlam's Marguerite Gautier is simultaneously both terribly funny and terribly moving, both ethereally beautiful and grotesque, both real and artificial, both a man in a dress and a woman...."[42] It was this quality that so enthralled his audiences and the critics, who did not know exactly what it was they were both laughing and crying at. Ludlam used ridiculosity to maintain a distance from the play, while at the same time investing all of his emotions into the tragedy of the character, ultimately creating a level of sympathy true to the original intent of the story.

As we have already observed, not only did Ludlam invest artifice in the physical trappings of his *Camille*, he also manipulated and used language and shtick to keep the story from wallowing in the already-inherent sentimentality. Some examples of Ludlam's ridiculous use of language and dialogue in *Camille* include:

MARGUERITE: I wear red camellias when I've got the rag on ... when the moon is not favorable to pleasure. I'll be wearing white ones tomorrow.[43]

* * * *

OLYMPE: I just found out today that Saint Gaudens is of Polish extraction.
MARGUERITE: No.
OLYMPE: His dentist is Polish.[44]

* * * *

SAINT GAUDENS: Your hollandaise was divine, my dear.
MARGUERITE: It's especially good around the Jewish hollandaise.[45]

* * * *

NICHETTE: You'll see, Marguerite. One of these days you'll fall like a ton of bricks.
MARGUERITE: Me, fall in love? *No, no, Nichette!*
NICHETTE: Toodle-oo Marguerite.
MARGUERITE: Ta-ta, Nichette.[46]

This last sequence of lines — "Toodle-oo" and "Ta-ta" — remained a running bit throughout the play; every time Nichette and Marguerite would part, this would be their send-off, even in the final scene of the play.

Perhaps the epitome of Ludlam's tragic/comic face-off occurs in the death scene, transfixed in many minds and hearts from the Garbo film. As Ludlam's production closely followed the action, theme, characterization, costuming, etc., of the original *La Dame aux Camellias*, the audience genuinely became emotionally involved in the increasingly pathetic situation of this pair of storm-tossed lovers. "Ludlam himself would get so carried away some nights that he would have to conceal his own deathbed sobs from the audience."[47] Ludlam set the stage perfectly for the final scene by staying fairly faithful to the original scene between Marguerite and Duval père, the turning point in the play, in which the father entreats her to stay away from his son:

MARGUERITE: One last favor.
DUVAL: Ask it.
MARGUERITE: Within a few hours, Armand will experience one of the greatest sorrows he has ever known, or perhaps ever will know. He will need someone who loves him. Will you be here, sir, at his side?
DUVAL: You are a noble girl. But I am afraid.
MARGUERITE: Fear nothing, sir. He shall hate me.
DUVAL: I shall never forget what I and my family owe you.
MARGUERITE: Make no mistake, monsieur, whatever I do is not for you. Everything I do is for Armand.
DUVAL: Is there nothing I can do for you in acknowledgment of the debt that I shall owe you?
MARGUERITE: When I am dead and Armand curses my memory, tell him that I loved him and that I proved it. We shall never meet again. Goodbye.[48]

This scene, despite some of the previous ridiculous antics, allows us to see the compassion and love in the character of Marguerite Gautier in universal terms, regardless of Ludlam's obvious maleness. As Ludlam himself said, "in the end you are either moved or won over. You believe in the character beyond the gender of the actor."[49]

The kind of heart-wrenching choice that Marguerite must make is something that anyone can relate to, and Ludlam's honest portrayal in this scene of genuine heartbreak was breathtaking. On her deathbed, Ludlam's Marguerite, just as in the original, summons her best friend Nichette to her:

> NICHETTE: Marguerite, you wrote me that you were dying, but I find you up and smiling.
> ARMAND: *(Aside)* Ah, Nichette, I am so miserable!
> MARGUERITE: I am dying, but I am happy too, and it is only my happiness that you can see... And so you are married! ... Look at that... What a strange life this first one is. What will the second be? ... You will be even happier than you were before. Speak of me sometimes, won't you? Armand, give me your hand. Believe me, it's not hard to die. That's strange.
> ARMAND: What?
> MARGUERITE: I'm not suffering anymore. I feel better, so much better than I have ever felt before... I am going to live. *(Appears to sleep)*
> GASTON: She is asleep.
> ARMAND: *(With anxiety at first, then with terror)* Marguerite! Marguerite! Marguerite! Don't leave me! Please don't leave me!
> GASTON: She loved you dearly, poor girl.
> NANINE: *(On her knees beside MARGUERITE)* Much will be forgiven you, for you loved much. Toodle-oo Marguerite.
>   CURTAIN[50]

Just as Ludlam takes the melodrama and sentimentality to their limits, Nanine ends the entire play with her endearing yet comic "Toodle-oo Marguerite," which brings the audience right back to the artificial and ridiculous play they are *really* watching. As New York critic Clive Barnes wrote in his initial review of the play, "You can, and possibly will, laugh until the tears run down your cheeks — but remember to question yourself whether all the tears are those of laughter."[51]

Ludlam's dramaturgical and theatrical sensibilities had evolved so that he was now much more in command of his writing skills. Throughout the plot of his *Camille*, he was able acutely to balance the comedy and the tragedy by creating a comic tension wherein the audience expected that, at any moment, no matter how tragic, something uproariously funny would tear them apart. It was this compatible fluidity of intentions, moving the audience from rippling titters to convulsive guffaws to sensitive silence and again back to rippling titters leading to convulsive guffaws leading to sensitive silence, that proved a breakthrough for Ludlam. For this reason, following the critical success of *Camille*, Ludlam was no longer merely an underground artist, but one whose ridiculosity was taken seriously by audiences and critics alike.

In February 1974, Ludlam and the Ridiculous Theatrical Company opened *Hot Ice*, patterned on the old-style Hollywood gangster films, particularly Raoul Walsh's 1949 *White Heat*, starring James Cagney. In Ludlam's *Hot Ice*, the forces of life, the Cryogenic Society, whose mission it is to stamp out death — "America's number one killer" — are pitted against the forces of death, the Euthanasia Police Force. Ludlam played crackpot ace detective Buck Armstrong, a member of EPF who goes undercover as a graduate with a degree in air conditioning and refrigerator repair to solve the mystery. The *New York Times* said *Hot Ice* was filled with "a manic collection of gags, wordplays and horseplay, with enough sense beneath the nonsense to make the evening frozen food for thought."[52] Although the play received a few good reviews, it attracted little audience and closed in four months. It is clear that with *Hot Ice*, Ludlam was still experimenting with dramatic structure, even to the point of including audience participation, but his efforts resulted in a confusing and often tedious plot. Ludlam's next project, *Stage Blood*, which opened on November 11, 1974, examined the very nature of acting through a ridiculous parody of *Hamlet*, using as his vehicle a theatre company's struggle to mount a production of the play.

STAGE BLOOD

Stage Blood, or "Highlights from Hamlet," as Ludlam gleefully referred to it, deliberately spotlights the artifice in acting; even its very title implies the illusion of theatrical blood used on stage rather than the real blood of life. It also represents the "stage blood" that flows through every actor's veins. Ludlam closely followed the plot of Shakespeare's *Hamlet*, except that in Ludlam's version the story unfolds in the real lives of the actors performing the play. The story of Hamlet is universal and, therefore, has been a part of the worldwide repertory since its inception. Ludlam adopts Shakespeare's "play-within-a-play" motif and uses that as the structure of *Stage Blood*. Throughout, he comments on the art of acting and declares that "To be or not to be" would be more precisely read as "To seem or not to seem."

The characters in *Stage Blood* include Carlton Stone, Sr., founder of the company, who has been relegated to the role of the ghost because of old age; Carlton Stone, Jr., the son, who has reluctantly inherited the lead role; Helga Vain, Junior's mother and Gertrude in the play; Edmund Dundreary, the practical joker of the troupe playing the role of Claudius, who is also the not-so-discreet lover of Helga; Jenkins, the stage manager and aspiring playwright; Elfie Fey, a starstruck young hometown girl who steps into the role of Ophelia; and Gilbert Fey, her strict and manipulative father. The plot revolves around a cash-starved, small-time traveling theatre troupe, the Caucasian Theatrical Company, who, because of booking errors and financial need, find themselves in Mudsville, U.S.A.— Everytown — performing their production of Shakespeare's *Hamlet*. They have just fired their Ophelia when in walks Elfie Fey, a local girl who just happens to know all of Ophelia's lines and is hired on the spot. Meanwhile, Jenkins, the stage manager, is attempting to convince Stone, Sr., to produce his 1,800-page play, *Fossil Fuel*, much to Stone, Sr.'s dismay. Eventually, night falls and the curtain goes up on Act I, Scene I of *Hamlet*, played with Shakespearean accuracy. However, at the end of the scene, a bloodcurdling scream is heard and Carlton Stone, Sr., is discovered dead, with his head in the toilet and a trickle of blood running from his ear.

In Act Two, Helga and Edmund, their affair no longer a secret, conspire to have Edmund take over the reins of the company instead of Carlton, Jr. Elfie's father, Gilbert, arrives and forbids his daughter to go on stage. He promises Carlton, Jr., that in return for discouraging his daughter from being an actress, he will reveal who murdered his father. Reluctantly, Carlton agrees to speak to Elfie after the evening's performance. After the two perform the scene where Hamlet chastises and abandons Ophelia, Carlton repeats precisely the same scene (minus the Shakespeare) in the dressing room trying to dissuade Elfie from acting. Previously in that same scene, when the Ghost enters as in *Hamlet*, another Ghost enters and chases the first Ghost off the stage.

Throughout the remainder of *Stage Blood*, the son, Carl, tries to find the culprit who murdered his father, eventually believing it to be his mother and her lover. As Elfie tells Carl, "You're just like Hamlet, seeking to avenge your father's death."[53] In the end we learn that Carlton, Sr., disguised as his twin brother Gilbert, has faked his own death and devised an elaborate charade as a way to teach his son how *really* to play the role of Hamlet. Instead of a stage littered with dead bodies, we find everyone happy, pairing off for sexual escapades: Stone, Sr., with his mistress, Elfie; Helga with Edmund; and Stone, Jr., with Jenkins, in what they call an "experimental relationship." As the actors leave the stage, we are left with an image of the "other" Ghost leaning against the proscenium, reading a copy of *Variety*, after Carlton, Jr., has just asked, "There's just one thing I can't figure out. Pop was playing dead in the dressing room, but we saw him go on as the

Ghost. How could he be in two places at the same time?"[54] Thus, the audience is left mystified, wondering if the supposed fake murder mystery was ever really solved.

Ludlam knew he wanted to write a parody of *Hamlet*, but he also desired to write a ghost story/murder mystery. In his usual unconventional, renegade manner, he revealed that he had borrowed a book from a friend called *How to Write a Murder Mystery* which contained a list of things you should *never* do when writing a murder mystery — and did them all.[55] He did, however, see *Hamlet* as a play about the nature of theatre and life, of acting and living, and felt it was necessary to weave in his own theories throughout the Danish tragedy as a way to heighten the sense of artifice. On another level, he felt that *Stage Blood* also epitomized the theme of an actor who is reluctant to play the famous and complex role of Hamlet, which opened the door for Ludlam to spring his ideas about acting on us.

Ludlam touches on the very nature of theatre via the juxtaposition of the onstage scenes with the ones off stage. Critic Elenore Lester points out,

> By moving back and forth between the stage on which the actors struggle with the classic lines and the miserable dressing rooms in which they eat their sandwiches (ham or turkey?), live out their private fantasies and prepare for the transformation into foreign psyches, Ludlam dramatizes basic questions about the very nature of theatre.[56]

Using that structure, the entire plot of *Stage Blood*, with Carlton, Sr., tricking his son into reacting and making choices as the character Hamlet, gives us some idea of Ludlam's desired approach to the art of acting. Early in the play, the father lectures his son on the rigors of being a thespian, based on Hamlet's speech to Rosencrantz and Guildenstern:

> STONE: Son, I can't tell you how to play Hamlet any more than I can tell you how to play this flute. In order to play Hamlet, you have to have *been* Hamlet. Why, look you now, how unworthy a thing you make of Hamlet! You would play Hamlet; you would seem to know his stops. You would pluck the heart of his mystery. You would sound him from his lowest note to the top of his compass; and there is much music, excellent voice, in this little organ, yet you cannot make it speak. 'Sblood, do you think Hamlet is easier to be played on than a pipe? Call Hamlet what instrument you will, though you can fret over him, you cannot play him.... *Hamlet* gave to the mystery story the one quality it had formerly lacked, the quality without which it could never attain greatness ... a streak of the irrational.[57]

Although at first this may sound a bit strange coming from Charles Ludlam, the master of artifice, he actually believed that absolute honesty was crucial to acting, and he committed to each and every one of his roles with equal vigor. The primary difference between the various characters in Ludlam's plays is merely in which particular world of illogic a given character resides. As long as the actor can believe the illogic to be logical and then truly live in that new logic, then any artistic choice would be justified. As Ludlam himself said, "If actors could seem to be possessed by their roles, they could justify any kind of theatrics, because the conviction of motivation was there to fill out this bigger form."[58]

Also, sprinkled throughout the play are lines which directly reflect Ludlam's innermost feeling about the theatre and acting. In Act One Jenkins, the playwright/stage manager, argues with Carlton, Sr., in favor of the Stanislavski system of acting that the previous Ophelia worked under, saying, "You didn't understand her acting because she was Stanislavski-trained. She works honestly and truthfully."[59] Carlton, Sr., interested more in magic and mystery, answers with, "What do you know of honesty and truth? I call it lies and deception. Deceiving the audience into believing in surface reality, illusion. The great actor gives you a glimpse beneath the surface. Something that lies beyond your honesty and truth."[60] Ludlam's credo on the theatre and acting is suggested throughout *Stage Blood*, as in the following exchange:

> EDMUND: I'm for a good story with a message you can take home with you. And I'm sure that everyone in this company will back me up.
> JENKINS: Of course, of course! Everyone will agree. But that's the M.D.R., baby, Minimum Daily Requirement: a good story that raises an issue. But what then, huh? Repeat the old forms? never! *(Shouting like Lear)* Recycle! Waste nothing! Do you hear what I'm saying? Cling to the Now through which all Future plunges to the Past!!![61]

At one point in Act One the character Carlton, Jr., gives the young ingenue Elfie some tips on acting after she asks him some pointed questions about the nature of the craft. Here Ludlam uses his script to blatantly proclaim his dictum on artifice versus reality on the stage, including the specific matter of how one produces real tears in a character:

> ELFIE: When you act, do you really become the character?
> CARL: *(Emphatically)* No, that would be dangerous. Acting is the art of seeming, not being.
>
>   * * * *
>
> ELFIE: There's something I've always wanted to know about acting. When you have to cry on stage, actually produce real tears, night after night, how do you do it?...
> CARL: Throughout the great ages of the theater, the greatest actors of every generation have, well, uh ... my mother always did it this way. *(Grabs a Kleenex from the dressing table and begins to cry violently)*

> ELFIE: *(Amazed)* Real tears!
> CARL: Would you like to try it?
> ELFIE: Yes!
> CARL: Take this onion, take this handkerchief. Now, holding the handker-
> chief in the right hand and the onion in the left (of course, if you're facing
> in the other direction, it's all reversed, but we'll get to that). Now, the hand-
> kerchief is like a little stage curtain, concealing the onion from the audi-
> ence's view.... Forget the play, the scene, the character, just go for the eter-
> nal thing; go for the emotion. Work yourself up.[62]

Aside from the use of artifice in acting, Ludlam also points to the
artifice of the theatre in the character of Edmund Dundreary, a practical
joker who, throughout the course of the play, constantly plays pranks on
his fellow thespians. When Elfie enters claiming she knows the role of
Ophelia, launching into the mad scene, Edmund offers her a rose in appreciation, which squirts in her face. At another point in the play, Edmund
and Stone, Sr., argue over the necessity of putting Shakespeare in modern
repertory:

> EDMUND: I always found Shakespeare too long and windy.
> STONE: Yes, you wouldn't want to break your wind! *(Sits on a "farting cush-
> ion," which Edmund has placed unbeknownst to the others)* A pooh-pooh
> cushion! *(Throws it at Edmund)* You practical joker![63]

At the top of Act Two, Edmund is seated on the toilet reading *Variety*, while Helga sits at her dressing table removing her makeup. When she
opens the cold cream, she screams as a snake jumps out at her, put there
by Edmund. When Carlton, Jr., confronts his mother about the mysterious death of his father, the scene parallels Act Three, Scene Four in *Hamlet*, in which, within the Queen's bedroom, Hamlet tests Gertrude's honesty and Polonius is stabbed while hiding behind the arras. In Ludlam's
version, however, Carlton, Jr. hears a noise behind the costume rack, picks
up a prop sword and plunges it into the clothes. As Helga shrieks, Edmund
suddenly falls through the dressing room door with a dagger stuck in his
back. As both mother and son gasp in horror, Edmund jumps up with a
laugh and pulls the dagger out, demonstrating his latest trick — a blade
which retracts into the handle. And, at the very end of the play, when all
the trickery has been revealed, Edmund continues with his jokes, giving
his new love Helga a jewel case, which she opens only to be greeted by a
mouse that pops out. Ludlam inserted these bits in *Stage Blood* as a
reminder that artifice in the theatre is sometimes used merely for the purpose of entertainment. Ludlam felt that above anything else, actor, writer,
director, etc., he was an entertainer, squeezing every laugh out of each play
with sublime indulgence.

Obviously, Ludlam borrows heavily from Shakespeare's *Hamlet* in his play, but he also transposes lines and scenes from other sources to create even more layers throughout *Stage Blood*. In Act Two when Carlton, Jr., alone and naked in his dressing room, ponders the death of his father, Ludlam inserts a passage from James Joyce's *Ulysses* about a father-son relationship from the point of view of the father which Ludlam inverts into the son's perspective. The ghost of his father appears unexpectedly and recites to Carlton, Jr., a speech taken directly from Thomas Kyd's *The Spanish Tragedy*, another father-son relationship passage that Joyce, curiously enough, was parodying in *Ulysses*.[64] Ludlam, though, maintains the father's perspective in this last example, thus giving us both sides of the coin. Here, Ludlam was not only giving voice to other playwrights, he was also speaking with his own voice. In an interview he once stated that while working on *Stage Blood*, he was remembering his feelings about his own father, whom he remembered saying, "Children! I should have raised pigs, I'd be better off!" He went on to state that "The real murderer of the father was me — killing my father in fantasy, working through and finally forgiving him. It was a milestone for me."[65] So Ludlam uses this commingling of textual references, *Hamlet*, *The Spanish Tragedy*, and *Ulysses*, to define his own artistic voice using his method of recycling and recombining, a main tenet of ridiculosity, through which he creates something completely fresh.

Ludlam also parodies the "play-within-the-play" scene in the first act of Chekhov's 1896 comedy *The Seagull*. Nina is performing with Treplev in a play that he wrote which is highly esoteric and symbolic, and the mother, Madam Arkadin, sits in the audience scoffing and ridiculing her son's work. Eventually Treplev storms off, hurt and offended. In Act Three of *Stage Blood*, Carlton, Jr., and Elfie perform a staged reading of Jenkins' 1,800-page play, *Fossil Fuel*, an avant-garde, nonverbal piece, for the company in hopes of eventually producing it. Ludlam transposes the conflict of mother and son in *The Seagull* onto Helga and Jenkins, the stage manager/ playwright in *Stage Blood*, although the son, Carl, is still very much involved.

By transposing Chekhov's scene into *Stage Blood*, Ludlam brilliantly layers his text with yet another classic scene, but one which allows his opinions on avant-garde art and theatre to surface, well in keeping with his vision of recycling established material. He rarely used outside material in his plays in a nebulous way, but rather he would incorporate and manipulate it in such a way that it would become a loudspeaker for his own voice.

Although the very title of the play *Stage Blood* implies artificiality, Ludlam and company remained fairly straightforward and sincere, perhaps a bit tame, in their approach to this script. Alas, this was to be its downfall.

Although many critics praised Ludlam's work, some were disappointed in its lack of outrageousness, including Marilyn Stasio of *Cue Magazine*, who wrote, "The usually inspired company is showing little of the invention that won them their honored name of Ridiculous."[66] It was a guest critic for the *New York Times*, Julius Novick, author of *Beyond Broadway: The Quest for Permanent Theaters*, however, who Ludlam felt did the most damage to the play. He wrote that "To do what Ludlam is trying to do in *Stage Blood* takes more wit, more intelligence, more talent, than he has been able to muster."[67] Unfortunately, many audience members seemed to agree with Mr. Novick's assessment, apparently disappointed that Ludlam had not included any ambiguous sexuality or perversity, no one was in drag, there was little nudity, and almost nothing vulgar was displayed or said. Nonetheless, Ludlam still believed in the validity of *Stage Blood* as part of the Ridiculous canon.

In hindsight, *Stage Blood* can be considered a vital rung in Ludlam's ladder of plays, heading onward toward a more defined and dramatic Ridiculous theatrical event. Compared with *Big Hotel*, *Camille*, or *Bluebeard*, *Stage Blood* must have seemed rather tame in nature; however, its text is far richer and more complex than anything Ludlam had attempted to that point. Unfortunately the play lasted only three months, stranding the Ridiculous Theatrical Company with a sizeable debt.

In the spring of 1975, shortly after *Stage Blood* closed, the company hurriedly produced a revival of *Bluebeard*, bringing back Mario Montez as Lampia the Leopard Woman. It received rave reviews and revived the company's spirits. While *Bluebeard* was running, Ludlam was fast at work on a new play, tentatively called *Fashionbound*, a spoof of the fashion industry. They also learned that the Baha'i Church had bought their home, the Evergreen Theatre, forcing them to leave. Before the move, though, Ludlam and troupe staged a fund-raiser on November 20, 1975, called *Tabu Tableaux*, which included scenes from his previous ten plays, plus a teaser from *Fashionbound*. A sold-out house at $25 per seat attended, easing the company's financial situation and also confirming Ludlam's growing popularity.

Fashionbound became *Caprice* and opened in February of 1976 at the Performing Garage, where it played for a few weeks before moving to the Provincetown Playhouse. The plot involves two conniving and famous clothes designers, Claude Caprice and Twyfford Adamant, who steal everything from each other, including lovers. *Caprice* was not well received by the critics or the audience and closed within weeks. Undaunted by the negative press, Ludlam and company had a work waiting in the wings, *Der Ring Gott Farblonjet*, a parody of Wagner's four-opera saga *Der Ring des*

Nibelungen, which opened a couple of weeks later in April of 1976 at the Truck and Warehouse Theater on East 4th Street.

DER RING GOTT FARBLONJET

The irony is immediately apparent in Charles Ludlam's parody of *Der Ring des Nibelungen* by Richard Wagner, an admitted anti–Semite. The very title contains a Yiddish word. Michael Feingold, critic for the *Village Voice,* translates *Der Ring Gott Farblonjet* into "The Ring Which Gets God Confused," or "lost or sent into a state of total confusion by God," or perhaps "so lost even God couldn't find it,"[68] already a ridiculous beginning for Ludlam's most expansive work yet. Feingold adds that putting a Yiddish title on a work by Wagner "suggests an intent to cut down not only the length of Wagner's work but also its lofty Aryan mythicizing."[69] Another critic wrote that, "[Ludlam] turned Richard Wagner's virulent anti–Semitism into a boomerang by sprinkling a truncated version of the Master's epic with shticks derived from the Yiddish theater."[70] There are no outright polemics throughout this play which speak directly to issues of race and religion, but the abundant use of Yiddish, or at least Yiddish-like words and phrases scattered throughout the play, along with the title, hinted at Ludlam's intended target.

In *Der Ring,* Ludlam remains fairly straightforward and accurate with his storytelling, condensing Wagner's four-opera, fifteen-hour magnum opus into a four-act, three-and-one-half-hour play, with each act representing one of the four operas: *Das Rheingold, Die Walküre, Siegfried* and *Götterdämmerung.* Wagner began each epic opera in the cycle (except, of course, the first) with a lengthy summary of previous events, which Ludlam discarded, allowing him to shorten the telling of this ancient Teutonic myth. Because of the scope of this ambitious project, Ludlam opted not to perform in *Der Ring Gott Farblonjet*'s cast of 16, but instead directed and designed the sets and costumes. The music was provided by Jim McElwaine.

Ludlam used *Der Ring* to explore his fascination with language. As Steven Samuels has written, "Of all contemporary American dramatists, only Ludlam had consistently concerned himself with the creation of a stage language that went beyond the diction of everyday speech. In *Der Ring Gott Farblonjet*— inspired by the Joyce of *Finnegans Wake*— Ludlam sought a comic, theatrical esperanto, hoping to make his work accessible to as broad an audience as Wagner's operas."[71] Ludlam, like the revolutionary Wagner, was intent on creating his own "Masterwork," one for the twentieth century. With this in mind, it is the language of *Der Ring* which provides most of the artifice in this theatrical event. According to Ludlam, "*Der Ring* abandoned literal speech and went into a completely abstract poetical language. Because it was about the evolution of man and thought, it was also the evolution of language."[72] In Wagner's opera each character is given a musical leitmotif, one that can be identified throughout the entire cycle. In Ludlam's version, he creates linguistic leitmotifs where "the Nihilumpens speak in potato-German; the Gibichungen speak an elevated revenge-tragedy Elizabethan speech; the Valkyries — chaste, heroic, virgin lesbians — have Gertrude Steinian speech."[73] By incorporating this method, Ludlam remains perversely true to Wagner's original intent, all the while using this pattern to his own ridiculous advantage. For example, in Act Three of *Der Ring*, the condensed version of Wagner's *Siegfried*, Siegfried and his adopted parent Ninny speak in their leitmotif of "potato–German," an invented language based on the English pronunciation of German and Yiddish words:

> SIEGFRIED: (*Threatening NINNY with the sword*) Tell mir who wast mein mutter und vater or ich will yer ass gekillen!
> NINNY: (*Trembling with fear*) Nay! Nay! Killt mir nicht! Und ich will sich tellen der truth. Dein mutter sar Sieglinda who died heir. Und left you in mein care! She gabe you yer name, und she gave me dis. (*Gives him the pieces of the sword*)
> SIEGFRIED: Dis ist mein onlisch heritage, ein broken sword? Gibt das pieces! Ich will siech schowen was einn gut sword really ist![74]

Although foreign sounding, Ludlam has crafted a language that sounds vaguely familiar, in a pseudo–German way, resulting in a ridiculous and highly artificial effect. And the absurdity is compounded when the same characters speak in the same manner every time they are on stage. Ludlam flamboyantly transposed Wagner's idea into a style which brought enormous amounts of attention to itself, thereby adding to the level of artifice.

Juxtaposed against this potato–German leitmotif and often clashing with it, Ludlam has the Gibichungen in Act Four of *Der Ring* speak in an elevated Elizabethan style:

> GUNTHUR: Did heresy keep the hangdog beggar? Anathema could ere be beautiful as thoughts strong and bold!
> HAGEN: Why touch upon such themes?
> GUNTHUR: Bring the victims to slaughter. I will reserve my best ability, my heart, my heart, my honor, only to thee. Only to thee.
> GUTRUNA: How might I bind this man to me?
> HAGEN: A potion precious, pleasant as ambrosia and red nectar. To his nostrils and he will turn to you.
> GUTRUNA: By the frozen and inconstant moon I will withdraw and prepare the magic draught.[75]

Another important element of artifice found in his Act Two version of *Die Walküre*, which Ludlam subtitles *The Dyke Bikers at Helgeland* (lifted directly from Henrik Ibsen's play *The Vikings at Helgeland*) allows Ludlam to saturate ridiculosity with overtones of pop culture. Here, Ludlam uses what he calls Gertrude Steinian speech, obviously parodying the stereotypical masculine image of lesbians. Not only is their speech "butch," but Ludlam uses this theme to comment on the lesbian's supposed feminist disgust with men:

> ORTLINDA: Brunnhilda. Brunnhilda? Where is Brunnhilda?
> VALTRAUTA: She eighty-sixed.
> ORTLINDA: With a hero?
> ROSSWEISSA and HELMVIGE: We saw her fly to the east.
> GRIMGERDA and SCHWERTLEITA: We saw her fly to the west.
> GERHILDA and SIEGRUNA: And she was carrying a woman!
> ORTLINDA: A straight woman?
> BRUNNHILDA: *(Enters hurriedly)* Lesbic sisters, save me! High Lord Val Father is after me. And this woman is pregnant!
> SCHWERTLEITA: Why have you brought a straight woman here? You know the rules.
> BRUNNHILDA: Shut up, Schwertleita. She carries in her womb the fetus of a hero.
> GRIMGERDA: Does she need help to get an abortion?
> BRUNNHILDA: This woman's seed must not miscarry. The genes are of the very highest quality.
> HELMVIGE: You're wasting your time. Try though you may, you'll never make a thoroughbred of mongrel Man.[76]

Ludlam also maximizes the sense of artifice with his sets and costumes, paralleling his sense of recycling of the script with the recycling of everyday objects to create mythic landscapes and images. Partly owing to a limited budget, but also as a deliberate means to promote his style, Ludlam fashioned his Nordic world out of junk, giving new meaning to the present-day concept of recycling garbage. Ludlam boasted that there was not a single natural fiber on his stage, with every object and garment being an ironic and fake antithesis of what it represented. Everything about *Der Ring* screamed artifice, from the three-piece band playing everything from Wagner selections and Rheingold beer commercials to the low-comedy sound effect of farting each time someone mentions "the bowels of the earth."

The level of artifice in *Der Ring Gott Farblonjet* is an allegory unto itself. It symbolizes, among other things, the artifice inherent within gay sensibility, which produced ridiculosity. On another level, Ludlam comments on his perception of the artifice of the commercial theatre in believing itself to be on the cutting edge of art, while in reality pandering to a lowering common denominator, spending ridiculously huge sums of money in the process. He also shows up the so-called avant-garde and its reduction of everything, including language, into an abyss of silence. On yet another level, Ludlam assimilates his sense of being an "outsider" because of his sexual orientation onto the stage in three dimensions via the sets and costumes. If commercial theatre and heterosexuality are the axioms imposed by those who feel they set the standards, then the level of artifice in *Der Ring* is a belligerent send-up to those self-appointed arbiters of theatrical "good taste." When Ludlam boasted that every physical element of *Der Ring* was synthetic, he was thumbing his nose at the imposters, deflating their biases by acknowledging and celebrating the artifice in a bold and ridiculous, up-front kind of way.

Der Ring Gott Farblonjet received mostly favorable reviews, but again that did not translate to the box office. Within a few months, it was performed only on Sundays, with *Stage Blood* brought back for the weekend evenings. During this time, though, Ludlam had become fascinated with ventriloquism after purchasing a dummy in Belgium. Needing a break from producing big ambitious shows, he teamed up with Black-Eyed Susan in *The Ventriloquist's Wife*, which he wrote. They performed it in various Greenwich Village nightclubs to packed houses. Based on the 1945 Michael Redgrave horror film *Dead of Night*, the play featured Ludlam as a down-on-his-luck actor who buys a wooden dummy in a pawn shop and names it "Walter Ego." He and his wife (Black-Eyed Susan) incorporate "Walter" in a nightclub act, where the dummy eventually begins to take over. The wife eventually amputates every wooden limb of Walter, which enrages the actor to the point where he becomes the dummy.

Early in 1978, Ludlam and his band of folly signed a ten-year lease on a theatre at 1 Sheridan Square in Greenwich Village. In December of that year, after months of renovations, he presented his new play, *Utopia, Inc.*, which he borrowed from Shakespeare's *The Tempest* and the Bob Hope–Bing Crosby movie *The Road to Utopia*, with additional parodies of lines, settings and business of such cult sagas as *Curse of the Mummy's Tomb*, *Forbidden Planet*, *Journey to the Center of the Earth* and *Lost Horizon*. It was poorly received by the critics and attracted hardly any audience. With no new production at hand, Ludlam decided to bring back past hits: *Camille*, *Stage Blood*, *The Ventriloquist's Wife* and *Corn* to play in repertory until he could figure out a new direction.

In April of 1979 Ludlam opened his new play, *The Enchanted Pig: A Fairy Tale for the Disenchanted*, based on a Romanian fairy tale by Andrew Long, with elements of *King Lear*, *The Frog Prince*, *Three Sisters* and *Cinderella* tossed in for good artificial measure, and finally found a success after a considerable dry spell. Mel Gussow of the *New York Times* wrote, "*The Enchanted Pig* is a pun-filled romantic adventure that cribs from a diversity of sources, spoofing but not debasing material ... it is easily in a class with such vintage Ludlam extravaganzas as 'Bluebeard' and 'Camille'."[77] Ludlam closed the 1979 season with a faithful rendition of Dickens' *A Christmas Carol*, which he planned to perform every year in the tradition of most established repertory companies. It was well received by both the critics and the audience. After closing the play in January of 1980, the company left on a tour of the West Coast, stopping in Vancouver, British Columbia and Seattle to perform *Bluebeard*, *Camille*, and *Stage Blood* in repertory before finally settling in San Francisco, where they had a contract for an indefinite run. Oddly enough, Ludlam was not well received in San Francisco, a city known for its large gay community, because, according to company manager Steven Samuels, "The stress of repetition had finally worn Ludlam and his cohorts down. The core of the acting ensemble, whose members had worked steadily together for thirteen years, finally broke up under personal and — not coincidentally — financially pressures."[78]

Both John Brockmeyer and Lola Pashalinski left the company to pursue other ventures. Ludlam came to the realization that the Ridiculous Theatrical Company "could no longer be a company with a past. We had to be a company with a present and a future as well. There are two ways for a theatre to grow: you can find new audiences for your old works, or you can create new work for your old audiences. We had been doing the former for a long time. Now it was time for something new."[79]

Upon his return from this disappointing tour, Ludlam regrouped and worked out a new artistic policy for the coming decade: he would remain at home and write new plays — farces — and reconstruct his company, supplementing the loss of Brockmeyer and Pashalinski with some fresh faces and talent.

— 6 —
The Ridiculous Plays, Part Two: 1980–1986

The start of a new decade marked the start of a new artistic policy for Ludlam and the Ridiculous Theatrical Company, with a vow to present only new, original works. He began in April of 1980 with a new play, a farce entitled *Reverse Psychology*, and a new actress, Charlotte Forbes, who was an old college friend of Charles and Black-Eyed Susan. As one critic noted, Ms. Forbes "has the look of a flamingo suffering severe pangs of conscience from being made to dress up as a lion."[1] *Reverse Psychology*, with a small cast of Forbes, Ludlam, Bill Vehr and Black-Eyed Susan, garnered rave reviews which translated into a thriving box office. Ludlam was intent on writing not just new farces, but also ones with plots which were structured more intricately and more tightly than his previous ventures, borrowing less dialogue from outside sources and relying more on his own writing talent. As Frank Rich of the *New York Times* wrote, "What Mr. Ludlam has written is an intricate, madcap farce of the old school — a conventional, contemporary sex comedy that plays by the rules of Georges Feydeu, Alan Ayckbourn and Preston Sturges."[2]

In *Reverse Psychology*, based on the premise and style of Noel Coward's *Private Lives*, Ludlam mocks the psychiatric community through a husband and wife, both therapists, who are each in love with the other's patient. Not until the end of the play do we discover that the two patients, Eleanor and Freddie, are actually married as well. Although this work was tamer than previous ridiculous plays, Ludlam managed to incorporate main-stays of the farcical machinery — mistaken identities, outrageous coincidences, and inopportune phone calls. *Reverse Psychology*'s long run lasted until mid–May of 1981 when the company began to preview Ludlam's new play, *Love's Tangled Web*, which opened on June 7, 1981.

Love's Tangled Web, a farce with various connected plots layered with multiple complexities, set in Long Island, swirled around mismatched lovers, psychic phenomena, an escaped gorilla, and the ambitions and greed of its characters: Sylvia Woodville, her mother Eve, Pastor Fenwick Bates (Eve's lover), Bertie (Sylvia's brother), Raeanne (a paranormal), Bram (the handyman), and a Gorilla. Unfortunately, it was not well received, either critically or at the box office. Nonetheless, Ludlam had still managed to further explore the style of classic farce, as evidenced in the end of the first scene in Act One:

> (*SYLVIA reenters and goes up the stairs. Doorbell rings and the PASTOR answers it. His voice is heard off.*)
>
> PASTOR: Gorilla? No, officer. We haven't seen any gorilla. When did it escape? Well, I certainly hope you catch it. Check the hedges down by the drive. Dangerous, eh? I'll be sure to lock all the doors and windows. Thank you.
>
> (*During the previous speech, GORILLA appears at French doors, opens them, and enters.*)
>
> SYLVIA: (*Voice from upstairs*) Bram, is that you? (*GORILLA goes upstairs*) Oh, Bram. Oh, oh.
>
> (*PASTOR, returning from off left, sees French doors left ajar and closes them. He tiptoes to the door of bedroom up center and knocks softly.*)
>
> PASTOR: (*Whispering*) Sylvia. Sylvia.
>
> (*Door opens. BERTIE, in drag as Sylvia, comes out wearing a veil and hiding behind a fan. PASTOR chases her around the sofa and back into the room. EVE enters sleepwalking. She opens the door to the balcony and goes out, balancing precariously out on the balustrade, as in Act I. A flashlight shines up into her face.*)
>
> RAEANNE: (*Voice*) Mrs. Woodville!
>
> (*EVE teeters and falls off the balcony. RAEANNE enters with EVE in her arms and goes to couch.*)
>
> EVE: Thank heavens you caught me. I would have ruined the rhododendrons. Raeanne, I've been sleepwalking more and more lately. I keep dreaming about my late husband. Do you think he's trying to contact me?
>
> RAEANNE: It's very likely. The departed often appear in dreams.
>
> EVE: Do you think you can contact him?
>
> RAEANNE: I'll try. Put your hands on the table. Are you there, Little Chief?
>
> EVE: Who's Little Chief?
>
> RAEANNE: He's my familiar. Are you there, Little Chief? (*Moaning upstairs*) You may speak to him now.
>
> EVE: Little Chief? Little Chief, I'm trying to contact my husband, Colonel Woodville. Is he there?
>
> (*Doors fly open. Sounds of banging and fisticuffs come from the master bedroom, SYLVIA's moaning orgasmically from upstairs.*)
>
> RAEANNE: I think we're making contact.
>
> (*BRAM enters from the kitchen in the Colonel's uniform. EVE, seeing him, screams.*)
>
> EVE: Bert! (*Faints*)[1]

Not wanting to lose money, Ludlam decided to close *Love's Tangled Web* three weeks after it opened, blaming the critics for not understanding its soap opera structure. In an interview regarding his new play he complained, "I suppose you could call it a critical failure. In other words, the critics failed it."[4] Not anticipating the abrupt closing, Ludlam was not prepared with a new play and decided to close the theatre for a short time. He was determined not to fall into the trap of reviving old hits when times got tough. Eight months after *Love's Tangled Web* closed, Ludlam and company opened a new production in February of 1982, *Secret Lives of the Sexists: The Farce of Modern Life.*

With this new play, Ludlam explored the absurdities generated by male chauvinism and militant feminism. The plot of *Secret Lives of the Sexists* is complicated, with subplots twisting and turning around each other continually, depicting well-bred people unintentionally forced to lead double lives. As one critic summarized, "These supposedly respectable people include: Buddy Husband (Bill Vehr) a man attempting to make his long lost mother-in-law an honest woman, his wife Nadine (Mink Stole) jealous of this unknown older woman, his impotent punkish brother (Everett Quinton), his horny frustrated sister-in-law (played by actor Georg Osterman), the mother-in-law (Black-Eyed Susan) a carney stripper turned beautician, and Phil Landers (Charles Ludlam), an over the hill, toupeed, physical therapist, impersonating a homosexual."[5] In jealous rages, they all accuse each other of infidelities, while they all plot and scheme, and in the process a raucous farce unfolds.

The highlight of the play occurs in act three, where Zena, the ex-burlesque stripper mother-in-law, gives a speech at a feminist rally called "Women Against Stenography." In the stage directions, Ludlam describes the set as "a dais for speech-making. An American flag. A feminist banner. The background has slogans in Gregg and Pittman shorthand as well as this inscription in speedwriting, 'i u cn rd ths u shd ern mo pa.'"[6] With an idea borrowed directly from Aristophanes' farce *Thesmophoriazusai*, Ludlam as Landers strips hair from the legs of his cohorts Buddy and Izzy with hot wax and dolls them up in drag in order secretly to invade this feminist rally and spy on the women. At the podium Zena is sharing her life story: she desperately wants to be reunited with her daughter, the product of a sexual seduction at the age of six by a circus freak known as "the Human Worm," a limbless monstrosity who can only slither on the ground. Unknown to her at the time, Zena's daughter Nadine, a militant feminist, takes the podium and lectures on the end of the "two sex system," championing her cause that soon words like mango and maniac will be renamed persongo and personiac.

Secret Lives of the Sexists was a critical and financial success, but Ludlam closed the show at the end of the summer in 1982, no longer desiring to run his plays so long that both the audiences and the actors tired of it. Keeping on track with his policy of presenting only new works, in October of the same year he opened his new play, *Exquisite Torture: A Romantic Ecstasy*, a surrealist comedy about the last of the Neros.

Inspired by Salvador Dalí's little-known novel *Hidden Faces*, which takes place in the nineteenth century, Ludlam's *Exquisite Torture* is set in Rome and San Diego and tells the story of Count Benito Neroni's search for true identity and true love. Ludlam also tosses in a bit of Genet's *The Maids* with his character Solange De Choisy, a performer whose stage name is Venus Veronica. As Allan Wallach pointed out in his review in *Newsday*, Ludlam pulled from the traditional farcical devices of "amnesia, a masked man who is mistaken for somebody else, marriage to the wrong man, a buried treasure, and a deathbed scene."[7] Because Ludlam was attempting to create a Daliesque, surrealistic mood, the play was slow and plodding and short on laughs. It did not receive favorable reviews and, again, Ludlam was forced into another short run. However, as company manager Steven Samuels pointed out, this "was Ludlam's last box office flop."[8] Undaunted, Ludlam continued writing new works, determined to rise above and take charge of his roller-coaster career. His next play, one of his most popular and successful, was a loving tribute to one of his idols, Molière, entitled *Le Bourgeois Avant-Garde: A Comedy Ballet After Molière*.

LE BOURGEOIS AVANT-GARDE

The fact that *Le Bourgeois Avant-Garde* was one of Ludlam's greatest successes is as much a tribute to Molière himself as it is to Ludlam. Ludlam closely followed the plot of Molière's *Le Bourgeois Gentilhomme* (*The Would-Be Gentleman*), sometimes quoting dialogue verbatim, translating Molière's satiric view of the upper-class, snobbish "gentlemen" into a not-so-subtle commentary on the pretentious affectations of the twentieth century avant-garde art movements. As Ludlam himself stated, "I wasn't attacking experimental theatre. I was, rather, criticizing the kind of work that masquerades as avant-garde but is, in reality, merely confusing...."[9]

The plot of Molière's farce revolves around Mr. Jourdain and his family, a middle-class merchant who desires to be thought of and treated as a gentlemen of fine breeding and part of the upper crust of society. Employed to help him achieve this are a Music Master, Dancing Master, Philosopher, Fencing Master and Master Tailor, all paid to keep Mr. Jourdain thinking that he is on the very cutting edge of class. Of course, each of these "Masters" only cares for the money that Jourdain throws his way, maintaining the charade only as long as Jourdain is fool enough to pay. He even disallows his daughter's marriage to a fine, upstanding middle-class lad, Cleonte, because his gentility is not refined enough, although it is clear from Molière's acid pen that Jourdain would not recognize fine breeding if it bit him on the nose. Mrs. Jourdain, his wife, is appalled at her husband's behavior, cautioning him that if a "gentleman" marries their daughter, he will look down upon their merchant/tradesman status and snub them. Jourdain will hear none of it; no noble is too good for his daughter and his family. Their maid, Nicole, aligned with Mrs. Jourdain, hatches a plot against Mr. Jourdain to let his own ridiculous behavior undo him. In disguise as a translator, Cleonte's valet, Covielle, enters with Cleonte, also in disguise as the Grand Turk's son, declaring that his royal patron wants to marry Jourdain's daughter Lucille, which turns Jourdain into a complete imbecile, stumbling over himself in an effort to make a noble impression on this supposed Turkish royalty. They all perform a Turkish dervish, using Jourdain as fodder to abuse and ridicule him — unknown, of course, to Jourdain, who revels in this absurdity. In the end, all the characters are paired off with their desired mates, leaving Covielle to say, "If there's a bigger fool than this anywhere, I'd like to meet him!"[10]

Molière subtitled his satiric farce "A Comedy Ballet" because in between each act was an interlude of music and dance which furthered the plot. In between the first two acts are the Dancing Master's pupils rehearsing for their performance for Jourdain. Between Act Two and Act Three, the Master Tailor and his boys dance for Jourdain after being handsomely paid for their charades. The third interlude has the cooks dancing together while they prepare the table for the magnificent feast that Jourdain has prepared in order to seduce a lady of false claim to royalty, and the final interlude is the erroneous Turkish wedding ceremony with bizarre invocations and turbaned whirling dervishes.

Ludlam subtitled his satiric farce "A Comedy Ballet After Molière" acknowledging his debt to Molière and hinting at the new ridiculous interpretation to follow. Ludlam does not utilize interludes in his version, but rather uses this opportunity to illustrate various confusing avant-garde performance art pieces. In fact, at the end of his play Ludlam turns the entire performance of *Le Bourgeois Avant-Garde* into its own parody of an avant-garde theatre piece, blurring the line between satiric commentary and all-out burlesque.

The Ludlam rendering takes place in Long Island, New York, at the home of Rufus Foufas, a middle-class green grocer, who specializes in tantalizing vegetables at his Friendly Foufas Food Stores. Mr. Foufas wants desperately to be one of the premier benefactors of the avant-garde, and strives shamelessly for their approval. Because the United States does not have the class structure such as Molière had in his day, Ludlam translates the target from membership in the upper crust of society to membership in the "in crowd" of the avant-garde art movements that began in the United States in the 1950s. These movements in the theatre began to throw out the script, throw out the logic of a story, and place more stress on the identity of the performer and creator. This movement in America was full of intellectual artists divorcing themselves from convention and claiming truly to understand the depths of human experience. The unbelieving Ludlam wrote that "the avant-garde has trouble communicating. When they have no plot, people can't understand what is going on, which is their limit. The avant-garde is wrong and the audience is right. The audience is supposed to know what is going on. If artists fail to communicate, it's their fault, not the audience."[11] In fact, Ludlam quipped that he was for "virtuoso maximalism," which certainly nobody could argue with.

Mr. Foufas has employed an avant-garde stage director, Percival Hack, whose very name should have given him away. In turn, Mr. Hack has brought in a Choreographer and Composer who are supposedly avant-garde geniuses, and together they are hoodwinking Foufas out of thousands of dollars. Much as in Molière's original, Ludlam's Foufas desires to seduce who he thinks is Poland's leading avant-garde actress, Maia Panzaroff, who in reality is Percival Hack's intended. Ludlam has great fun with names in this play. Merely reading the name Maia Panzaroff on the page might be deceiving; one needs actually to say the name to get Ludlam's full satiric bent.

Mrs. Foufas wants their daughter Prue Foufas to marry their next door neighbor, Newton Entwhistle, a local banker, while Mr. Foufas has a celebrated graffiti artist, known as Moderna 83, in mind for Prue. When we meet Moderna 83, we find that he speaks a new language, as illustrated in Chapter 4. Here Ludlam is not-so-subtly mocking such avant-garde artists as Samuel Beckett, Robert Wilson, Mabou Mines, Peter Brook and Richard Foreman who often stretched their theatrical visions to absurd, vacuous limits.

As in Molière's play, Ludlam also has a maid, Violet, who appears in an utterly politically incorrect manner as a stage personification of Aunt Jemima. This maid also schemes to make a fool out of Foufas by exploiting his own stupidity, thereby helping Mrs. Foufas to secure Prue's marriage to Newton Entwhistle. Violet gets Mr. Foufas to believe that *the* most advanced avant-garde artist, Nicky Newfangle, is coming to meet him.

Newfangle (Newton Entwhistle in disguise) is allegedly the founder and leading theorist of the post-avant-garde movement. As Hack explains:

> HACK: Well it's a kind of antimovement. He synthesized subsurrealism and unsound structuralism and came out with repressed expressionism. He's heard about you and wants to meet you.[12]

Foufas falls all over himself in anticipation of meeting Newfangle, who has promised to indoctrinate Foufas into the "avant-derrière" movement as its leading patron. The initiation consists of a nutrient enema, as avant-derrières do not eat through their mouths. Instead of a Turkish dervish as with Molière, Ludlam's "comedy ballet" involves the entire cast performing an avant-garde piece where "they all pair off doing mechanical Susy-Q movements. Then in ballroom dance positions, they do a rocking movement. Then all stop."[13] True to the original, everyone is happily paired off at the end, and all are satisfied with their derision of Foufas. Ludlam gives Percival Hack the line directly from Molière's play, "And if there's a bigger fool than this anywhere, I'd like to meet him."[14] But then the ultimate touché at the avant-garde movement is delivered by Maia Panzaroff, who, when asked by Mrs. Foufas what avant-garde really means, replies, "Avant-garde is French for bullshit!"[15]

Ludlam uses the premise of the pretentiousness of the avant-garde to have a field day with the sense of artifice in the play. When Mr. Foufas first enters he wants to see the play the avant-garde trio have concocted for him for that evening's soirée, designed to impress the phony Maia Panzaroff. When he asks to see the play, the director Hack responds with:

> HACK: Mr. Foufas, the avant-garde don't do plays. We do pieces.
> FOUFAS: You shouldn't just do pieces. You should do the whole thing.
> HACK: You misunderstand me. A play is a piece and a piece is a play.
> FOUFAS: I mean your prologue or dialogue or whatever it is. Your singing and dancing.
> HACK: Mr. Foufas, we do not say, "Let me see your play." Among the avant-garde. It would be more appropriate to say, "Let me see your piece."[16]

Later, Ludlam takes this theme further, developing the entire finale of *Le Bourgeois Avant-Garde* in the style of avant-garde performance. As Violet enters disguised as the Translator, she passes out plastic buttocks to everyone, who promptly attach them to their front sides. As noted before, they are all moving in a Suzy-Q motion, side-stepping across the stage, when Prue enters, bound and gagged in a wedding dress, with her father intending to give her to Nicky Newfangle. She looks around at the bizarre assortment of characters in her house and asks:

> PRUE: Really, Father, why are you dressed like that? Is this supposed to be a play?
> FOUFAS: No, this isn't a play. This is a piece![17]

Interestingly, it could be speculated that Ludlam has Foufas almost stepping out of character here; perhaps the reference is as much to *Le Bourgeois Avant-Garde* itself as it is to the performance within the performance. This was one of Ludlam's not-so-subtle criticisms of the chaotic and ludicrous nature of much of the avant-garde movement.

At another performance interlude in the play, when Foufas asks Hack about the "piece" they are to perform that night at dinner, the Composer, Choreographer, and director Hack give a preview for him after explaining the nature of abstract art. However, when we arrive at the dinner scene in Act Two, the performance that actually occurs is nothing like the preview. Ludlam takes the absurdity to a far higher level as the Choreographer, Composer, and Moderna perform for Foufas, Hack and Panzaroff, who are sitting at the table dining on Foufas' artichokes. The stage directions call for the Composer to dip his finger into water, run it around the rim of a glass until it rings, which continues to the end. Then Moderna enters in Greek costume, carrying a lyre and a cage with a live chicken. The cage has a roll of sheet music in it. As the sheet music is pulled through the cage, the chicken's footprints are to become the music which the composer is playing. Moderna then draws the sheet music across the stage, in front of the dining table. The Composer chants and drones strangely. The Choreographer then enters, skipping and spinning in place. The Composer sets off a toy monkey which bangs cymbals throughout the remainder of the scene. When the piece has finally ended Foufas, Hack, and Maia Panzaroff snap their fingers in applause.

Of course, the fact that most avant-garde theatre is abstract allows Ludlam to illustrate his opinion by showing that it doesn't really mean anything at all and is, more often than not, pure pretense.

Earlier in the play, in attempting to explain to Foufas the definition of "abstract," the Composer and Hack create a definition that is as abstract as the subject:

> COMPOSER: Abstract has to do with pure form removed from any representational content. It is form liberated from content.
> FOUFAS: In other words if it doesn't represent anything it's abstract.
> COMPOSER: Yes.[18]

Of course the preview of the performance is so intentionally unclear and convoluted that Mr. Foufas falls fast asleep, but when he suddenly awakens, in order to appear avant-garde, states that he understood everything perfectly. As one critic noted, "Ludlam's inspired silliness makes a fine mockery of arts patrons who affect the dress, manner, and lingo of the artists they admire."[19]

Mr. Foufas continually attempts to dress in what he believes to be the latest avant-garde fashions. In Act One, he models his latest fashion for the trio of "post-talent" artists, as they call themselves, putting on an outfit with tentacles sprouting from the arms and legs, Frank Rich of the *New York Times* wrote that Ludlam "looked like a white octopus in heat."[20] In Act Two, for the dinner party held in honor of Maia Panzaroff, Foufas enters in a leisure suit made entirely out of artificial turf, creating the effect of an oversized, hairy pickle. Then, over that already ridiculous outfit, Foufas applies big plastic buttocks to his frontside for the avant-derrière initiation, layering the visual absurdity a step further.

Ludlam mocks not only the avant-garde with this broad satire, but verbally spoofs every "ism" imaginable. The play opens and closes with the Choreographer and Composer in heated discussions about avant-garde terminology. A portion of the opening scene goes as follows:

> CHOREOGRAPHER: I consider myself to be much more advanced. I am a Postmodern.
> COMPOSER: You mean you are a Futurist?
> CHOREOGRAPHER: No, the future was over by the early thirties.
> COMPOSER: Well I am a *Post*postmodernist.
> CHOREOGRAPHER: And what may I ask is that?
> COMPOSER: A Neomodernist.
> CHOREOGRAPHER: *(Indignantly)* Hurmph!
> COMPOSER: When Postmodernism died, a Modernist revival ensued. *(Triumphantly)* And we're right back where we started!
> CHOREOGRAPHER: How pretentious! You've done nothing but revive Futurism.
> COMPOSER: You ass! The future cannot be revived until it has been lived, and when it has been lived it is no longer the future!
> CHOREOGRAPHER: Do you know what I think? I think you're nothing but a lapsed Surrealist posing as a Postmodernist.
> COMPOSER: And I think you're a Constructivist posing as an Expressionist.
> CHOREOGRAPHER: Dadaist!
> COMPOSER: Fauve!
> CHOREOGRAPHER: Cubist!
> COMPOSER: Surrealist!
> CHOREOGRAPHER: Pop artist!
> COMPOSER: Op artist!
> CHOREOGRAPHER: Conceptualist!
> COMPOSER: Realist!
> CHOREOGRAPHER: *(Reeling as if from a blow)* Ouch![21]

Ludlam cleverly builds this battle from "ist" to "pseudo-ist" to what surely must be the pinnacle of insults to any true avant-garde artist — "realist" — causing the Choreographer to double over in pain at the mere thought. Of course, Ludlam does not stop there. He adds one more insult for the record when the Choreographer viciously retaliates, calling the Composer a Minimalist, which, as we have already noted, Ludlam found particularly offensive to his aesthetic sensibility.

After the avant-derrière ceremony and the pairing off of mates, the Choreographer and Composer close the show with what could be considered a *da capo*:

> CHOREOGRAPHER: You know, I think he really has something there. It strikes me as a reaction to Cubism.
> COMPOSER: Spherism!
> CHOREOGRAPHER: A kind of unimpressionablism!
> COMPOSER: No, I think it's rejectivism.
> CHOREOGRAPHER: Abstract rejectivism.
> COMPOSER: No, nonplussed rejectivism.
> CHOREOGRAPHER: Anarcho-formalism.
> COMPOSER: Formal anarchy?
> CHOREOGRAPHER: Passive positivism.
> COMPOSER: Postpremodernism.
> CHOREOGRAPHER: Prepostmodernism
> COMPOSER: Aushaus School — dissallows function as a design criterion.
> CHOREOGRAPHER: Excellerationism.
>
> *(Music swells and lights fade as the exchange becomes more manic.*
>
> COMPOSER: Energism.
> CHOREOGRAPHER: Lethargism.
> COMPOSER: Inhibitionism.
> CHOREOGRAPHER: Precisionism.
>
> *(Ad infinitum.)*
>
> *The End*[22]

Another example of Ludlam's relentless attack on the avant-garde occurs in Act One, this time on literary forms when he asks Hack to help him compose a letter to Maia Panzaroff, to declare his undying affection:

> FOUFAS: ...I don't want anything in the letter except my exact words. But I want them arranged so that they sound avant-garde. What would you advise me to do?
> HACK: Then I'm afraid there's nothing to do but deconstruct the text.
> FOUFAS: Deconstruct the text?[23]

Hack then has Foufas put each word on a separate piece of paper. Hack pulls them out of a hat, and reads them in the order pulled. After three attempts,

Foufas, unhappy with the results, becomes desperate to find another method, and Hack quickly informs him that he could always just send it in its original order, causing Foufas to declare, "I can't believe it. I've only just discovered the avant-garde, and I got it right the first time!"[24] Clearly Ludlam thinks such literary devices are meaningless and often too obscure to communicate anything intelligent whatsoever.

To counter the absurd and foolish Mr. Foufas, Ludlam writes Mrs. Foufas as a simple, straightforward, honest woman, with clear objectives and unalterable opinions, who wastes not a word and feels no need for external embellishments in her life. When she confronts her husband about the marriage of their daughter Prue, she describes why she prefers the banker next door, Newton Entwhistle, all after Foufas has refused to give him Prue's hand because Newton doesn't even know the meaning of the words avant-garde.

Ludlam dramatizes the absurd mythology in this scene that all avant-garde artists, because of their self-proclaimed heightened artistic sensibilities, either are misunderstood or hire prostitutes who give them sexually transmitted diseases, all of which helps make them truly insightful "artists." In reality, documentation proves that most so-called artists of the avant-garde persuasion, when not on public display, put on their pants one leg at a time just like the rest of the world, which is precisely Ludlam's point.

Le Bourgeois Avant-Garde was undeniably one of Ludlam's biggest hits, with critics and audiences alike. With *Le Bourgeois Avant-Garde*, Ludlam was able to create a truly literary work combining parody with satire, but always maintaining his focus on the intent. As Don Nelsen wrote in his *New York Daily News* review, "Yet despite all its stylized shenanigans, 'Bourgeois' ... does not patronize its audience because it is intelligently conceived and goes after phoniness that is quite fashionable in our society. The ubiquitous Ludlam, ... Black-Eyed Susan, Bill Vehr and Quinton lead a cast which keeps its eye on the point even though the eye may be rolling toward the ceiling."[25]

Perhaps the scene which best exemplifies Ludlam's voice underneath the play occurs in Act One, after Foufas has donned his ridiculous "octopus" outfit, which he thinks is cutting-edge. Violet the maid enters and, upon seeing her boss, starts to laugh boisterously. She continues her belly-laughing throughout the entire scene, although at times she tries her best to contain herself. She looks at Foufas and laughs hysterically into his ridiculous face, just as Ludlam is laughing in the ridiculous face of his avant-garde colleagues. When the play closed in the summer of 1983, it was still attracting large crowds, but Ludlam and company had already opened their new play *Galas: A Modern Tragedy*, based on the life of Maria Callas.

GALAS

In the opening moments of Ludlam's *Galas*, with the stage dark, taped interviews of Maria Callas are played, then an aria from *Madama Butterfly* is heard, in Callas' unique voice. Although the play is cleverly titled *Galas*, it is clear whose life is to be ridiculously portrayed. As Ludlam wrote in the program, "The characters in the play are real. Only their names have been changed to protect the playwright." In fact, *Galas* highlights specific, well-known moments from Callas' life, creating a biography of sorts with, naturally, a ridiculous slant: the marriage of Callas and an older Verona brick dealer, Meneghini; her humbling of the La Scala management; her brazen audience with the Pope; her mid-performance flight from a production of *Norma* in Rome; her affair with Aristotle Onassis; and her sad and lonely departure from this world.

Ludlam structured *Galas* very much like the bel canto operas that made the diva famous. With a somewhat thin script, Ludlam's new play provided the perfect arena in which his own "diva" qualities could shine forth. As Michael Feingold wrote in the *Village Voice*, "As drama the piece is no more than the merest gossip, enlivened occasionally by an emotional outburst or a gag line. As a vehicle for Ludlam's exquisitely showy performance, it does exactly what Rossinni, Bellini, Puccini do for a diva who knows how to work her opportunities to the hilt."[26] And as Frank Rich wrote in his *New York Times* review, "We cease to watch a man playing a woman and instead see a comic heroine who is completely consistent on Mr. Ludlam's own terms. To do this takes total conviction as well as talent, and it is that fierce conviction that elevates the performance from the realm of caricature to that of inspired clowning."[27]

Although Charles Ludlam became known for gender-bending and performing in drag, *Galas* was actually the first play since *Camille* in 1973, ten years earlier, in which he had appeared in a dress. And not surprisingly, both women were of mythic proportions. Ludlam felt he had a lot in common with the tortured Maria Callas, both as an artist and as a personality. As an artist, Ludlam writes that[28] "Like Maria Callas sometimes things you do that seem terribly new and daring and revolutionary are really traditional things. In fact, Callas was considered revolutionary because she almost single-handedly revived the Italian bel canto opera, long thought to be passe. Her singing was not thought of as beautiful in the orthodox sense, but she possessed a power and a presence that electrified and seduced audiences into rapture. She epitomized the meaning of prima donna and diva.

As a personality, Maria Callas was hounded by the press during most of her career, and gossip about her private life, according to writer David A. Lowe, "created an image of Callas that relied more on fantasy than on fact."[29] Ludlam received a taste of this tabloid journalism himself, understanding fully the risk one takes in being in the public eye.

Perhaps this is the one area which Ludlam understood perfectly: the loneliness, frustration and anxieties which lie beneath the surface of any truly gifted artist, the need to be perfect, not to compromise, for the sake of the art. It is indeed true that Ludlam had a devoted following of critics and fans alike, but there were also critics who, he felt, did not understand his intentions and thus wrote negative, even nasty, reviews about him and his work. John Simon of *New York Magazine*, for example, wrote about *Galas* that "There are a few facts, and some Callas records are played; the rest is mostly facile, old, unfunny jokes.... I see very little point — and less daring — in travestying this unlovable, unhappy woman, except that it affords Ludlam a chance to be outrageous and, by surrounding himself with rank amateurs, to look professional."[30] But as Eleanor Blau discovered when she interviewed Ludlam in the *New York Times*,

> Mr. Ludlam, who says he's an opera fan but not fanatic about it, identifies with Miss Callas as a victim of attacks that miss the point. Some critics, he noted, complain about "amateurish" acting by members of his company, failing to understand that at the Ridiculous Theater: "You know there is the pretense of acting. It's part stereotypic and part original — the vivid quirkiness, the actors' eccentricities. The illusion is something we play with and step in and out of."[31]

This is precisely why Ludlam studied and clung to Goethe's three principles of criticism: What was the artist trying to do? Did he succeed in doing it? Was it worth doing? In Ludlam's opinion, "'What was he trying to do?' is the great question which nobody dares ask anymore. It has gone out of fashion to ask that."[32]

In the first scene of Act One of *Galas*, Ludlam shows us an opera diva's rise to stardom and her struggles to be accepted into elite society. Closely mirroring Callas's life, Ludlam's Maria Magdalena Galas arrives in Verona as a young, rather unattractive and overweight American singer, and is met at the train station by Giovanni Baptista Mercanteggini, an older industrialist who owns a string of brick factories. Ludlam's transposition of Meneghini to Mercanteggini reveals his clever wit at play, in creating a name which incorporates his occupation, but which is also easily recognizable to any knowledgeable Callas fan. When we first see Ludlam on stage as Galas, according to the stage directions, "She wears sensible oxfords, a severe suit, and a cloth coat. She carries a covered birdcage and (forgive me for saying so) she is fat. She looks around the train station wearily and sits down at a small table."[33] After this visual prelude, Ludlam gives himself a first line that sets the satiric tone of the play: "*(To the waiter)* I'd like the veal cutlet, please."[34] Upon meeting Mercanteggini and discovering that he is to be her host, she begins to discuss with him their mutual passion for music, and again Ludlam uses factual elements of Callas's difficult and egotistical reputation to his satirical advantage:

> MERCANTEGGINI: We are both music lovers.
> GALAS: I am not a music lover. I am a musician.
> MERCANTEGGINI: But surely you love music.
> GALAS: I am a musician. And because I am a singer I am a musical instrument. A music lover, no. I am music.[35]

In Scene Two, we await the arrival of the new Mrs. Maria Mercanteggini from her South American tour, at their grand villa in Verona. Ludlam exercises some poetic license here with the introduction of the Cassandra-like maid Bruna Lina Rasta, an ex-diva who has been employed by Mercanteggini for a long time. In Bruna, played by Everett Quinton, Ludlam created a theatrical device similar to the Greek chorus, whose function it was to comment on the action and to fill in plot details. Bruna not only makes declamatory speeches in the style of a Greek chorus, she also enters and exits in ridiculously caricatured Greek-like movements.

Soon, two officials from La Scala appear to offer Galas a guest-artist contract, which she refuses to sign, vowing to sing at La Scala on her terms, (namely full membership in the company for her) or no terms at all. Eventually, through a comic misunderstanding, the two gentlemen agree to the terms, but her salary is quite a bit higher than even she expected:

> MERCANTEGGINI: Magdalena, they have agreed to the million lire.
> GALAS: How is that possible?
> MERCANTEGGINI: You said, "Not for a million lire," and they agreed.
> GALAS: But I didn't really mean a million lire. That was only a figure of speech. I used it merely to emphasize my point about *La Traviata*.
> MERCANTEGGINI: Oh, they've agreed to *La Traviata*. But what's more important, I've stumbled on an amazing discovery. We can get virtually anything we ask for.[36]

In this scene, Ludlam also shows us how the press began to manipulate Maria Callas' privacy by reporting rumor and innuendo, which caused her to encase herself in an iron cocoon:

MERCANTEGGINI: They say you lost weight because you had a tapeworm.
GALAS: Aaagh! But it's not true. How could they lie about me like that? How could they lie? It's horrible! It's too too horrible!"

Maria Callas was plagued her entire career by false rumors and sensationalistic reporting from the press, against which she constantly battled, which further added to her aura of being "difficult."

Perhaps the funniest scene in *Galas* is Ludlam's spoof on Callas' private audience with the Pope in Rome. In the actual account, Callas, being Greek Orthodox, considered the Pope to be just another bishop and felt it unnecessary to treat this man as if he were holy. After all, the church initially disavowed her marriage to Meneghini, causing them to threaten mere civil marriage at the Town Hall. Eventually, the Pope relented and the marriage proceeded at the tiny Church of the Philippines in Verona. Later in her life, when the Pope requested a meeting with the famous diva, Callas, not forgetting her initial snub, argued with His Holiness about the merits of Wagner. Of course the press had a field day with this cheeky behavior.

Ludlam doesn't waste a satiric beat in his version, in Scene Four of the first act, where we first meet the Pope and a Prelate:

POPE: Deus benedicte tutti homine.
PRELATE: Forgive me, Your Holiness. It is very well to bless all men. But do you think you could expand your blessing to include women as well?
POPE: Deus benedicte tutti homine et tutti dame.
PRELATE: With your permission, Your Holiness. It would perhaps be better if you could make a more general and all-inclusive blessing.
POPE: Deus benedicte tutti homine, tutti dame, et tutti fruitti.[38]

Ludlam begins this scene by showing us, in a comic way, the inherent bias of the Catholic Church against women and homosexuals and, in doing so, puts us on the side of Galas before she even enters. Ludlam also uses this scene to show us, once again, the artifice which is intrinsic to his ridiculous style when the Prelate motions for Galas, Bruna and Mercanteggini to come forward and kiss the Pope's ring. When it is Bruna's turn, as the stage directions indicate, and as Quinton so unabashedly followed, "Bruna removes her coat revealing sackcloth and ashes, dons a crown of thorns, and crawls to the POPE on her knees, flagellating herself with a flail she takes from her bag."[39] Ludlam continues the use of artifice for comic effect when it is Galas' turn to step forward and kiss the Pontiff's ring: "When LA GALAS goes forward proudly to kiss his ring he lowers it by degrees, forcing her to bow very low. She crosses herself with a gesture of contempt."[40] Then, later in the scene, vowing not to be upstaged by even the

Pope, Galas uses a rosary given to her by His Holiness and "lassoes his hand to prevent him from lowering it again, kisses the ring, and steps back with hands clasped angelically in prayer."[41] Not only does Ludlam reveal more of the determined and brazen character of Galas/Callas, he simultaneously makes fun of the Pope and the Catholic Church, the church of his upbringing, longtime oppressors of homosexuals and women.

In the final scene in Act One, Ludlam portrays the real-life account, albeit in his ridiculous manner, of Callas' refusal to continue a performance of *Norma* due to vocal problems. Sympathetic to the artist, Ludlam reveals the valid reasons behind this decision through the Greek chorus, Bruna, who emphatically says, "Leave her alone. When the voice goes it is no use to call it back. Believe me, if she could finish the performance tonight, she would."[42] In the true account, Callas did not, in fact, finish the performance, but she was aware of the ramifications of her decision. She opted for the lesser of two evils. If she did not sing she would disappoint, and if she sang badly she would also disappoint. Rome Opera thereupon sued the Meneghinis, forcing Maria and her husband into a court battle, which they won. But the public relations damage was done. She was harshly criticized in the press, which accused her of being an egotistical and selfish star. Ludlam's final tag in Act One, offering proof that his was a loving and sympathetic satire, was Mercanteggini's final line to the Rome Opera management: "Well, you have your scandal."[43] Ludlam portrays the incident fairly factually, but with his ridiculous slant he was able to dramatize the true reasons behind the scandal which, at the same time, heightened his identification with this misunderstood talent.

Act Two of *Galas* has only two scenes and shows the descent into loneliness and solitude that befell Maria Callas. The first scene begins on a yacht owned by Aristotle Plato Socrates Odysseus, a wicked spoof on Aristotle Onassis, complete with sailors singing the opening of Act Two of Ponchielli's *La Gioconda*. Here, Ludlam reminds his audience that he is using the very ingredients of opera to tell his story of Maria Callas. Again, as in the true story, Galas and Odysseus begin an affair, which results in the dissolution of her marriage to Mercanteggini. At one point, Odysseus throws an elegant costume party on his yacht, which excites Galas' theatrical sense, but which leaves her husband, Mercanteggini, dejected as he senses his position as lover and husband to be dwindling rapidly. Throughout the drama, however, Ludlam manages always to elicit a ridiculous tone such as when, at one point, Mercanteggini says with great agitation:

> These people are disgusting. They're like animals. I'm in a pigsty! (*ILKA crosses in a pig mask. A passenger in gorilla costume passes with cocktail in hand*)

> Excuse me, have you seen my wife? *(GUEST snorts and exits. To other GUESTS)* Pardon, have you seen my wife?
>
> *(Each time he asks a guest this question they laugh a nightmarish laugh and exit. Weird laughter is heard coming from all sides. Enter ATHINA, nude, except for her hair which falls below her waist, partially covering her body. She is weeping)*
>
> ATHINA: You have lost your Magdalena.
> MERCANTEGGINI: What?
> ATHINA: I came upon them in the dark. They had hidden in the lifeboat. I heard sounds and lifted up the tarp. And there the two great fishes lay, flopping in the net. Then twisting, turning head to tail, I heard her laugh and say, "It will open up my throat!"[44]

After Athina, the current wife of Odysseus, tells Mercanteggini what she has witnessed, Ludlam turns to opera again to dramatize the moment. He has Mercanteggini open a box Odysseus has given him and take out a Pagliacci costume, which he puts on. He smears his face with clown white, while muttering unintelligibly. We hear the voice of Caruso singing "Vesti la Giubba" from Pagliacci. Mercanteggini lip-syncs the aria and makes the appropriate gestures.

In the final scene, Maria Galas, alone and depressed in her Paris apartment, having lost her first husband, her lover Aristotle, and her voice, says to Bruna, "I need some good news," to which Bruna replies, "Madam, your dog is dead."[45] Ludlam undercuts the drama of the moment here with a joke, keeping the audience at an emotional distance while still furthering the plot. Continuing in this vein, in response to the dead animal, Ludlam parodies the graveyard scene from *Hamlet*, with Galas holding the deceased ball of fur in her hands, rather than a skull.

However, in the final moments of the play, Ludlam doesn't just undercut a serious moment with a joke, he sets up the entire tragic ending of the play using comedy, once again incorporating opera to dramatize the impact. In a bit borrowed directly from the opera *Madama Butterfly*, Galas asks Bruna to bring her the kimono that was given to her by the female impersonator of the Kabuki Theater. She takes it, and snaps open a fan, which conceals a knife. She blindfolds Bruna and asks her to sing the "Vissi d'arte," from Tosca, which she does.

> GALAS: What do I do from morning to night if I don't have my career? I have no family, I have no husband, I have no babies, I have no lover, I have no dog, I have no voice, and there's nothing good on television tonight. What do I do, what do I do from morning to night? I can't just sit around and play cards or gossip — I'm not the type. *(Suddenly her gaze falls on the fan. She looks to heaven as if for permission, smiles, takes fan, rises, opens fan, and exits toward the screen. Before she disappears behind the screen, she looks*

> *back at BRUNA and smiles in affirmation. She throws a scarf over the screen, then raises her hand with the dagger)* Grazie, Bruna. *(Her hand comes down with great force. As the last notes of the "Vissi d'arte" fade away, the scarf is dragged down behind the screen...)*[46]

Fittingly, Ludlam ends the life of Galas as tragically if it were an actual scene from *Madama Butterfly*, creating layers of artifice. Not only does he use satire and parody to comment on the artifice inherent in grand opera, he also takes poetic license with the life of Maria Callas, by ending it in the grand, theatrical manner in which she lived her life. If Maria Callas could have rewritten her own story, it would not be surprising, given her nature, that she might have chosen to leave this world in this very way — as befitting the prima donna and diva that she had become.

Galas was a huge success for Ludlam, causing both the *New York Times* and *Time* magazine to list it as one of the best plays of 1983 before it finally closed in the spring of 1984. Indeed, most critics commented on the limitations within the script, but gave honors to Ludlam anyway due to his brilliant "diva-like" performance as the quintessential opera star. For the first time in years, the Ridiculous Theatrical Company was in the black financially, and Ludlam felt closer than ever to his ultimate dream.

That same spring, Ludlam and company mounted his new play, *How to Write a Play*, giving only three sold-out performances in order to satisfy the requirements for funding from the various foundations. *How to Write a Play: An Absolute Farce* was Ludlam's personal testimony to writing a play under a deadline in order to acquire government funding, and Ludlam threw in everything but the proverbial kitchen sink. The main characters are Charles and Everett, based on the obvious. Charles is sitting at his typewriter trying desperately to write a new play to meet an important deadline. In the course of the play, everything and anything that could keep him from this task occurs. A mistake in the trade papers lists their apartment as the audition site and everyone from their very overweight maid, Natalie, to a group of gay seniors shows up. Natalie gets stuck trying to jump out the window, a gorilla appears on a leash, a South American general appears, the Emperor and Empress of Humidia desire an audience with Charles, and last but not least, Orville Titwilly comes to audition as a balloon folder. At one point Ludlam has the character of Charles dress as Magdalena Galas, and to layer the artifice even further, pretends that another character is himself, Charles. This gives Ludlam the chance to wax poetic concerning his own merits as playwright and actor:

> CHARLES: *(Clutching at straws)* Here he is everybody! America's foremost comic playwright, Charles Ludlam ... a real genius! ... One of the great

minds of the theater! ... A man whose profound understanding of human nature has made him a modern bard! ... A man with a consummate ear for dialogue ... Mr. Eloquence himself, Charles Ludlam![47]

After all of the distracting events have occurred, in a quiet apartment once again, the character Charles expresses his panic to Everett that he will not finish his play by the deadline. Everett, in a calm manner, makes a simple suggestion:

> EVERETT: Why don't you just write about all the distractions and interruptions that happen to you when you're trying to write a play?
> CHARLES: (*Brightening*) That's a brilliant idea! I'll do it! (*He sits down at the typewriter, threads it with a piece of paper, and with a faraway look in his eye, begins to giggle and type.*)[48]

After the *real* Ludlam successfully met the deadline, though, the funding did come through and Ludlam immediately began previews of the new play he had been crafting, *The Mystery of Irma Vep*, based on the lurid potboiler novels of nineteenth century Victorian England called "penny dreadfuls."

THE MYSTERY OF IRMA VEP

Out of the entire canon of Ludlam's plays, *The Mystery of Irma Vep* was perhaps the most highly acclaimed by the critics. And it is, today, the one Ludlam play that is consistently being produced in theatres all across the country. It is, arguably, the pinnacle of Ludlam's concept of ridiculosity realized in theatrical form. It combines a tightly structured plot with full and complete character development and is driven by potent conflict on many levels. It is stuffed with lines lifted directly from nineteenth century literature. It also possesses the sensibility of the cinematic gothic horror/melodrama, which is fairly unavoidable since major components of its storyline are lifted directly from several of these movies, yet it is chockfull of burlesque gag lines and the kinds of self-conscious stage effects which had become so firmly associated with Ludlam's Theatre of the Ridiculous.

One major criticism of Ludlam throughout his career was that he always seemed to surround himself with bad actors. Some critics even ventured that it was a calculated ploy to make himself shine all the brighter. However, Ludlam wrote *The Mystery of Irma Vep* for a cast of two — himself and Everett Quinton, each playing four different characters. This was an aesthetic choice, reflecting Ludlam's unshakable belief in his own vision, rather than a reaction to any criticism of his casting choices, for Ludlam's overall concept for the structure of *Irma Vep* was the old burlesque notion of the quick-change. His fascination with magic and illusion went back to his childhood, and the idea of creating the illusion of an actor exiting out one door and immediately entering through another across the stage dressed as a different character was the hook around which Ludlam built the show.

The quick-change as a theatrical device dates back to the days of burlesque and melodrama. Once again, Ludlam felt compelled to breathe new life into a virtually extinct theatrical genre, proving that with the appropriate sensibility, it is possible to probe the past and find inspiration, rather than mere anachronism. Ridiculosity proved to be the very sensibility that could revive the nineteenth century gothic horror and fashion a theatrical event that would hilariously recreate it for the twentieth century.

In *The Mystery of Irma Vep*, Ludlam and Quinton, each playing four characters, changed costumes — and roles — in as little time as it took the audience to adjust themselves in their seats. The curtain opens on the drawing room of Mandacrest, a sprawling manor on the English Moors. Edgar Hillcrest, the lord of the manor, has just returned with his new bride, ex–chorus girl Enid, after losing his first wife, Irma Vep, in a mysterious mishap at the millcreek. He still keeps a candle burning on the mantelpiece in front of Irma's large, dominating portrait, as a memorial to his first love. It seems Irma drowned mysteriously after she discovered their son, Victor, with his neck torn open, apparently by some wild beast, possibly her pet wolf, who was also named Victor.

The maid Jane Twisden and the one-legged stableboy Nicodemus Underwood, still devoted to their former mistress Irma, find it difficult to accept Enid as the new lady of the house and are only coldly cordial to her, barely even acknowledging her presence. While Lady Enid and Jane are awkwardly getting acquainted, the howling of a wolf is heard in the distance, raising the hair on Jane's manly arms. It turns out that the wolf that killed the boy Victor was never caught. Lord Edgar decides once and for all to find the wolf and kill it, finally putting to rest the tragedy that occurred at the millcreek. In a short while, he enters dragging a dead carcass, supposedly the wolf Victor, and orders Nicodemus to take down the picture of Irma and blow out the candle. Jane enters, horrified at what Nicodemus is doing, and approaches the carcass slowly, ending Act One, Scene One with the melodramatic cliffhanger line, "It's no rejoicing there'll be this night, Nicodemus Underwood. He's killed the wrong wolf."[49]

Later that evening, Enid comes downstairs, unable to sleep, and encounters Jane, who launches into the history of Mandacrest and the mysterious goings-on that have occurred. After they finish their toddies Jane retires to bed, suggesting that Enid read one of Lord Edgar's treatises on Egyptology. Suddenly a terrifying intruder appears at the French doors and chases Enid around the room, until it catches her and drags her out the French doors, amidst her shrill screams for help. Lord Edgar knows that it is none other than Victor the wolf come back to haunt him. He takes his pistol, vowing to kill it for sure this time. Meanwhile, Nicodemus enters carrying the limp body of Lady Enid and takes her off to another room as Jane enters, awakened by the commotion. Informed of the return of Victor, Nicodemus retrieves a gun from the wall which, in a struggle with Jane, goes off unexpectedly, causing the picture of Irma Vep on the mantlepiece to ooze blood.

The following day Lord Edgar, observing the numbed and quasi-catatonic Lady Enid, fears that what his Egyptian studies have taught him may actually be true, that there are really creatures who never die, known as vampires. He decides to journey to the tomb of the Princess Pev Amri, who was preserved in a state of suspended animation and was known as She Who Sleeps But Will One Day Wake.

Act two opens in Egypt. Lord Edgar has hired the services of Alcazar, a treasure seeker's guide to the tombs, who leads him to the Princess Pev Amri's tomb. Lord Edgar slowly opens the sarcophagus, revealing a mummified woman with one stone-cold breast exposed and a scroll in her hand which reads "She Who Sleeps But Will One Day Wake." Edgar has found his treasure. Suddenly the mummified woman comes to life speaking in ancient gibberish. He runs to find Alcazar while the mummy returns to her sarcophagus, leaving the room deserted when they return. Lord Edgar decides to take the mummy home and hauls the sarcophagus out.

Back at Mandacrest, Lady Enid has just returned from a short vacation to a sanitarium. She sleeps all day and she stays up all night, evidence of her insanity according to Jane. Jane finishes her rounds of gossip and chores, and leaves Nicodemus alone in sight of the full moon glowing outside the window. He begins a magical transformation into a wolf, exposing his true supernatural essence to the audience, and flees through the French doors, looking for his next victim.

Later that night, Lady Enid and Jane spend a quiet evening playing duets on their dulcimers and drinking toddies. Enid complains to Jane that Edgar is ignoring her, so Jane talks her into wearing one of the pretty dresses in the closet to surprise him, knowing full well that if Edgar were to see Enid in one of Irma's old dresses, he would explode. As she exits, Lady Enid explores the room briefly, discovering a pretty ornament on the fireplace which triggers a sliding panel, revealing behind a bookcase a cage with a shrouded figure. She claims to be Lady Irma, held prisoner because she, and she alone, knows where the secret jewels are hidden. Hearing Lord Edgar approach, Enid quickly closes the panel, hiding the mysterious figure. Of course, Lord Edgar is aghast at Lady Enid for having on one of Irma's dresses. They argue and Edgar leaves in a huff. Left alone, Lady Enid, who now has the keys to the cage, pulls the figurine, revealing again the shrouded figure. Enid unlocks the cage, and the figure leaps out and begins choking her. She struggles with the stranger and pulls off a mask exposing Jane, the real vampire, who admits to killing Lady Irma and the boy Victor. Enid flees with Jane in hot pursuit. As Enid flies back into the room, Nicodemus enters briefly and tries to calm and comfort her, leaving hastily as he feels the effect of the full moon outside. Suddenly Jane flies through the mummy case wielding a meat cleaver, intent on killing Lady Enid. Enid hurries for the door, snagging her robe in it as she exits. While Jane pounds on the door, Nicodemus the werewolf rushes in, attacking Jane and carrying her out through the French doors. He immediately returns with only Jane's dress, when Lord Edgar dashes in and shoots Nicodemus, killing him, thereby ending the reign of terror at Mandacrest.

In the final scene, Lord Edgar and Lady Enid are seated comfortably in their Victorian drawing room, contemplating the recent events. Soon the conversation turns to Edgar's trip to Egypt and his invaluable discovery. Unable to bear it any longer, Lady Enid sheepishly admits that it was she in the sarcophagus. She also confesses that the tomb was, in fact, in an Egyptian restaurant in London, and her father is really Professor Lionel Cuncliff, the leading Egyptologist and sarcophagologist at Cambridge University. Enid begs his forgiveness and professes that she did it only to win Edgar over from the spirit of his first wife. Lord Edgar lovingly forgives Lady Enid, as they both walk, arm-in-arm, toward the French doors. Swinging the doors wide, Lord Edgar turns to Lady Enid, both silhouetted by moonlight, and they ardently end the story with lines borrowed directly from the last speeches in Henrik Ibsen's play, *Little Eyolf*.

Ludlam once remarked that he had worked backwards in *Irma Vep*, starting with the theatrical devices and then developing the story, he meant in order to create a logical and linear story. By this he had first to work out all of the technical elements necessary to enable that story to unfold. Chief among these was the demanding technical structure of the play. In order for two actors successfully to play four characters apiece with quick changes, Ludlam had to map out the end and work backward toward the beginning, carefully planning each exit and entrance to avoid an actor colliding with himself on stage. According to Ludlam:

> A playwright can usually bring on any character at any time that he wants, but I couldn't because it involved a change — an exit which had to be justified

and covered — and then you had to think of where the various characters had gone and where you had left them and how you could get them back on. It's really a kind of Rubik's Cube effect. Every time you try to change one element, all the other elements go out of whack. It's that precise.[50]

By this stage of Ludlam's career however, he was very much in command of his playwriting skills, having already written and produced over twenty plays. His challenge was not only to tell a gothic horror story with a coherent beginning, middle and end, but also to carefully plot that story so that the actors would exit as one character and miraculously reappear across the stage as another. After he had successfully accomplished this logistical task, he then began working vigorously with Quinton, who designed the costumes, to systematize the quick-changes, often spending a disproportionate amount of the rehearsal period working out this complex detail. As he revealed in an article in *Theatre Crafts*:

> Quick-change is a branch of magic, and a lot of what happens is based on misdirection. The changes are possible, but they don't seem possible. When I'm walking offstage at a leisurely pace, I burst into an incredible run the minute I'm out of sight. Everything goes at a much faster tempo backstage. It deceives you, because you see the person exit slowly and you're still hearing the voice.
>
> Ventriloquism creates the illusion that the actor is disappearing into the distance on one side of the stage, while he's actually already on the other side being dressed as a different character. The three dressers operate balletically, like a Bunraku team, so we almost don't have to look while we're flying through. We worked with a stopwatch when rehearsing the changes. Those were nine-second costume changes! You can't even be handed something from a different side than you're used to.
>
> It's up to the actor to create the illusion that this madness did not just happen, that you're coming from a place where something other than a quick-change occurred. It takes tremendous concentration to avoid coming on looking like you've just been through a car wash. We sweat so profusely, in fact, that we have paper towels — whole rolls — to use as blotters, so that we can enter looking fresh.[51]

Technically speaking, the set had to be rigged intricately for the execution of the many supernatural effects that were to be presented. For instance, when Jane and Nicodemus struggle with the gun and shoot Lady Irma's portrait, the picture is supposed to appear to be bleeding. Lighting designer Lawrence Eichler described the creation of this special effect as follows:

> The bleeding effect is [like] an upside down thermometer. You know, on a telethon, as they strive toward their goal, they have a red stripe moving up a slot behind a placard. Here, the red slot drops down from above, so it looks like blood dripping. The portrait is painted on canvas glued to a thin aluminum

sheet, which enables us to cut a hole shaped like a thermometer. Behind this long slot a stick with its bottom half painted in a neutral tone slides down. As the top red half is revealed, we see blood dripping.[52]

Eichler also incorporated the use of footlights which, in their period, would merely have illuminated the stage. Instead, they became horror lights to which the actors played when appropriate. According to Everett Quinton, "When I say, 'You left red marks on my wrist,' I put my wrist right into the red. I'm strangled by the invisible Irma in blue light, so it looks like I'm turning blue."[53] The set, which Ludlam designed and painted, was thoroughly researched; the Victorian interior incorporated rich and diverse colors, including decorative finishes creating *trompe l'oeil* effects. It was authentic looking, in an artificial and excessive way. Through the back French doors was a canvas painted to look like the English moor, stark and darkly mysterious. Of course, Ludlam made no attempt to hide the fact that this was merely a canvas, so at the very end of the play, when Enid and Edgar, waxing overly romantic and sentimental, walk arm-in-arm toward the doors reciting the *Little Eyolf* dialogue, the juxtaposition of the obviously artificial canvas outdoors provides the precise clash of styles and genres which propelled the parody and satire in Ludlam's work.

When Ludlam as Nicodemus turns into a werewolf on stage at the end of the play, the elements of ventriloquism and misdirection combine to accomplish the task cheaply and simply. As Ludlam tells it, "It took millions of dollars for Michael Jackson to turn into a werewolf, but it only cost me forty dollars for costume pieces and props. I have things hidden behind the draperies and I just pull them out. I distract you with my body movements. I stagger, and meanwhile I'm putting on the gloves behind the drapes and the lights are flashing."[54]

The film which became the basic plot framework for *Irma Vep* was *Rebecca*, directed by Alfred Hitchcock, based on Daphne du Maurier's gothic novel. It is the story of a young, innocent girl who falls in love with a wealthy older gentleman who has recently lost his wife under mysterious circumstances. He marries her and brings her to his enormous and opulent estate, Manderley, transformed by Ludlam into Mandacrest for *The Mystery of Irma Vep*. Perhaps the most striking resemblance to the film is found in the character of Mrs. Danvers the maid, played by Judith Anderson, who, in Ludlam's play, became the maid of Mandacrest, Jane Twisden. Mrs. Danvers adored Rebecca, the first wife of wealthy Maxim, and will not adjust to having a new mistress of the house, much like Jane's relationship with the new Lady Enid. Both Mrs. Danvers and her colleague Jane are icy cold, with a stare that can freeze the blood. In the movie, Mrs.

Danvers goes mad in the end, sets Manderley ablaze, and perishes in the fire. Ludlam takes this a step farther in his play, making Jane the villainess and the source of the evil curse upon Mandacrest.

Ludlam directly lifted from *Rebecca* and also Henrik Ibsen's *Rosmersholm* the theme of the spirit of the dead first wife who remains alive and haunts the first husband. In fact, in Ibsen's play, the character which could be linked to Lady Enid is named *Rebecca* West, a young girl who falls in love with the older widower Rosmersholm. Theatre critic Michael Feingold of the *Village Voice* was the only reviewer to catch this link of *Irma Vep* to playwright Henrik Ibsen:

> In the midst of the horror wildness and the vaudeville spoofery, he has pasted in, so as to demonstrate their links with the basic Gothic-horror plot structures, excerpts from the most sublime works of the most gravely dignified of modern playwrights. Yes, that's right, Henrik Ibsen. If you've never been aware of the connection between *Rosmersholm* and *Rebecca*, or the possible source of Lon Chaney Jr.'s Wolf Man movies in *Little Eyolf*, prepare to meet thy doom and go down laughing.[55]

Indeed, Ludlam even takes dialogue from the film and play and implants it verbatim in *The Mystery of Irma Vep*:

> LADY ENID: They cling to their dead a long time at Mandacrest.
> JANE: I think it's the dead that cling to us. It's as if they just don't want to let go. Like they can't bear to leave us behind.[56]

Another cinematic source indirectly used for *The Mystery of Irma Vep* is the gothic romance film *Wuthering Heights*, based on the novel by Emily Bronte. Directed by William Wyler and starring Laurence Olivier and Merle Oberon, this movie takes place on the same English moors where Ludlam placed his Mandacrest tale. Ludlam did not directly use the story of this film in his play, but used instead the romantic and dangerous milieu of the stark, barren moors. Ludlam does, however, at one point lift a line directly from the movie where a young Cathy is encouraging a young, indigent Heathcliff, and recycles it in *Irma Vep* to the characters of Jane and Nicodemus. But Ludlam indulges his sense of ridiculosity by adding a tag line to his scene, thus creating the level of comedic artifice which makes it impossible for either the actors or the audience to become too sentimentally enmeshed:

> NICODEMUS: I was abandoned. Found on the doorstep of a London doss house. My own mother didn't want me.
> JANE: Who knows but your father was emperor of China and your mother was an Indian queen, each of them able to buy up Mandacrest with one

week's income. And you were kidnapped by wicked sailors and brought to England. Were I in your place, I would frame high notions of my birth, and the thought of what I was should give me courage and dignity.
NICODEMUS: Thank you, Janey. In the future while I'm shoveling shit I'll try to think of myself as a prince in disguise.[57]

By switching the lines from the young, romantic leads to the maid and stableman/grounds keeper, Ludlam displays the tactics of ridiculosity. Through the many levels, the concept of recycling need not necessarily result in a literal transference from the original source. Rather, Ludlam begs, borrows and steals from anything he deems appropriate, and applies it within his play wherever it suits his ridiculous purpose, regardless of whether it remains accurate in context or true to the intent of the original.

The third film Ludlam borrowed from was the gothic horror melodrama *The Hounds of the Baskervilles*, based on the novel by Sir Arthur Conan Doyle and starring Basil Rathbone. Again, Ludlam drew upon this film's aura of mystery and fascination with the dank moors of England. He used this film for its sense of the supernatural, where a vicious hound, thought to be a werewolf (recast in *Irma Vep* as Victor the wolf), has haunted the Baskervilles' manor for the last 200 years. Ludlam has effectively cross-referenced all three of these films, while adding fleeting moments from *The Wolfman*, *The Mummy*, and Charlotte Bronte's novel and the Orson Welles film of *Jane Eyre*, specifically the bit with the shrouded figure in a cage. In Welles' film, the character Grace Poole is the insane wife of Mr. Rochester, whom he keeps confined in an attic room of his castle.

As previously noted, one of Ludlam's major literary heists used in *Irma Vep* was the "penny-dreadful," a mainstay of bad, melodramatic Victorian literature of the nineteenth century. Chief among these was *Varney the Vampyre: The Feast of Blood*, a gothic horror novel which provided Ludlam rich fodder for spoofing the genre. Ludlam also synthesized into his play the ambience of Louis Feuillade's silent-movie serials, as well as the collage novels of surrealist Max Ernst. In addition, Ludlam distinctly recalls H. Rider Haggard's classic *She*, with just a hint of Hilton's climactic ending in Shangri-La lifted from *Lost Horizon*, with Lord Edgar's departure for Egypt to unravel the mystery of the ancient royal princess who sleeps but will some day awaken. But as we have seen, Ludlam did not use this literature for mere general impressions and atmospheric references; he also seized upon specific lines from a variety of literary sources, using them in ways that subtly displayed his continued ability to paste together a collage. There is no metaphoric or symbolic meaning implied with their use outside of Ludlam's exercising his sense of ridiculosity for purely comic effect. Some few examples follow.

In Act One, Scene Three of *Irma Vep*, after Lady Enid returns from being dragged off by the mysterious intruder, Ludlam collages a number of lines from Act Two, Scene Two, of Shakespeare's *Macbeth*, where Macbeth begins to uncoil as he recounts to Lady Macbeth his killing of the king. The scene from Shakespeare goes as follows:

> MACBETH: Methought I heard a voice cry "Sleep no more!
> Macbeth does murder sleep!" — the innocent sleep,
> Sleep that knits up the ravelled sleave of care,
> The death of each day's life, sore labour's bath,
> Balm of hurt minds, great nature's second course,
> Chief nourisher in life's feast.
> LADY MACBETH: What do you mean?
> MACBETH: Still it cried "Sleep no more!" to all the house:
> "Glamis hath murdered sleep, and therefore Cawdor
> Shall sleep no more, Macbeth shall sleep no more!"[58]

In *Irma Vep* it appears as:

> LORD EDGAR: Now, you'd getter get some sleep.
> LADY ENID: No sleep! No sleep for me! I shall never sleep again! Sleep is dead. Sleep is dead. She hath murthered sleep. I dare not be alone to sleep. Don't leave me alone. Don't ever leave me alone again. For sleep is dead. Sleep is dead. Who murthered sleep?[59]

Near the end of *The Mystery of Irma Vep*, when Lord Edgar shoots Nicodemus, thinking he is killing the vicious werewolf, Ludlam lifts a bit of Oscar Wilde's *Ballad of Reading Gaol*. A dying Nicodemus lies in the arms of his master, Lord Edgar, and the following dialogue ensues:

> NICODEMUS: Each man kills the thing he loves. The coward does it with a kiss, the brave man with a sword. Yet, Nicodemus did love.
> LORD EDGAR: Nicodemus, Nicodemus, I've killed you. In earnest.
> NICODEMUS: Thank you. *(Dies)*[60]

This is Wilde's original:

> Yet each man kills the thing he loves,
> By each let this be heard,
> Some do it with a bitter look,
> Some with a flattering word.
> The coward does it with a kiss,
> The brave man with a sword![61]

One final illustration of Ludlam's filching from past literary works occurs near the end of the play, where he miraculously appears as Lady

Enid and Nicodemus simultaneously, virtually performing the scene with himself as the two separate characters, lifting the concept of the quick-change to new heights. The following borrows cleverly from Edgar Allan Poe's *The Raven*:

> LADY ENID: *(There is a tapping at the window, as in Act 1)* There it is again. The rapping! The rapping! As if someone gently tapping. Tapping at my chamber door!
> NICODEMUS: *(Off)* Hey Lady Enid! What's going on? *(Poking his head through the door)* What's going on here? *(Ducks out)*
> LADY ENID: Oh Nicodemus. I heard a rapping, a rapping, as if someone gently tapping, tapping at my chamber door! *(She ducks out)*
> NICODEMUS: *(Popping in)* There there, Lady Enid. 'Tis the wind and nothing more.[62]

Along with the cinematic and literary references, *The Mystery of Irma Vep* is rife with Ludlam's usual bad jokes and corny lines, another mainstay of ridiculosity. Although his skills as a playwright had become more refined, Ludlam still implanted these groaners into *Irma Vep* to produce the distance he always strove to create between the actor and role. This glaring artifice not only provides an abundance of comedic theatricality, but also it allows the audience to experience momentarily the actor's viewpoint. When these ludicrous lines of dialogue appear, the actor, in essence, steps briefly out of his role and comments on the ongoing theatrical event, creating a window for the audience to relate directly to the actor, as well as to the role portrayed. This, in part, accounts for the great success and loyal following Ludlam experienced with the Ridiculous Theatrical Company. He injected his personality into every role he played. He was constantly creating the character of Charles Ludlam as much as he was creating any of the fictional ones, and he did this by calling attention to the inherent artifice of the theatre.

A marvelous example of this in *The Mystery of Irma Vep* occurs in the second scene of act two, when Lady Enid and Jane sit down with their toddies and strum a duet of "The Last Rose of Summer" on their dulcimers. At one point Lady Enid says:

> LADY ENID: Where is Nicodemus? I want to have a word with him.
> JANE: I'm afraid that's not possible, Lady Enid.
> LADY ENID: And why not? Send for Nicodemus. I demand to see him at once.
> JANE: Nicodemus can't come, Lady Enid. For obvious reasons.
> LADY ENID: Obvious reasons? *(The light dawns)* Oh! Oh! For obvious reasons.
> JANE: Are you fond of Nicodemus?

LADY ENID: Fond of Nicodemus? Sometimes I feel that I am Nicodemus. That Nicodemus and I are one and the same person.[61]

What makes this scene so funny and, simultaneously, so dramatically intriguing is that the roles of Lady Enid and Nicodemus are played by the same actor. Given the mechanics of the play where two actors play numerous roles, with rapid costume changes, the audience is intentionally let in on the joke before the actor, and waits patiently to see how this will resolve itself. Of course, as the light dawns, the actor realizes, right in the midst of the play, what the audience already knows: that this is a physical impossibility for the very fact of the quick-change, the theatrically technical element which is at the very heart of the aesthetic of this play. Ludlam clearly set this theatrical device up from the first scene of the play. Obviously the actor did not inadvertently forget he plays both these parts; rather it is just Ludlam's way of calling even more attention to the already blatant artifice. It also did no harm to have the last speech of Lady Enid echo Cathy's line from *Wuthering Heights*: "Ellen, I *am* Heathcliff!"

At another moment, Ludlam calls attention to the artifice by making overt references to dressing in drag, a key ingredient in ridiculosity. This exchange takes place in the second act when Jane convinces Lady Enid to wear one of Irma's old dresses, still hanging in the closet:

LADY ENID: How do I look?
JANE: Lovely, Lady Enid. It's sure to put Lord Edgar into a romantic mood. This dress was always his favorite.
LADY ENID: Are you sure he really likes it?
JANE: Positive. He's even worn it himself when in an antic mood, in younger, happier days. *(Exits)*.
LADY ENID: Well any man who dresses up as a woman can't be all bad![64]

The obvious irony here is that the audience knows full well that Ludlam, a man, is in fact dressed as Lady Enid while reciting these lines, further heightening the duplicity.

Another example of Ludlam's calling attention to the inherent theatricality of the event occurs when Lord Edgar travels to Egypt to decipher the mystery of She Who Sleeps But Will One Day Wake. Upon unwinding the mummy Pev Amri (which we clearly see is actually Lady Enid in disguise), and after performing a ridiculous ritual, she comes to life. Ludlam creates the comedy here both visually and verbally. When unwrapped, Ludlam, as Pev Amri, wore a plastic breast-plate with two enormous protruding breasts. As she comes to life, the mummy and Lord Edgar carry on the following ridiculous conversation:

PEV AMRI: Habebe? Habebe tay?
LORD EDGAR: Oh God!
PEV AMRI: *(Dances, then)* Fahouta bala bala mem fou ha ram sahadi Kar-
nak!
LORD EDGAR: Oh exquisite! Exquisite beauty!
PEV AMRI: Han fu bazaar danbazaar.
LORD EDGAR: Forgive me divine one, but your spoken language is lost on
me.
PEV AMRI: Mabrouka. Geza. Ankh! Ankh!
LORD EDGAR: Ankh! Life! Ankh! Life! Life!
PEV AMRI: Ankh ... life?
LORD EDGAR: Ankh ... life.
PEV AMRI: Life. Life!
LORD EDGAR: Life!
PEV AMRI: *(Writhing indicates stiffness of spine)* Cairo! Cairo! Practor![65]

Of course, Ludlam had worked it into the script that if the audience were
to boo and hiss at his ridiculously trite gag, he, as Pev Amri, would respond
sharply with "Asp!"

The critical response to *The Mystery of Irma Vep* when it opened in
1984 was unanimous in its praise, and Ludlam won a myriad of awards for
the production, thus cementing his position in the theatrical community
of New York City. Having finally broken through into national critical status, the Ridiculous Theatrical Company had a production reviewed in *Time*
magazine for the first time. Critic Richard Corliss wrote in the October 15,
1984, edition, "As author and director, Ludlam moves the melodrama with
ferocious precision; this is high-voltage comedy, not low Camp. But it is
as an actor that this supernaturally gifted jackanapes-of-all-trades shines
brightest ... it's penny wonderful."[66]

In the local New York press, Mel Gussow of the make-or-break *New
York Times* acknowledged the extraordinary acting talent of Charles Ludlam in his review of the play: "He shifts from an ominous, one-legged
haunter of the heath to the new mistress of Mandacrest. In one slightly
offstage extremely offcenter scene, he simultaneously plays both the heroine and her assailant, changing profiles and voices like a hermaphroditic
ventriloquist."[67] Renowned New York theatre critic Clive Barnes of the *New
York Post* wrote in his review entitled "Calling All Vampires to Sheridan
Sq.," "The literary tone is poised between the Brontes, Sherlock Holmes,
and the *Rocky Horror Show*. It makes Gothic seem historic, and gives fresh
blood to ghoulish. Lovely, funny, affectionate stuff. Beautifully written,
beautifully acted, and most of all, beautifully crafted."[68] Sy Syna of the *New
York Tribune* ventured deeper into the text and performance in his review,
noting that, "Ludlam usually has something serious to say tucked away
under his razzle-dazzle parodies. This is a play about transformations, not

merely of the actors into various roles, or characters within their 'stations in life' as the British like to call it, but those transformations we undergo under the force of fate or fad or societal pressures which may make us monsters or turn us into types of twinkling delight."[69]

To top off an already smashing success, *The Mystery of Irma Vep* was named among the year's best plays for 1984 by both *Time* magazine and the *New York Times*. Both Ludlam and Quinton won Drama Desk and Obie awards for their performances and Ludlam received a Maharam Foundation Award for Excellence in Design for his sets. It appeared as if Ludlam had truly hit his stride as artistic director and driving force behind the Ridiculous Theatrical Company, deftly synthesizing his roles as director, playwright, designer, producer and actor. *Irma Vep* was the perfect blend of ridiculous farce and articulate, literary borrowings. Ludlam balanced on a tightrope, teetering between the ridiculous and the sublime by juxtaposing crude, corny bits taken from burlesque and vaudeville, gothic cinematic melodramas, and erudite passages from William Shakespeare and such luminaries of literature as James Joyce, Edgar Allan Poe, Oscar Wilde and Henrik Ibsen. Michael Feingold, in his *Village Voice* review, was correct in his assessment that anyone from a "total ignoramus to a super sophisticate" could enjoy *The Mystery of Irma Vep*. This broad accessibility is surely the main reason this particular Ludlam play is produced so often in regional theatres across the country.

By the way, in case there is still any mystery about *Irma Vep* left untold, the name Irma Vep is, in Ludlam's words, vampire "anagrammatized." Of course, the same is true of Pev Amri. For the truly perceptive, Ludlam cleverly buried the mysterious plot twist of *The Mystery of Irma Vep* in its very title. Following the enormous success of *Irma Vep*, Ludlam followed with his next production, *Salammbo*, in the fall of 1985, and played the two in repertory.

SALAMMBO

Freely adapted from the novel by Gustave Flaubert, Ludlam's ridiculous version of *Salammbo*, subtitled "An Erotic Tragedy," provided him with a decadent atmosphere ripe for satire and parody. As Ludlam wrote in the printed program of the production:

> Flaubert's extravagant novel, *Salammbo*, has exerted a certain fascination since it first appeared in 1862. It was both an immediate success and scandal ... In dramatizing Flaubert's novel, it was necessary to evoke the sense of the extreme within the finite frame of an evening in the theatre. While the play

may seem shocking to those unfamiliar with the original, we hope that we have found in essence what Flaubert gave us in such comprehensive detail. But isn't our task in staging such a work, identical to the dilemma of the play's protagonists? To accomplish in art what is unattainable in life.[70]

The play, like the novel, is set in the Carthage of 300 B.C. where Salammbo is priestess of the high moon and keeper of the Sacred Veil of Tanit. Her nemesis, Matho, chief of the barbarians, camps (in more ways than one in Ludlam's version) with his men outside the city gates, hoping to get revenge on Salammbo's father Hamilcar Barca, Suffete of Carthage, by stealing the Sacred Veil. Matho's mission is successful and a panicked Salammbo flees from her opulent and guarded world to retrieve the stolen veil. In the process, Matho and Salammbo develop a raging passion for each other and Salammbo loses her virginity to her enemy, but she does successfully retrieve the veil, after performing the Dance of the Seven Veils.

Flaubert's novel, written in 1848, was a metaphorical reaction to political and bureaucratic corruption and excess, as well as the revolutions mounted to seize back the people's power in nineteenth century France. Carthage is portrayed as a diseased and decadent place, where power is given to a corpulent few and wealth is the sole key to public office. The love and passion between Salammbo and Mathos are pitted against this dire background, providing a forum for the argument that love conquers all — even greed, lechery and evil. As Robert Heide wrote in the *New York Native*, "It was about the official religion, which was a state religion, a fascist state, that stated, 'All who touch the veil must die!' And then you had to die to prove that they were right — in the play — that society always has to be right, even if they're dead wrong in actuality."[71]

Ludlam's interest in the story was layered with political and social intent. It allowed him to comment on the hypocritical style of conservatism that Ronald Reagan brought to the White House in the 1980s, with his paternalistic posturing on moral issues, done to appease the religious right, which took the spotlight off of the unfair redistribution of the country's wealth, done to appease big business and big money. Ludlam continually saw his fellow gays being persecuted and slandered in the name of "traditional family values." Although he never considered his company a gay theatre, he wanted to give the gay community something — a play of their own.

Throughout Flaubert's novel, the barbarians are described as huge men with bulging veins in their arms. As Ludlam wrote, "I often have thought about those old paintings of heroes with their incredible bodies. It seemed to me, on consideration, that this was the way these characters should be represented in the theatre, not by having scrawny actors who looked silly in tights in those roles."[72] To solve this problem, Ludlam hired the biggest bodybuilders he could find, and used them in erotic and sensual ways. It did not matter that none of them had ever acted before. That had never been a problem for Ludlam. It was the sheer physical decadence that Ludlam desired to match, a quality found in Flaubert's original. Also, he knew that the gay community, in particular, would converge on the theatre, as if drawn by magnets, to see these well-oiled, well-developed male specimens. According to Ludlam, "I was trying to create something decadent while making it at the same time almost a spoof of decadence, I wanted to create something very exotic that would also be erotic."[73]

As Ludlam's *Salammbo* begins, the stage lights slowly rise out of the darkness, with mysterious Egyptian-like music playing, onto a set of marbled columns, representing Hamilcar's gardens. On the tiny stage at Sheridan Square were scantily clad, well-oiled bodybuilders, posing and flexing their gigantic muscles, with their swords, sheathed at their sides, becoming playful phallic symbols as the eroticism built. The images harken back to the Steve Reeves Hercules movies of the 1950s and 1960s, which many gay men remember vividly from their youth. We learn that the barbarians are angry at Hamilcar's refusal to pay them for saving Carthage, and their frenzy mounts to a fever pitch. At just the point where the collective chant appears the most raucous, Ludlam undercuts the moment with a comic gag line:

> THIRD BARBARIAN: We've earned our pay. Where is it?
> OTHER BARBARIANS: Yes, where is it?
> THIRD BARBARIAN: Bring us wine, meat, and women!
> *(Others take up the chant)*
> BARBARIANS: Wine meat women! Wine meat women! Wine meat women!
> FIRST BARBARIAN: Just wine and meat for me, thanks.[74]

Not only does Ludlam interrupt with comedy, he tantalizes his gay audience with what could be considered gay erotic art. Ludlam continues in this manner as in the scene where Salammbo and Matho make love: they roll in on a bed with four of the bodybuilders posing as bedposts, flexing and gyrating. The entire physical surrounding is immersed in a sexual soup. In Act Two, just prior to Salammbo's Dance of the Seven Veils, four bodybuilders enter following a papier-mâché golden calf, which they admire in a lustful, ritualistic manner. All of the sudden a fifth muscleman enters — in high heels — and all five begin a daisy-chain of a blatantly homoerotic nature.

Ludlam got plenty of ridiculous comedy out of the bodybuilders' functioning as sexual statues, but he scored a ridiculous coup with the man he cast as Matho — Philip Campanaro — who made no attempt whatsoever to hide a very thick Brooklyn accent. The juxtaposition of such an overtly masculine man with a perfectly muscled physique, dressed in classic Hercules garb, with a nasal, whiny voice which turned every "th" in the English language to "d," caused critic Terry Helbing of the *New York Native* to write, "Campanaro gives new dimension to the term 'bad acting'."[75] Don Nelsen of the *New York Daily News* reviewed the play and wrote, "When [Ludlam] performs opposite Philip Campanaro's solid-oak Matho, the result is something like a mischievous nightingale singing to a giant clothespin."[76]

Many of the critics were dismayed by Ludlam's choice of Campanaro as the hero Matho, writing that after the success of *Irma Vep*, Ludlam had taken a giant step back into amateurism. But there were some who championed Ludlam's design, such as James Magruder, who wrote that, "Campanaro's body — the inverted triangle of myth — and his borough accent, combined with a lack of dramatic training, create a stage presence of such stupefying gaucheness that it can *only* be sincere."[77] Magruder and a few other critics were aware that Ludlam had consciously and purposefully cultivated this so-called amateurish style. Bad acting had always been a part of Ludlam's aesthetic, but some critics thought he had crossed the line from "so bad it's good" into "so bad it's just bad."

Perhaps one of Ludlam's most controversial casting decisions was in *Salammbo*, where he cast a 500-pound woman, Katy Dierlam, in the role of Hanno, an evil and corrupt general afflicted with leprosy. Bending the gender the other way by having a woman play a man was not unusual for Ludlam, but some thought this bordered on misogyny. The following is Flaubert's description of Hanno in the original novel:

> He wore boots of black felt set with silver moons. His legs were swathed in linen bands like a mummy's, and the flesh bulged forth between the crossings; his belly stood out from the scarlet jerkin which covered his thighs, and the folds of his neck drooped down upon his breast like the dewlaps of an ox; his flower-painted tunic was bursting at the arm-pits; he wore a scarf, a girdle, and a wide black cloak with laced double sleeves. The wealth of his robes, his great necklace of blue stones, his golden clasps and heavy earrings did but enhance the hideousness of his deformity. He might have been some grotesque idol rough-hewn from a block of stone; for a pale leprosy covered all his body and gave him a semblance of some lifeless thing.[78]

Ludlam knew that he needed the same visual excess with Hanno that he had with the bodybuilder barbarians, and since Dierlam had already performed as Natalie, the maid, in *How to Write a Play*, it seemed only natural to him that she play Hanno. Outside of cross-gender casting, which had been a staple with the Ridiculous Theatrical Company, there was certainly no hidden agenda of misogyny on Ludlam's part in this casting choice.

The sight of this massively overweight, half-naked body sitting on the stage, his/her body covered with oozing sores and a bloody bandage covering the stump on his right arm where a hand should be, was startling. The actress wore a bald cap and thick, bushy eyebrows and was swathed in what could best be described as extra-extra-large diapers. She was surrounded by the musclemen, fanning her and feeding her flamingo lips and peacock tongues. At one point in the scene, her other hand falls off and she nonchalantly tosses it over her shoulder as she continues decadently stuffing her face. Ludlam also used Dierlam's size to its maximum comic effect when these obviously strong men attempt to get her to her feet. Again, Ludlam takes us from tragedy to burlesque in the blink of an eye, as what unfolds is similar to an old vaudeville routine. It takes five minutes to get the hefty Hanno stabilized on his feet, proving once again that nothing is sacred, not even the circus fat lady, when it comes to the ridiculous. By having an obese woman portray a man, not only was Ludlam commenting on the socially constructed gender roles that society manipulates, but he was also clearly exposing the pervasive social prejudice against fat people. Why should Dierlam's nudity on stage be considered any more "grotesque" than Black-Eyed Susan's, or Ludlam's? Because she was such the antithesis of the classical definition of beauty, some critics and audience members were horrified, but Ludlam's aesthetic was always utterly inclusive, and devoid of any kind of arbitrary bias whatsoever. All in all, it was a much more humanistic approach to theatrical representation than most conventional theatres dared to offer.

It should be noted that *Salammbo* was only Ludlam's third complete character in drag at the Ridiculous Theatrical Company; the first two were *Camille* and *Galas*. Although he was often stigmatized as a drag performer, the facts do not bear this out. As the High Priestess Salammbo, Ludlam looked like Cleopatra, covered in silk, chiffon, jewels, beads and bangles and wearing a jet-black, page-boy wig. His voice, as one critic wrote, "is a roller coaster that ascends to the innocent tones of an ingenue and descends precipitously to a Tallulah growl."[79]

The climax of the play, the Dance of the Seven Veils, allowed Ludlam's ridiculous imagination to run wild as he entered swathed in layers of chiffon pastels. His "dance" resembled something out of a Martha Graham modern dance workshop, with Ludlam gyrating and genuflecting to bizarre Oriental music. At precisely appointed times, he would strip himself of the veils one at a time, and at one point, to prove that he was anatomically correct, he lifted the veils to reveal a hairy vagina strategically applied between his legs. As the music became more frenzied, so too did the dance, except that Ludlam was now tap-dancing as if he were starring in *42nd Street* on Broadway. At just the moment when the final veil was removed, Ludlam ran offstage and a *real* woman appeared naked and collapsed on the stage. She was carried off by the barbarians and with a not-so-subtle sleight-of-hand, Ludlam reappeared, as if to say, "See, I told you I was really a woman."

Although many critics did not think *Salammbo* one of Ludlam's best plays, they unanimously praised his abilities as a comic actor. For example, Frank Rich of the *New York Times* wrote, "If Mr. Ludlam has failed to merge the sublime and the ridiculous in his writing and directions, he has, as usual, accomplished the trick in his acting. His Salammbo is masterfully comic ... the characterization achieves a dignity unknown to the jokier realms of female impersonation."[80]

Confident of his approach, Ludlam always took the negative criticism in stride. He realized that the revulsion some felt over the visual decadence in *Salammbo* was more a reflection of their own sexual and erotic fears and insecurities than a genuine criticism of the production itself. In *Salammbo*, more than in any other Ludlam production in recent years, he shoved the diversity of the human body directly into the audience's face, forcing people to grapple with their own preconceptions and bigotry. As he stated in an interview regarding *Salammbo*,

> You see these magnificent physical specimens and you have to deal with it. You have to either admit that they have a power over you or deny it. Some people are horrified by bodybuilders, which is an interesting reaction. I think horror is a perfectly legitimate thing to evoke. The play is an assault, an assault on bourgeois values, and it's an attack of fascism."[81]

Despite the controversies and the negative reviews, *Salammbo* ran in repertory with *The Mystery of Irma Vep* until the end of the season. The Ridiculous Theatrical Company closed its season with a preview of Ludlam's new play, *The Artificial Jungle*, a *film noir* for the theatre, which officially opened in September of 1986.

THE ARTIFICIAL JUNGLE

In what would be Charles Ludlam's final Ridiculous production, *The Artificial Jungle* recombines the 1940s *films noirs The Postman Always Rings Twice* and *Double Indemnity* with the pet shop locale and man-eating plant of the Off Broadway musical *Little Shop of Horrors*, all encased in the nineteenth century naturalist novel and play by Emile Zola, *Thérèse Raquin*.

Unlike *Salammbo*, this new play relied far less on visual humor and more on the style and content of its genre. In fact, *The Artificial Jungle* appears rather tame when placed against other Ludlam plays like *Bluebeard*, *Le Bourgeois Avant-Garde*, *Stage Blood* or *Big Hotel*. But Ludlam had refined his playwrighting craft, and instead of allowing the performances to inform the script, he wrote a tightly structured suspense thriller with crisp reversals that propel the action toward its end.

Ludlam's plot in *The Artificial Jungle* revolves around Chester Nurdiger ("Nurd" for short); his hot and steamy wife Roxanne; his mother; Frank Spenelli, a local cop and Chester's best friend; and Zachary Slade, a drifter who happens by and answers a "help wanted" sign that Chester has just placed in the window of his pet shop, aptly named the Artificial Jungle. We learn in the first scene that Chester will do anything to make a sale, even fake the voice of a muted parrot, tricking his best friend, Frankie, into believing the bird talks. Roxanne (Roxy for short) is bored with her life, finding little if any joy in retrieving tubifex worms, cleaning the gerbils' cages, and feeding the piranhas. As Mrs. Nurdiger dotes over her "mama's boy" son, Roxy feels even more like a caged animal than the actual pets in the shop. In strolls Zachary Slade, a Pee Wee Herman type dressed as James Dean, with mischief written all over his face. Immediately, he puts the moves on Roxy, seducing her with promises of happiness and sexual satisfaction. Although reluctant at first, Roxy realizes her tedious life is unbearable. She and Zack begin to make plans to do away with Chester so they can be together forever. But first Zack compels Chester to fix up the shop a little with a new sign, a television commercial and some new decorating. Then, after tricking him into signing a new life insurance policy, Zack enters Chester's and Roxy's bedroom late one night and suffocates Chester by holding a pillow over his face. They both drag the limp, lifeless body out to the pet shop, intent on feeding him to the lethal piranhas, but Frankie, the cop, stops by after noticing the lights are on. Roxy and Zack declare that Chester is drunk after celebrating the new shop sign, and they get Frankie to help them drag the corpse to bed, realizing that they now have the perfect alibi. When Frankie leaves, Zack and Roxy immediately drag Chester back to the shop and plunge his head into the piranha tank as the curtain closes on Act Two and the audience files out for intermission, left with the sound of piranhas voraciously gorging.

Mrs. Nurdiger, devastated over the loss of her son, does not suspect anything until she overhears Zack and Roxy talking about their roles in the murder, upon which she is seized by a paralyzing stroke left unable to move anything except her eyes, which she exercises with a vengeance. Knowing that Mrs. Nurdiger is now aware of who killed her son, Zack and Roxy begin unraveling in their paranoia; Zachary continually sees apparitions of Chester with his face eaten away all throughout the shop. However, they attempt to maintain as normal an appearance as possible, down to the ritual of Thursday night dominoes with Frankie. They leave Chester's seat vacant in his memory. Eventually, Mrs. Nurdiger begins signaling danger with her eyes and actually starts implicating Zack and Roxy by spelling their names on the table. Roxy and Zack look on in panic and fear, but Frankie misinterprets the mother's meaning and assumes she is speaking lovingly of her daughter-in-law and Zack. What Zachary and Roxanne have not taken into consideration, though, is that the heretofore mute parrot actually can talk, and it begins incriminating them by mimicking what they said at the time of the murder. Roxy steals Frankie's gun and blows the parrot off its perch, and Zack struggles with her to get the gun away. In the scuffle Roxanne is shot and slowly slides down Zach's body. Zachary reveals that he put malachite green in his drink, a cure for "ich" in fish, and falls dead from the poison. *The Artificial Jungle* ends with two tiny spotlights focused on Mrs. Nurdiger's condemning eyes, as a blues melody is heard wailing through a saxophone, and then a fade to black.

It was not coincidental that Ludlam drew from Emile Zola, father of the naturalist movement in literature and drama in the nineteenth century. Many of the underpinnings of the doctrines of naturalism rise indirectly from Charles Darwin's scientific theory of evolution propounded in *The Origin of Species*, originally published in 1859. Darwin stated that man is identical in nature to every other living species on the planet and is subjected to the same laws of nature, including the concept of evolution through survival of the fittest. The idea of the survival of the fittest is the defining principle of Darwin's theory of natural selection, which argues that the weaker individuals of a given species will be either eliminated or subordinated while the stronger, better adapted individuals will thrive and reproduce. A social ideology emerged from this scientific theory in the late nineteenth century and came to be known as Social Darwinism; it asserted that those whom society deemed as culturally and socially superior were somehow biologically superior and therefore were better equipped to rule over and dictate to those deemed less advanced. This assumption was used to explain and establish the righteousness of a variety of heinous social injustices and arbitrary class stratifications. Although Social Darwinism was short-lived as a sociological and philosophical movement, it seemed to re-emerge in the United States in the 1980s with the election of Ronald Reagan. The concept of Social Darwinism has became an integral part of the style of conservatism which developed during that decade and, indeed, continues to this day.

Given the political climate which had developed by 1986 when Ludlam opened *The Artificial Jungle*, he was surely commenting on the state of the American political landscape, especially the unjustifiable free rein given to bigotry and bias. More directly, Ludlam was referring to the unnecessary hardship of being gay in this so-called civilized society, as well as the equally artificial perspective a homosexual must adopt in order to exist within a heterosexual majority. Social Darwinism did not contemplate the homosexual's role in the evolution of mankind. This omission led to the classification of homosexuals as subhuman, inviting the predominantly heterosexual world, fortified by the alleged laws of nature, to attempt to suppress this perceivably weaker minority. Ludlam's artistry in conveying this theme lies in clever parody cloaked in the style of 1940s *film noir*, in which, not coincidentally, unbridled heterosexual lust can be found at peak levels.

In the scene from *The Artificial Jungle* when Roxanne and Zachary first admit their sexual attraction, Ludlam cleverly parodies the artificial natures of both lust and seduction in those old movies, and he also sets up classic heterosexual seduction from a homosexual perspective. In Act Two, when Roxy and Zack are finally left alone, he makes his move:

> ZACHARY: You like me, don't you?
> ROXANNE: Oh yes. I like you. I like you fine. You smell like a man. He smells like a bar of soap.
> ROXANNE: Now kiss me, Zack. Kiss me till I bleed.
> ZACHARY: You're like a wild animal.
> ROXANNE: In an artificial jungle. *(They kiss.)*[82]
> Later in the same act, as they plot the death of Chester, Roxanne and Zachary continue their pseudo-steamy love talk, furthering the obvious artifice by mimicking the dialogue of those 1940s films. Roxy is in dark glasses and Zack wears a leather jacket and jeans:
> ROXANNE: Listen, Zack, he's accident-prone. We have to plan it better, that's all. Throw 'em off our trail. Put the blame somewhere else.
> ZACHARY: Like where?
> ROXANNE: Like on the piranhas. They can strip a body in half an hour and they do a clean job. Nobody ever sent a piranha up the river.[83]

Ludlam was also satirizing the entire genre of suspense in *The Artificial Jungle*, mocking the devices of frustration which are frequently used to create suspense. Ludlam builds up his suspense in a logical manner, but the elements of shock and surprise intended to make audiences jump in their seats are usually conveyed by something absurdly ridiculous. For instance, when Frankie returns to the pet shop in Act One to return the parrot that won't talk, the conversation turns to murder:

FRANKIE: They found a woman's body cut up in four pieces.
CHESTER: Cut up in four pieces. Now how would you do that? A wing and a breast or a leg and a thigh? (*Draws imaginary lines on ROXANNE, then, as she speaks, on himself*)
ROXANNE: Stop that!
MRS. NURDIGER: Horrible.
ZACHARY: They found the pieces in a trunk some guest had left behind.
FRANKIE: No, they don't have any idea who did it.
CHESTER: (*Laughs*)
ZACHARY: And who was the victim?
FRANKIE: I'm afraid they don't know that either.
MRS. NURDIGER: You mean they can't even identify the victim?
FRANKIE: Her identity is a little hard to establish. You see, the body was naked and the head was missing.
CHESTER: Perhaps it was mislaid.

* * * *

ZACHARY: Do many crimes go unpunished?
FRANKIE: Are you kidding? Stranglings, poisonings, drownings, and fatal falls — they disappear without a scream or so much as a drop of blood. And no weapon found. The police search. But they find no clues. And the murderer is walking around free as a bird.
PARROT: (*Screams, all jump with fright*)[84]

In the scene where Roxanne and Zachary decide to go through with their plan to murder Chester, Ludlam uses the technique of excess to effect a comic, yet gruesome, outcome:

ZACHARY: Now what?
ROXANNE: Like we planned.
ZACHARY: Are you sure you want to go through with it?
ROXANNE: I'm sure if you're sure.
ZACHARY: I'm sure if you're sure.
ROXANNE: Then do it. Here's a pillow.
ZACHARY: (*Takes pillow and raises it over CHESTER's sleeping face*) Here goes. (*Pauses*) I can't go through with it.
ROXANNE: You've got to do it. We've come this far. We can't turn back now.
ZACHARY: I can't.
ROXANNE: Listen, Zack, we're on this train together and we're not getting off until the last stop.
CHESTER: (*Suddenly waking and not fully realizing where he is sees ZACK standing over him*) Hi, Zack, want some more wine — Hey, Roxanne, get another glass. A toast to ... Hey, wait a minute. What time is it? I must have ... What are you doing here? What are you doing? (*ZACHARY smothers CHESTER with the pillow*) Hey, Zack, cut it out! Ha! Ha! Stop it. That isn't funny. I can't breathe. I CAN'T BREATHE! Stop! Help! Zack! Roxanne, help me! Roxanne! (*He manages to get out from under the pillow and sees that ROXANNE is staring at him coldly*) Roxanne. Roxanne. (*ZACHARY holds the pillow over CHESTER's face again*) Mamma! Mamma! Roxanne! (*He coughs and we hear his muffled cries through the pillow. Finally the sounds*

*fade and he stops. ROXANNE and ZACHARY exchange a look. She nods.
ZACHARY removes the pillow from CHESTER's face. CHESTER jumps up
and starts screaming again)* Help! Help! Aahhhgh! *(ZACHARY smothers him
again. This time he dies.)*[85]

The final, and most hilarious, example of Ludlam's satirical treatment
of suspense in *The Artificial Jungle* occurs in the third act, after the murder, when Zachary begins seeing the dead Chester as if he were Banquo's
ghost in *Hamlet* in the worst B-grade horror movie.

In Ludlam's actual ridiculous production of *The Artificial Jungle*, the
role of Mrs. Nurdiger was played in drag by the male performance artist
Ethyl Eichelberger, who physically towered over everyone else in the cast.
At the moment in the play, when the mother discovers who really murdered
her son, Eichelberger displayed her climactic state of shock by jumping up
and doing a flip in the air, landing on the ground in the state of a stroke,
with only her eyes movable. Most critics who reviewed the show pointed
to this moment as one of the comic highlights in the play. Of course, underneath the burlesque is a serious undercurrent — the death of Chester. Ludlam conveys the horror of the events using ridiculous comic invention,
simultaneously creating layers of parody.

Apart from the parodies of suspense, Ludlam also manages to incorporate artifice purely for its comic effect, such as in Act Two when Chester
is filming a commercial for his newly refurbished pet shop. Not only does
Ludlam parody bad late-night local commercials, he also uses visual images
to accentuate the comedy. He has Chester dressed in a Tarzan costume as
Zachary videotapes him. After attempting a Tarzan cry, Chester dully
drones the lines of his copy. Meanwhile, his mother leaves and returns in
a sarong, proclaiming herself the Artificial Jungle mother. Chester lets out
his Tarzan cry again. His mother exclaims, "My son the orangutan," and
Zachary, the director, yells, "Cut! That's a good one."[86]

In performance, Ludlam's Chester was a mild-mannered nerd whose
Tarzan yell looked and sounded like a young, effeminate boy trying to
impersonate masculinity. His "pitch" also sounded like every bad used-car
salesman who should never have been put in front of the camera, causing
critic James Magruder to write, "[Ludlam's] performance captures, all at
once, the non-professional bathed in flop sweat, over-pronouncing his
lines, the huckster sincerely committed to his product, the child forced to
recite the lines of Longfellow in front of his classmates, the neighbor who
goes overboard every year making his costume for the Halloween party, and
the accountant who is wondering how much all this is going to cost."[87]

The Artificial Jungle was well received by both the critics and the public and played through April of 1987. It closed only because Ludlam had to

be hospitalized due to complications from the AIDS virus. He died on May 28 at the age of 44. On July 13, 1987, the remaining members of the Ridiculous Theatrical Company held what Tish Dace called "an extraordinary, three-and-a-half-hour celebration of Charles Ludlam's life and art" called *Tabu Tableaux* at the Second Avenue Theatre.[88] In this marathon performance, seven scenes from his plays were presented that night, including *Salammbo*, *Secret Lives of the Sexists*, and *Eunuchs of the Forbidden City*, along with slides and excerpts from films which Ludlam had been in. The evening closed with a scene from a play he had been working on at the time of his death called *Houdini: A Piece of Pure Escapism*, which sadly will never see the light of the stage.

Ludlam's life partner Everett Quinton has since taken over the reins as artistic director of the Ridiculous Theatrical Company, mixing revivals of Ludlam's works with new works of his own, created within the traditions of the ridiculous. The spirit of ridiculosity is being kept alive.

— 7 —

Charles Ludlam
at the End

Charles Ludlam was simultaneously a Renaissance man and a traditionalist, cleverly fusing a modern sensibility into classical forms. His entire career was spent in the pursuit of becoming the *enfant terrible* of America's first nationally recognized comic repertory theatre. Despite many financial setbacks and creative roadblocks, he managed to assemble and develop a core of virtually untrained actors who matured artistically and grew to understand each other's nuances and timings so intimately that they functioned as a truly dynamic working ensemble. In the American theatre, this was, and continues to be, a rarity indeed.

Ridiculosity, as Charles Ludlam defined it through his work, was about values — establishing, and in fact revaluing values, both finding value in something considered worthless or passé and poking holes in things that are held to be sacred without question or examination, which Ludlam saw as worthless. He strove to shake up society's rigid, intractable system of values. His listing in the *1986 Current Biography Yearbook* noted, "If one theme emerges as the central force in Ludlam's work, it concerns liberation. Ludlam urge[d] people to free themselves from society's preconceived notions of what makes happiness, what determines morality and what is proper."[1]

Given his penchant for breaking down barriers, Ludlam, not surprisingly, established a Saturday morning children's theatre wing of his Ridiculous Theatrical Company, hoping to stimulate and unleash the vivid imaginations of the audiences of the future. His first venture into this new market was called *Professor Bedlam's Punch and Judy Show*, wherein he created historically accurate depictions of the legendary wooden puppets. Ludlam poured himself into the history of Punch and Judy and even hunted down an old puppeteer named Al Flossi who instructed Ludlam in the manipulation of the puppets. Actually, this was probably one of a very few children's theatre events which adults could truly enjoy as well. Even though the children may not have understood all of the subtle innuendos and double entendres, Ludlam provided enough visual and verbal stimulation to keep them utterly enthralled. In the *New York Times* review, Mel Gussow wrote, "With amazing dexterity, [Ludlam] manipulates this cast of zanies, rapidly switching characters and voices (as an added gift, Judy throatily bears the voice of Tallulah and that devil sounds suspiciously like Bela Lugosi) and offering a pyrotechnic display of verbal and technical gymnastics."[2]

His other venture into children's theatre was the Ridiculous Science Fiction Serial Puppet Theatre's production of *Anti-Galaxie Nebula*. Ludlam drew upon the old movie serials such as *Flash Gordon*, which were designed to keep the audience hanging on the edge of a cliff until the next week's installment. He also remained true to his concept of recycling materials as the sets and costumes in this science fiction gallery of farce consisted of styrofoam, popsicle sticks and various beaded odds and ends, all held together with glue and tape. As Glenn Loney observed in his review:

> Out of the most ordinary items — strands of green beads on a wooden rod make the Green Bead Man — Ludlam create[d] a Universe of marvelous fantasy. Old bits of styrofoam, painted with fluorescent colors and moved on sticks or with black-gloved hands, become mysterious spaceships, floating in an endless void inside the puppet theater's bubble. Madam X's dreaded space dirigible looked more like a deformed salami than a supersonic craft, but so what?[3]

Along with Madam X, the other super-heroic and super-evil villains in this science fiction serial included Flora the Princess from Planet Zorch, Maria Calyx, Princess Gloria, and Dr. Zesterone. Ludlam began each episode by recapping the prior episode's plot, catching the children (and adults) up with the current plot twist. He, too, would end each episode with a cliffhanger, hoping to generate enough intrigue with the kids so that they would return again and again. One of his "codas" might have sounded something like: "Will Madame X have her brain sucked and return to temporary goodness, or will she release the poison gas that will put the entire universe to sleep?" Ludlam knew that humor was humor, whether high or low, and both children and adults alike would, if nothing else, be thoroughly entertained. And Charles Ludlam was, at the very core of his being, an entertainer. His was a synthetic art in both senses — art whose goal is synthesis, or art that synthesizes. As one critic observed at a performance of *Anti-Galaxie Nebula*, "Ludlam lifted the skirt of one of the puppets, exposing the bare flesh of his wrist and palm — and the audience was shocked."[4] Ludlam's children's theatre was an instant success because he approached it from the mindset and perspective of a child, creating something magical out of Styrofoam and sticks in much the same way an imaginative child might do, playing in his or her backyard. It was a blessing for children and adults alike that Charles Ludlam never lost his childhood connection with creativity.

Sadly, that same six-year-old, wide-eyed Charlie Ludlam who wandered off at the fair and wound up at the freak show, totally mesmerized and changed forever, who watched Broadway matinees dressed as a suburban matron, who paraded as Norma Desmond on stage, who wrote, produced, directed and acted in twenty-nine plays for twenty years with a fairly stable repertory company, and who left indelible memories embedded in the minds of his fans, died from complications due to AIDS on May 28, 1987, cutting short the run of his play *The Artificial Jungle*. As longtime friend Richard Hennessy recalled, "[Charles] was very impressed by the fact that Molière's last play was about his illness and that he virtually died on the stage. Molière had worked his lung problems into the script, and coughed up blood on the stage. During *The Artificial Jungle*, "Charles was getting skinnier and skinnier, and he worked that into the play."[5] Photographs of this production depict a much thinner, gaunter Charles Ludlam, evidence of the effects of the debilitating virus. Thomas M. Disch noted in a memorial tribute in *The Nation*:

> No doubt the dead are all of equal degree. But when an artist of Ludlam's stature dies in the prime of life, the loss of what more he might have achieved becomes a common loss, and our futile regrets for the great performances we now will never enjoy — how I wish I'd seen his *Salammbo* (while I could!) are like the futile regrets we feel for other times we have been negligent of the demands of love.[6]

The weekend after his death, hundreds of mourners turned the theatre at Sheridan Square in Greenwich Village into a shrine for the departed Ludlam. Hundreds more stopped by, leaving flowers, notes and memories. The remaining members of the company and close friends gave tribute to Ludlam with another *Tabu Tableaux*, depicting highlights from his plays. Needless to say, the evening was sold out; many of his admirers felt cheated by the death of someone who strove so diligently to redefine the very barriers that he had worked so hard to break down.

At the time of Ludlam's death, he had not only negotiated a Broadway production of *Der Ring Gott Farblonjet*, but he had also been hired by the late Joseph Papp to direct a ridiculously bloody version of Shakespeare's

Titus Andronicus (à la *The Texas Chainsaw Massacre*) at the Public Theatre. In addition, Ludlam also had many ideas for new, ridiculous plays at the time of his death, leaving some as mere titles, and a few others with a brief summary:

Making Ends Meet
Tabloid Tragedy
The Boobytrap
Dr. Jeckyl and Mrs. Hyde
Voodoo Rhapsody
Voodoo Woman
IM1. RU12?
Terror of the Tongs
Murder at the Trocadero
Mission Dolores
The Critic Misbehaves
Dawn of the Brain Picklers: A Farce
The Brain That Wouldn't Die: A Chamber Opera
Withered Moonwarts or Fun and Feasting Among the Fuscias
A Fairy Frolic by Bharrells o' Funlam
Dote & Antidote: Aphrodisiamania
Copelia: The Girl with the Enamel Eyes

* * * *

Amnesia — a day in the life of a typical boring family, the Mutts, where Mr. Mutt forgets his anniversary.

The Elephant Woman — the discovery of the Elephant Woman in darkest Africa under a pile of peanuts by Dr. Livingston.

The Arrival of Godot — A play about putting on a play. The director and actors are in actual rehearsal when the director gets knocked out by a salami that was supposed to be foam rubber (the director has demanded realism). All freeze. The lights down to a pinpoint. The director wakes up and begins rehearsing The Arrival of Godot. Gogo, Didi, and Godot go into a tavern to drink.

Ludlam had also intended to write and produce an accurate recreation of the crass but tantalizing popular entertainment of an old vaudeville theatre using a small corps of comedians and rotating "specialty" acts. *Vaudeville* was intended to be an ongoing theatrical enterprise, running indefinitely. His plan was to keep an air of nostalgia and authenticity while simultaneously capturing the imaginations of a contemporary audience with the latest wonders of the world. The following is a sample program:

1. Country & Western singers
2. Lady wrestlers
3. Transvestite ballerina
4. Escape artist
5. Boa constrictor dance
6. Fire-eater or juggler
7. Calypso dancer
8. Geek-man eats live fish
9. Petomane-farting champion
10. Midget opera company

11. Armless piano player
12. Punch and Judy puppets
13. Ventriloquist
14. Tap dancers in wheelchairs
15. Magic act
16. Big production numbers
17. Animal act — trained poodles

Throughout his career, Ludlam did, from time to time, briefly branch out into other media. For years he had been working on screenplays for two films in his spare time, *The Sorrows of Dolores*, a parody of *Perils of Pauline*, and *Museum of Wax*, to be filmed entirely at the wax museum at Coney Island, which has subsequently been torn down. Ludlam desperately wanted to document this incredible piece of American folk art before its demise. In fact, he started his own production company called Shadowgraph Photoplays, the umbrella under which he created these projects.

In 1984, Ludlam appeared in the title role in Henrik Ibsen's *Hedda Gabler* at the American Ibsen Theatre in Pittsburgh, directed by Mel Shapiro. As he recalled in a journal he kept during that time, "[My] first meeting with Mel Shapiro and Leon Katz. I ask, 'What's the concept?' Mel answers, 'You are the concept.' I mention her lesbianism.... I will not seek to blend, smooth out or reconcile the contradictions in the character so much as accentuate them ... Hedda is the great sphinx."[7]

In 1985, he was hired to stage Hans Werner Henze's *The English Cat* for the Santa Fe Opera, while simultaneously flying back and forth from Florida to film his appearance as a guest star on the season premier of *Miami Vice*. Later that same year, he adapted Johann Strauss' *Die Fledermaus* for the Santa Fe Opera. In these, as in every project Ludlam undertook, he remained loyal to his ridiculous vision, infusing a modern sensibility into a time-honored form.

The project that Ludlam was closest to completing at the time of his death was a new play, *Houdini: A Piece of Pure Escapism*. As friend and business associate Steven Samuels wrote in the introduction to Ludlam's anthology of plays,

> *Houdini*, particularly, was intended to be his noblest creation, a masterful blend of history, comedy, and stage illusion, a philosophical disquisition on the tragedy of Harry Houdini's desperate attempts to escape the bonds of this life. Ludlam had received a generous grant to make a film of himself creating *Houdini*, a documentary which would have opened still more doors for him and the company.[8]

Charles Ludlam was a short, thin, balding man with no shortage of big ideas. Although his lover, Everett Quinton, has since taken over as artistic director of the Ridiculous Theatrical Company, the absence of Ludlam leaves a gigantic tear in the fabric of ridiculosity. Understandably, Quinton was unsure of his ability to fill this gap, so on his deathbed, Ludlam tried to put his lover's mind at ease by revealing his technique to Quinton as concisely as possible:

> CHARLES: You must continue the theatre.
> EVERETT: But I can't write. I don't know how.
> CHARLES: Steal lines. Orchestrate platitudes. Hang them on some plot you found somewhere else.
> EVERETT: But I don't know how to make it funny.
> CHARLES: You don't have to worry about that. Funny is in the eye of the beholder. You know yourself from doing the same play every night. Some audiences are solemn and others laugh. Let the audience be the judge of what is funny.[9]

Charles Ludlam always did have big ideas about the theatre, hoping to make an impact on a much larger scale, while not compromising even an inch of his sense of ridiculosity. In one of his very last interviews, Ludlam revealed some of those big ideas, creating a sense of anticipation for what actually might have been:

> I'd love to do the Houdini story as a big tent show. Tour the country. I also thought *Salammbo* would be great at Madison Square Garden. They have this thing called "Night of the Champions," where all the bodybuilders are in this giant show. And I was thinking of staging that, and having them all enter on zebras. All these naked musclemen on ponies painted like zebras. And thousands of dancing girls. I think it's just what the doctor ordered. I have it! The Beaumont. Human sacrifices at the Beaumont![10]

Given Charles Ludlam's track record, it is certainly plausible that these ideas would eventually have come to fruition, in one form or another. There was no vessel so large that his outrageous bounty would not fill it to overflowing.

Perhaps the most fitting way to conclude a work on the theatrical achievements and philosophy of Charles Ludlam is to recall the words of distinguished playwright, scholar and teacher Leon Katz, a dear friend and devoted fan of Ludlam, who offered these thoughts in a eulogy he delivered at Ludlam's funeral:

> He celebrated life for all of us with a comic art that amounted to genius, a revelation of comedy at the limit of what is comically conceivable. All of us remember those incredible moments of laughter so convulsive as to be almost unbearable, moments that will stay with us for the rest of our lives…. One of the greatest curtain lines in dramatic literature occurs in *Camille* when Everett, as Nichette, stands over the body of Marguerite and speaks her eulogy: "Much can be forgiven for love, and you have loved much. Toodle-oo, Marguerite."
> Our beloved, beloved Charles, toodle-oo.[11]

Charles Ludlam did love much. He loved and was beloved by the theatre; it was truly his home. He never strayed from his ambitions, despite an often bumpy ride. In addition to his 29 plays and wonderfully ridiculous way of interpreting life, perhaps his ultimate legacy will simply be that he made us laugh. This was his gift and he shared it lovingly. His innate comic genius was such that often he caused those who experienced him live on stage literally to laugh until they ached.

The chronicle of American theatre will surely provide a lasting place for Charles Ludlam. His contributions to the art of creating theatre were artistically provocative and stimulating. His works were always performed with an acute social conscience. Yet, they were also hilariously silly and child-like. If it holds true that sublime clowns and comedians tickle the collective soul, then Charles Ludlam is indeed responsible for giving the theatre-going public a wild, rollicking belly-laugh by showing us our reflections in the circus funhouse mirror of ridiculosity. In the throes of this convulsive laughter, he has taught us difficult and valuable lessons about our society and ourselves.

APPENDIX
Manifesto: Ridiculous Theater,
Scourge of Human Folly
(by Charles Ludlam)

Aim: To get beyond nihilism by revaluing combat.

Axioms to a theater for ridicule:

1. You are a living mockery of your own ideals. If not, you have set your ideals too low.

2. The things one takes seriously are one's weaknesses.

3. Just as many people who claim a belief in God disprove it with their every act, so too there are those whose every deed, though they say there is no God, is an act of faith.

4. Evolution is a conscious process.

5. Bathos is that which is intended to be sorrowful but because of the extremity of its expression becomes comic. Pathos is that which is meant to be comic but because of the extremity of its expression becomes sorrowful. Some things which seem to be opposites are actually different degrees of the same thing.

6. The comic hero thrives by his vices. The tragic hero is destroyed by his virtue. Moral paradox is the crux of the drama.

7. The theater is a humble materialist enterprise which seeks to produce riches of the imagination, not the other way around. The theater is an event and not an object. Theater workers need not blush and conceal their desperate struggle to pay the landlords their rents. Theater without the stink of art.

Instructions for use:
This is farce not Sunday school. Illustrate hedonistic calculus. Test out a

dangerous idea, a theme that threatens to destroy one's whole value system. Treat the material in a madly farcical manner without losing the seriousness of the theme. Show how paradoxes arrest the mind. Scare yourself a bit along the way.[1]

Notes

Introduction

1. The slang term "blue-rinse" set, or crowd, is theatrical lingo referring to all of the elderly suburban-minded, women's club members who throng to matinees of Broadway shows in their Gucci shoes, carrying Bergdorf bags. Their hair is, more often than not, an unusual shade of light blue, sometimes purple.

2. "Charles Ludlam: Ridiculous & Outrageous." *After Dark Magazine*, Sept. 1981, p. 84.

3. Steven Samuels. "Charles Ludlam: A Brief Life." *The Complete Plays of Charles Ludlam*. New York: Harper & Row, 1989, p. xx.

4. Victor Hugo. *Preface to Cromwell*, as reprinted in Bernard Dukore, ed., *Dramatic Theory and Criticism*. New York: Harcourt Brace Jovanovich College Publishers, 1974, p. 691.

5. Charles Ludlam. "Manifesto: Ridiculous Theater, Scourge of Human Folly." *The Complete Plays of Charles Ludlam*. New York: Harper & Row, 1989, p. iix. For complete Manifesto, see Appendix.

6. Richard Schechner. *Public Domain*. New York: Avon Books, 1970, p. 211.

7. Elenore Lester. "The Holy Foolery of Charles Ludlam." *New York Times*, 14 July 1974, sec. 2, p. 1.

8. Steven Samuels, ed. *Ridiculous Theatre: Scourge of Human Folly; The Essays and Opinions of Charles Ludlam*. New York: Theatre Communications Group, 1992, p. 221.

9. Sam H. Shirakawa. "The Eccentric World of Charles Ludlam." *New York Times*, July 3, 1983, p. H3.

Chapter 1

1. Steven Samuels, ed. *Ridiculous Theatre: Scourge of Human Folly. The Essays and Opinions of Charles Ludlam*. New York: Theatre Communications Group, 1992, p. 7.

2. *Ibid.*, p. 7.

3. *Ibid.*, p. 6.

4. *Ibid.*, p. 6.

5. Calvin Tomkins. "Profiles: Ridiculous." *The New Yorker*, Nov. 15, 1976, p. 61.

6. Samuels, p. 8.

7. *Ibid.*, p. 9.

8. Tomkins, p. 65.

9. Samuels, p. 9.

10. *Ibid.*, p. 65.

11. Gautam Dasgupta. "Interview: Charles Ludlam." *Performing Arts Journal,* Spring-Summer 1978, p. 69.

12. Shirakawa, Sam H. "The Eccentric World of Charles Ludlam." *New York Times,* July 3, 1983, p. H3.

13. Tomkins, p. 65.

14. Samuels, p. 11.

15. Tomkins, p. 65.

16. *Ibid.*, p. 11.

17. Michael Bronski. *Culture Clash.* Boston: South End Press, 1984, p. 131.

Chapter 2

1. Gerald Rabkin. "An Introduction." *Performing Arts Journal,* Spring/Summer 1978, p. 41.

2. Charles Ludlam. *The Complete Plays of Charles Ludlam.* New York: Harper & Row, 1989, p. 87.

3. James Fisher. *The Theatre of Yesterday and Tomorrow: Commedia Dell'Arte on the Modern Stage.* New York: The Edwin Mellen Press, 1992, p. 2.

4. William Dean Howells. "The New Taste in Theatricals." *Atlantic Monthly,* May 1989, pp. 642–643.

5. Robert C. Allen. *Horrible Prettiness.* Chapel Hill: The University of North Carolina Press, 1991, p. 147.

6. *Ibid.*, pp. 185–186.

7. Todd Gitlin. *The Sixties.* New York: Bantam Books, 1987, p. 6.

8. George Chauncey. *Gay New York.* New York: Basic Books, 1994, p. 34.

9. *Ibid.*, p. 56.

10. Barry D. Adams. *The Rise of the Gay and Lesbian Movement.* Boston: Twayne Publishers, 1987, p. 58.

11. Chauncey, p. 329.

12. *Ibid.*, p. 333.

13. *Ibid.*, p. 244.

14. *Fulton Bar & Grill v. State Liquor Authority,* SLA Hearing Officer's Report, Feb. 16, 1960, Exhibit "G" Annexed to Answer, Papers on Appeal from an Order, 67–74, at 68. As cited in Chauncey, p. 344.

15. Bernard Weintraub. "Thousands Line Up to View Judy Garland's Body." *New York Times,* June 27, 1969, p. 46.

16. Martin Duberman. *Stonewall.* New York: Plume, 1994, p. 189.

17. Lucian Truscott IV. "Gay Power Comes to Sheridan Square." *Village Voice,* July 3, 1969, pp. 1, 18.

18. Jonathan Black. "Gay Power Hits Back." *Village Voice,* July 3, 1969, pp. 1, 3, 44.

19. Neal Weaver. "Slow Burn: The Long Road to Stonewall." *LA Village View,* June 24–30, 1994, p. 32.

20. David Bergman. "Strategic Camp: The Art of Gay Rhetoric," in *Camp Grounds.* David Bergman, ed., Amherst: University of Massachusetts Press, 1993, p. 103.

21. Gerald Rabkin. "Theatre of the Ridiculous." *Performing Arts Journal,* Spring/Summer 1978, p. 41.

22. Patrick S. Smith. *Andy Warhol's Art & Films.* Ann Arbor, Mich.: UMI Research Press, 1986, p. 143.

23. Ronald Tavel. "The Theatre of the Ridiculous." *Tri-Quarterly,* No. 6, 1966, pp. 94–95.

24. Calvin Tomkins. "Profiles: Ridiculous." *The New Yorker,* November 15, 1976, p. 59.

25. Rabkin, p. 42.

26. *Midnight Movies.* J. Hoberman and Jonathan Rosenbaum, eds. New York: Harper & Row, 1983, p. 74.

27. Dan Issac. "Ronald Tavel: Ridiculous Playwright." *The Drama Review,* Vol. 13, No. 1 (T-41), Fall 1968, p. 106.

28. Tomkins, p. 60.

29. Tavel, p. 95.

30. Tomkins, p. 60.

31. *Ibid.,* p. 60.

32. Bonnie Marranca. "Introduction," Bonnie Marranca, ed. *Theatre of the Ridiculous.* New York: Performing Arts Journal Publications, 1979, p. 6.

33. Tavel, p. 108.

34. Bonnie Marranca. *American Playwright: A Critical Survey.* New York: Drama Book Specialists, 1981, pp. 194–195.

35. Bonnie Marranca. "The Plays of Ridiculous Theatre." *Performing Arts Journal,* Spring/Summer 1978, p. 60.

36. *Ibid.,* p. 55.

37. Jack Smith, in Hoberman and Rosenbaum, p. 48.

38. *Ibid.,* p. 37.

39. Issac, "Ronald Tavel," p. 110.

40. Dan Issac. "I Come from Ohio: An Interview with John Vaccaro." *The Drama Review,* Vol. 13, No. 1 (T-41), Fall 1968, p. 142.

41. Tomkins, p. 68.

42. Issac, "Ronald Tavel," p. 113.

43. Tomkins, p. 72.

44. Dan Issac. "Charles Ludlam/Norma Desmond/Laurette Bedlam." *The Drama Review,* Vol. 13, No. 1 (T-41), Fall 1968 (no page number available).

45. Tomkins, p. 73.

46. *Ibid.,* p. 73.

47. David Kaufman. "From the Sublime to the Ridiculous." *Interview,* Vol. XIX, No. 12, December 1989, p. 82.

48. Tomkins, p. 74.

Chapter 3

1. Bonnie Marranca. *American Playwrights: A Critical Survey.* New York: Drama Book Specialists, 1981, p. 194.

2. Ronald Argelander. "Ridiculous Theatrical Company." *The Drama Review,* Vol. 18, No. 2, 1974, p. 82.

3. Stefan Brecht. *Queer Theatre.* New York: Methuen Books, 1986, p. 55.

4. Gautam Dasgupta. "Interview: Charles Ludlam." *Performing Arts Journal,* Spring/Summer 1978, p. 69.

5. Frank Browning. *Culture of Desire.* New York: Crown, 1993, p. 9.

6. Michael Bronski. *Culture Clash*. Boston: South End Press, 1984, p. 191.

7. *Ibid.*, p. 8.

8. Mark Thompson. *Gay Spirit*. New York: St. Martin's Press, 1987, p. xiv.

9. Mel Gussow. "In the Ridiculous Theatrical Troupe, Ludlamania Knows No Bounds." *New York Times*, Oct. 24, 1980, p. C3.

10. Michael Feingold. "The Bold Soprano." *Village Voice*, Feb. 27, 1983, p. 95.

11. *Ibid.*, p. 93.

12. Terry Helbing. "Charles Ludlam Finds Utopia." *Where It's At*, Jan. 8, 1979, p. 20.

13. Laurence Senelick. "Glamour Drag & Male Impersonation." In Lesley Ferris, ed., *Crossing the Stage: Controversies On Cross-Dressing*. New York: Routledge Press, 1993, p. 85.

14. George Chauncey. *Gay New York*. New York: Basic Books, 1994, p. 299.

15. Esther Newton. *Mother Camp*. New Jersey: Prentice-Hall, 1972, p. 102.

16. Judith Butler. *Gender Trouble: Feminism and the Subversion of Identity*. New York: Routledge Press, 1990, p. 6.

17. Newton, p. 103.

18. Laurence Senelick. "Introduction." In Laurence Senelick, ed., *Gender in Performance*. New Hampshire: University Press of New England, 1992, p. ix.

19. Jan Kott. *Theater of Essence*. Evanston: Northwestern University Press, 1984, p. 124.

20. Dasgupta, p. 79.

21. *Ibid.*, pp. 78–79.

22. Jill Dolan. "Gender Impersonation Onstage." In Senelick, p. 6.

23. Frank Scheck. "20 Ridiculous Years." *Stages*, March 1986, p. 22.

24. Michael Shepherd. "Charles Ludlam." *Christopher Street*, No. 62, March 1982, p. 16.

25. Charles Ludlam. "Monograph." In Steven Samuels, ed., *Ridiculous Theatre: Scourge of Human Folly. The Essays and Opinions of Charles Ludlam*. New York: Theatre Communications Group, 1992, p. 53.

26. Clive Barnes. "Galas: Tragedy Turned Comedy." *New York Times*, Sept. 26, 1983, p. 20.

27. Elenore Lester. "The Holy Foolery of Charles Ludlam." *New York Times*, July 14, 1974, pp. 8–9.

28. Kate Davy. "Fe/Male Impersonation." In Moe Meyer, ed., *Politics and Poetics of Camp*, New York: Routledge Press, 1994, p. 137.

29. Samuels, p. 39.

30. *American Heritage Dictionary of the English Language*, Third Edition. Houghton Mifflin, 1992. (As retrieved electronically via Compuserve.)

31. Chauncey, p. 290.

32. Scott Long. "The Loneliness of Camp." In David Bergman, ed., *Camp Grounds*. Amherst: University of Massachusetts Press, 1993, p. 90.

33. Bronski, p. 46.

34. Samuels, p. 130.

35. David Bergman. "Strategic Camp." In Bergman, p. 106.

36. Susan Sontag. *Against Interpretation*. New York: Doubleday, 1966, p. 287.

37. *Ibid.*, p. 279.

38. *Ibid.*, p. 290.

39. *Ibid.*, p. 290.

40. Rosalyn Regelson. "Up the Camp Staircase." *New York Times*, March 3, 1968, pp. 13–14.

41. Jack Babuscio. "Camp and the Gay Sensibility." In Richard Dyer, ed., *Gays and Film*. New York: Zoetrope, 1984, p. 40.

42. *Ibid.*, p. 43.

43. *Ibid.*, pp. 40–41.

44. *Ibid.*, p. 41.

45. *Ibid.*, p. 44.

46. *Ibid.*, p. 44.

47. *Ibid.*, p. 48.

48. Newton, p. 106.

49. *Ibid.*, p. 119.

50. Samuels, p. 226.

51. *Ibid.*, p. 225.

52. *Ibid.*, p. 226.

53. *Ibid.*, p. 227.

54. *Ibid.*, p. 202.

55. Wayne Koestenbaum. *The Queen's Throat*. New York: Poseidon Press, 1993, p. 145.

56. Bronski, p. 135.

57. Koestenbaum, p. 46.

58. *Ibid.*, p. 32.

59. Samuels, p. 202.

Chapter 4

1. Clive Barnes. "Galas: Tragedy Turned Comedy." *New York Post*, Sept. 26, 1983, p. 20.

2. Louis Montros. "The Purpose of Playing: Reflections on a Shakespearean Anthropology." *Helios*, NS, 1980, p. 7.

3. Gautam Dasgupta. "Interview: Charles Ludlam." *Performing Arts Journal*. Spring/Summer 1978, p. 79.

4. *Current Biography Yearbook*. New York: H.W. Wilson, 1986, p. 315.

5. Richard Schechner. *Public Domain*. New York: Avon Books, 1969, p. 198.

6. Eileen Blumenthal. "Mild Kingdom." *Village Voice*, Sept. 30, 1986, p. 97.

7. Michael Feingold. "Let Ludlam Ring!" *Village Voice*, May 9, 1977, p. 83.

8. Robert Thomas Wharton III. "The Working Dynamics of the Ridiculous Theatrical Company" (unpublished dissertation). Florida State University, 1985, p. 180.

9. Calvin Tomkins. "Profiles: Ridiculous." *The New Yorker*, Nov. 15, 1976, p. 551.

10. Mel Gussow. "Stage: The Grand Tarot." *New York Times*, March 4, 1971, p. 28.

11. Ross Wetzsteon. "Sex Acts on Stage: Where Does Art Get Off?" *Village Voice*, March 22, 1976, p. 76

12. *Ibid.*, p. 77.

13. Tish Dace. "From the Ridiculous to the Sublime." *Theatre Crafts*. March 1986, pp. 68–69.

14. Ricki Fulman. *New York Daily News*, Nov. 11, 1984 (quoted in *Current Biography Yearbook 1986*. New York: H.W. Wilson, 1986, p. 318).

15. Schechner, p. 201.

16. Steven Samuels, ed. *Ridiculous Theatre: Scourge of Human Folly. The Essays and Opinions of Charles Ludlam*. New York: Theatre Communications Group, 1992, p. 107.

17. *Ibid.*, p. 206.

18. Sam H. Shirakawa. "The Eccentric World of Charles Ludlam." *New York Times,* July 3, 1983, p. H3.

19. Samuels, p. 18.

20. Tomkins, p. 83.

21. Tish Dace. "Rampantly Ridiculous." *Other Stages,* Oct. 19, 1978, p. 3.

22. Ron Argelander. "Ridiculous Theatre Company." *The Drama Review,* Vol. 18, No. 2, 1974, p. 83.

23. Dasgupta, p. 77.

24. Bonnie Marranca. *American Playwrights: A Critical Survey.* New York: Drama Book Specialists, 1981, p. 193.

25. Charles Ludlam. *Reverse Psychology.* New York: Samuel French, 1989, pp. 36–37.

26. Charles Ludlam. *The Complete Plays of Charles Ludlam.* New York: Harper & Row, 1989, p. 822.

27. Ludlam. *Bluebeard.* New York: Samuel French, 1971, p. 17.

28. Ludlam, *Complete Plays,* pp. 710–711.

29. *Ibid.*, p. 420.

30. Samuels, p. 160.

31. "Charles Ludlam: Ridiculous and Outrageous." *After Dark.* Sept. 1981, p. 84.

32. Argelander, p. 85.

33. David Sterritt. *Christian Science Monitor,* March 13, 1981, p. 19.

34. Stefan Brecht. *Queer Theatre.* New York: Methuen Books, 1986, p. 33.

35. James MaGruder. "Three Gags in Ludlam." *Performing Arts Journal,* Spring/Summer 1987, p. 33.

36. Howard Kissel. "Salammbo." *Women's Wear Daily,* Nov. 8, 1985, p. 18.

37. Constant Coquelin. *Art and the Actor,* trans. Abby Langdon Alger. New York: Dramatic Museum of Columbia University, 1915, pp. 46–47.

38. *Ibid.*, p. 45.

39. Argelander, p. 86.

Chapter 5

1. Steven Samuels. "Charles Ludlam: A Brief Life." In Charles Ludlam, *The Complete Plays of Charles Ludlam.* New York: Harper & Row, 1989, p. xiii.

2. Charles Ludlam. *The Complete Plays of Charles Ludlam.* New York: Harper & Row, 1989, p. 5.

3. Albert Bermel. "All Out Ridicule." *The New Leader,* March 13, 1967, p. 28.

4. Sam H. Shirakawa. "The Eccentric World of Charles Ludlam." *New York Times,* July 3, 1983, p. H3.

5. Ludlam, p. 6.

6. *Ibid.*, p. 9.

7. *Ibid.*, p. 20.

8. *Ibid.*, p. 18.

9. Original script in the Charles Ludlam Archives.

10. *Ibid.*, p. 22.

11. A.D.C. "Theatre: Big Hotel." *Village Voice,* Jan. 18, 1968, p. 26.

12. "Order in the Court." *Soho Weekly News.* Oct. 25, 1979, p. 48.

13. Martin Washburn. "Theatre: Turds in Hell." *Village Voice,* Dec. 5, 1968, p. 47.

14. Martin Gottfried. "Martin Gottfried Looks at New York's Ridiculous Theatre, Now Tarot-turned." *Vogue,* June 15, 1971, p. 84.

15. Calvin Tomkins. "Profiles: Ridiculous." *The New Yorker,* Nov. 15, 1976, p. 83.

16. Charles Ludlam, *Bluebeard.* New York: Samuel French, 1971.

17. *Ibid.,* p. 7.

18. Robert Thomas Wharton III. *The Working Dynamics of the Ridiculous Theatrical Company.* Ph.D. dissertation, Florida State University, 1985, p. 222.

19. Tomkins, p. 80.

20. Ludlam, *Bluebeard,* p. 8.

21. Martin Gottfried. "Bluebeard." *Women's Wear Daily,* May 11, 1970, p. 14.

22. Sylviane Gold. "Look for Gray Matter in Ludlam's Bluebeard." *New York Post,* May 9, 1975, p. 31.

23. David Sears. "Ludlam Stages Bluebeard." *Villager,* April 24, 1975, pp. 5–6.

24. Mel Gussow. "Laughs Pepper Ghoulish Bluebeard." *New York Times,* May 5, 1970, p. 59.

25. Ludlam, *Bluebeard.*

26. Jan Stuart. "Sex with a Sense of the Ridiculous." *Newsday,* Nov. 15, 1991, p. 83.

27. Steven Samuels, ed. *Ridiculous Theatre: Scourge of Human Folly. The Essays and Opinions of Charles Ludlam.* New York: Theatre Communications Group, 1992, p. 25.

28. Ludlam, *Bluebeard,* p. 13.

29. *Ibid.*

30. Ludlam. *Bluebeard,* pp. 17–18.

31. Tish Dace. "Rampantly Ridiculous." *Other Stages,* Oct. 19, 1978, p. 3.

32. Ludlam, *Complete Plays,* p. 224.

33. Alexandre Dumas *fils. La Dame aux Camellias,* trans. Henrietta Metcalf. New York: Samuel French, 1989, p. 69.

34. Ludlam, *Complete Plays,* p. 234.

35. *Ibid.,* p. 246.

36. Clive Barnes. "Stage: An Oddly Touching Camille." *New York Times,* May 14, 1974, p. 22.

37. Ludlam, *Complete Plays,* p. 236.

38. Tomkins, p. 85.

39. Samuels, *Ridiculous Theatre,* p. 37.

40. Elenore Lester. "Camille." *New York Times,* July 14, 1977, p. 8.

41. Tomkins, p. 85.

42. Misha Berson. "A Moving and Funny Camille." *The San Francisco Bay Guardian,* Feb. 28, 1990, p. 29.

43. Ludlam, *Complete Plays,* p. 232.

44. *Ibid.,* p. 225.

45. *Ibid.,* p. 230.

46. *Ibid.,* p. 225.

47. Tomkins, p. 84.

48. Ludlam, *Complete Plays,* p. 239.

49. Gautam Dasgupta. "Interview: Charles Ludlam." *Performing Arts Journal,* Spring/Summer 1978, p. 78.

50. Ludlam, *Complete Plays,* p. 251.

51. Barnes, p. 31.

52. Mel Gussow. "The Theater: Hilarious 'Hot Ice'." *New York Times,* Feb. 11, 1974, p. 48.

53. Ludlam, *Complete Plays,* p. 314.

54. *Ibid.*, p. 316.

55. Samuels, *Ridiculous Theatre*, p. 50.

56. Elenore Lester. "To Be or to Seem." *Soho Weekly News*, July 14, 1977 (no page number).

57. Charles Ludlam. *Stage Blood.* New York: Samuel French, 1974, p. 11.

58. *Ibid.*

59. *Ibid.*

60. *Ibid.*

61. *Ibid.*, p. 21.

62. *Ibid.*, pp. 25–26.

63. *Ibid.*, p. 20.

64. *Ibid.*, p. 300.

65. Tomkins, p. 95.

66. Marilyn Stasio. "Not So Ridiculous." *Cue Magazine*, Dec. 23–30, 1974, p. 31.

67. Julius Novick. "Stage Blood Is Anemic Parody." *New York Times*, Jan. 12, 1975, Sec. 2, p. 5.

68. Michael Feingold. "Let Ludlam Ring!" *Village Voice*, May 9, 1977, p. 83.

69. Michael Feingold. "Der Ring Gott Farblonjet: A Masterwork." *Village Voice*, April 24, 1990, p. 103.

70. Shirakawa, p. H10.

71. Samuels, "Charles Ludlam," p. xvi.

72. Samuels, *Ridiculous Theatre*, p. 63.

73. *Ibid.*, p. 63.

74. Ludlam, *Complete Plays*, p. 422.

75. *Ibid.*, p. 430.

76. *Ibid.*, p. 418.

77. Mel Gussow. "Stage: Black-Eyed Susan Wed to 'Enchanted Pig'." *New York Times*, April 24, 1979, p. C10.

78. Samuels, "Charles Ludlam," p. xvii.

79. Dennis Powers. "Ludlam! The Ridiculous Theatrical Company Stalks the Primitive Child — And Audiences." *Theatre Communications*, Dec. 1981, p. 4.

Chapter 6

1. Michael Feingold. "Charles' Ark." *Village Voice*, Sept. 17, 1980, p. 80.

2. Frank Rich. "Stage: Ludlam's 'Reverse Psychology'." *New York Times*, Sept. 16, 1980, p. C1.

3. Charles Ludlam. *The Complete Plays of Charles Ludlam.* New York: Harper & Row, 1989, pp. 620–621.

4. Dennis Powers. "Ludlam! The Ridiculous Theatrical Company Stalks the Primitive Child — And Audiences." *Theatre Communications*, Dec. 1981, p. 4.

5. Arch Brown. "Review: A Wonderfully Wacky Ludlam." *Villager*, March 4, 1982, p. 15.

6. Ludlam, p. 657.

7. Allan Wallach. "A Satirical Piece with an Apt Title." *Newsday*, Oct. 12, 1982, Part 2, p. 24.

8. Steven Samuels. "Charles Ludlam: A Brief Life." In Charles Ludlam, *The Complete Plays of Charles Ludlam.* New York: Harper & Row, 1989, p. xviii.

9. Steven Samuels, ed. *Ridiculous Theater: Scourge of Human Folly. The Essays*

and Opinions of Charles Ludlam. New York: Theatre Communications Group, 1992, p. 116.

10. Molière. *The Miser and Other Plays,* trans. John Wood. New York: Penguin Books, 1962, p. 62.

11. Samuels, *Ridiculous Theatre,* p. 223.

12. *Ibid.,* p. 721.

13. *Ibid.,* p. 729.

14. *Ibid.,* p. 729.

15. *Ibid.,* p. 729.

16. *Ibid.,* p. 701.

17. *Ibid.,* p. 726.

18. *Ibid.,* p. 703.

19. Marilyn Stasio. "Ludlam Hilarious as an Ass of the Arts." *New York Post,* June 25, 1983, p. 19.

20. Frank Rich. "Stage: 'Le Bourgeois,' Comedy After Moliere." *New York Times,* April 15, 1983, p. C3.

21. Ludlam, pp. 699–700.

22. *Ibid.,* p. 729.

23. *Ibid.,* p. 706.

24. *Ibid.,* p. 707.

25. Don Nelsen. *New York Daily News,* March 19, 1983, p. 57.

26. Michael Feingold. "The Bold Soprano." *Village Voice,* Feb. 27, 1983, p. 95.

27. Frank Rich. "Stage: Galas, New Play by Ridiculous Company." *New York Times,* Sept. 16, 1983. p. C3.

28. Samuels, *Ridiculous Theatre,* p. 119.

29. David A. Lowe, ed. *Callas: As They Saw Her.* New York: Ungar Publishing Company, 1986, p. 3.

30. John Simon. "Galas." *New York Magazine,* Sept. 26, 1983, p. 103.

31. Eleanor Blau. "Galas." *New York Times,* Nov. 25, 1983, p. C2.

32. Samuels, *Ridiculous Theatre,* p. 188.

33. Ludlam, p. 734.

34. *Ibid.,* p. 734.

35. *Ibid.,* pp. 734–735.

36. *Ibid.,* p. 744.

37. *Ibid.,* p. 745.

38. *Ibid.,* p. 746.

39. *Ibid.,* p. 746.

40. *Ibid.,* p. 746.

41. *Ibid.,* p. 747.

42. *Ibid.,* p. 749.

43. *Ibid.,* p. 750.

44. *Ibid.,* p. 757.

45. *Ibid.,* p. 762.

46. *Ibid.,* pp. 763–764.

47. *Ibid.,* pp. 840–841.

48. *Ibid.,* p. 843.

49. Ludlam, p. 774.

50. Samuels, *Ridiculous Theatre,* p. 122.

51. Tish Dace. "From the Ridiculous to the Sublime." *Theatre Crafts* March 1986, p. 36.

52. *Ibid.,* p. 68.

53. *Ibid.*, p. 68.

54. Samuels, *Ridiculous Theatre*, p. 125.

55. Michael Feingold. "Undead Awaken." *Village Voice*, Oct. 16, 1984, p. 113.

56. Charles Ludlam. *The Mystery of Irma Vep*. New York: Samuel French, 1984, p. 14.

57. *Ibid.*, p. 48.

58. William Shakespeare. *The Tragedy of Macbeth*, ed. R. A. Foakes. New York: Bobbs-Merrill, 1968, pp. 43–44.

59. Ludlam. *Irma Vep*. New York: Samuel French, pp. 31–32.

60. *Ibid.*, p. 65.

61. Oscar Wilde. "The Ballad of Reading Gaol." As quoted in . Angela Partington, ed., *The Concise Oxford Dictionary of Quotations*. Oxford: Oxford University Press, 1994, p. 350.

62. Ludlam. *Irma Vep*. New York: Samuel French, pp. 63–64.

63. *Ibid.*, p. 50.

64. *Ibid.*, pp. 53–54.

65. *Ibid.*, pp. 44–45.

66. Richard Corliss. "Tour de Farce." *Time*, Oct. 15, 1984, p. 113.

67. Mel Gussow. "Stage: The Mystery of Irma Vep." *New York Times*, Oct. 4, 1984, p. C16.

68. Clive Barnes. "Calling All Vampires to Sheridan Sq." *New York Post*, Oct. 8, 1984, p. 50.

69. Sy Syna. "The Secret Is Out — Campy Irma Vep Is Howlingly Funny." *New York Tribune*, Oct. 6, 1984, p. 3B.

70. Charles Ludlam. "Notes: Salammbo." *Showbill*, Nov. 4, 1985, p. 16.

71. Robert Heide. "From the Ridiculous to the Sublime." *New York Native*, Oct. 27, 1986, p. 53.

72. Frank Scheck. "20 Ridiculous Years." *Stages*, March 1986, p. 7.

73. *Ibid.*, p. 7.

74. Ludlam, *Complete Plays*, p. 847.

75. Terry Helbing. "Taking the Veil." *New York Native*, Nov. 18, 1985, p. 43.

76. Don Nelsen. "All Dressed Up and No Place to Go." *New York Daily News*, Nov. 15, 1985, p. 15.

77. James MaGruder. "Three Gags in Ludlam." *Performing Arts Journal*, Spring/Summer 1987, p. 32.

78. Gustave Flaubert. *Salammbo*, trans. E. Powys Mathers. London: Chiswick Press, 1947, pp. 35–36.

79. Allan Wallach. "Charles Ludlam Takes On Flaubert." *Newsday*, Nov. 8, 1985, p. 13.

80. Frank Rich. "Theater: Ridiculous's 'Salammbo'." *New York Times*, Nov. 12, 1985, p. C13.

81. Scheck, p. 7.

82. Charles Ludlam. *The Artificial Jungle*. New York: Samuel French, 1986, pp. 28–29.

83. *Ibid.*, p. 32.

84. *Ibid.*, pp. 21–23.

85. *Ibid.*, pp. 41–42.

86. *Ibid.*, pp. 25–26.

87. MaGruder, p. 33.

88. Tish Dace. "Ludlam Memorial Draws Capacity Crowd." *New York Native*, Aug. 3, 1987, p. 9.

Chapter 7

1. "Charles Ludlam." *1986 Current Biography Yearbook.* New York: H.W. Wilson, 1986, p. 315.

2. Mel Gussow. "The Stage: Puppets and Pyrotechnics." *New York Times,* Oct. 26, 1974, p. 37.

3. Glenn Loney. "Fora Flees Fiends." *Other Stages,* Oct. 5, 1978, p. 5.

4. Robert Chesley. "Dialogue with the Ridiculous." *Omega One,* Jan. 19, 1979, p. 23.

5. David Kaufman. "From the Ridiculous to the Sublime." *Interview,* Vol. XIX, No. 50 (Dec. 1989), p. 120.

6. Thomas M. Disch. "Titus Andronicus." *The Nation,* June 20, 1987, p. 863.

7. Steven Samuels, ed. *Ridiculous Theatre: Scourge of Human Folly. The Essays and Opinions of Charles Ludlam.* New York: Theatre Communications Group, 1992, pp. 169–170.

8. Steven Samuels. "Charles Ludlam: A Brief Life," in Charles Ludlam, *The Complete Plays of Charles Ludlam.* New York: Harper & Row, 1989, p. xix.

9. Samuels, *Ridiculous Theatre,* p. 263.

10. Frank Scheck. "20 Ridiculous Years." *Stages,* March 1986, p. 22.

11. Reprinted as "In Memory" in *Drama Review,* Winter 1987, pp. 8, 9.

Appendix

1. As quoted in *The Complete Plays of Charles Ludlam.* New York: Harper & Row, 1989, p. viii.

Bibliography

Books

Adams, Barry D. *The Rise of the Gay and Lesbian Movement*. Boston: Twayne Publishers, 1987.

Allen, Robert C. *Horrible Prettiness: Burlesque and American Culture*. Chapel Hill: University of North Carolina Press, 1991.

American Heritage Dictionary of the English Language. Third Edition. New York: Houghton Mifflin, 1993.

Bergman, David, ed. *Camp Grounds*. Amherst: University of Massachusetts Press, 1993.

Brecht, Stefan. *Queer Theatre*. New York: Methuen Books, 1986.

Bronski, Michael. *Culture Clash*. Boston: South End Press, 1984.

Browning, Frank. *Culture of Desire*. New York: Crown, 1993.

"Charles Ludlam." *1986 Current Biography Yearbook*. New York: H.W. Wilson, 1986, p. 315.

Chauncey, George. *Gay New York*. New York: Basic Books, 1994.

Coquelin, Constant. *Art and the Actor*, trans. Abby Langdon Alger. New York: Dramatic Museum of Columbia University, 1915.

Duberman, Martin. *Stonewall*. New York: Plume, 1994.

Dumas, Alexandre, *fils*. *La Dame aux Camellias*, trans. Henrietta Metcalf. New York: Samuel French, 1989.

Ferris, Lesley, ed. *Crossing the Stage: Controversies on Cross-Dressing*. New York: Routledge Press, 1993.

Fisher, James. *The Theatre of Yesterday and Tomorrow: Commedia Dell'Arte on the Modern Stage*. New York: The Edwin Mellen Press, 1992.

Flaubert, Gustave. *Salammbo*, trans. E. Powys Mathers. London: Chiswick Press, 1947.

Gitlin, Todd. *The Sixties*. New York: Bantam Books, 1987.

Hoberman, J. and Jonathan Rosenbaum, eds. *Midnight Movies*. New York: Harper & Row, 1983.

Hugo, Victor. *Preface to Cromwell*. As reprinted in Bernard Dukore, ed., *Dramatic Theory and Criticism*. New York: Harcourt Brace Jovanovich College Publishers, 1974, p. 691.

Koestenbaum, Wayne. *The Queen's Throat*. New York: Poseidon Press, 1993.

Kott, Jan. *Theater of Essence*. Evanston IL: Northwestern University Press, 1984.

Lowe, David A., ed. *Callas: As They Saw Her*. New York: Ungar Publishing Company, 1986.

Ludlam, Charles. *The Complete Plays of Charles Ludlam*. New York: Harper & Row Publishers, 1989.

Marranca, Bonnie. *American Playwrights: A Critical Survey*. New York: Drama Book
    Specialists, 1981.
_____. *Theatre of the Ridiculous*. New York: Performing Arts Journal Publications, 1979.
Meyer, Moe, ed. *Politics and Poetics of Camp*. New York: Routledge Press, 1994.
Molière. *The Miser and Other Plays*, trans. John Wood. New York: Penguin Books, 1962.
Partington, Angela, ed. *The Concise Oxford Dictionary of Quotation*. Oxford: Oxford
    University Press, 1994.
Samuels, Steven, ed. *Ridiculous Theatre: Scourge of Human Folly. The Essays and Opin-
    ions of Charles Ludlam*. New York: Theatre Communications Group, 1992.
Schechner, Richard. *Public Domain*. New York: Avon Books, 1969.
Senelick, Laurence, ed. *Gender in Performance*. New Hampshire: University Press of
    New England, 1992.
Shakespeare, William. *Macbeth*. ed. R.A. Foakes. New York: Bobbs-Merrill, 1968.
Sontag, Susan. *Against Interpretation*. New York: Doubleday, 1966.
Thompson, Mark. *Gay Spirit: Myth and Meaning*. New York: St. Martin's Press, 1987.

Articles

"Charles Ludlam: Ridiculous & Outrageous." *After Dark Magazine*, Sept. 1981 (no author
    or page listed).
Argelander, Ronald. "Ridiculous Theatrical Company." *The Drama Review*, Vol. 18.,
    No. 2., 1974, pp. 81+
Babuscio, Jack. "Camp and the Gay Sensibility." In Richard Dyer, ed. *Gays and Film*.
    New York: Zoetrope, 1984, pp. 40+.
Bermel, Albert. "All Out Ridicule." *The New Leader*, March 13, 1967, p. 28.
Black, Jonathan. "Gay Power Hits Back." *Village Voice*, Vol. XIV, No. 42. (July 3, 1969),
    pp. 1+.
Chesley, Robert. "Dialogue with the Ridiculous." *Omega One*, Jan. 19, 1978, p. 22.
Dace, Tish. "From the Ridiculous to the Sublime." *Theatre Crafts*, March 1986, pp. 68+.
_____. "Rampantly Ridiculous." *Other Stages*, Oct. 9, 1978, p. 3.
_____. "Ludlam Memorial Draws Capacity Crowd." *New York Native*. 3 August 1987.
    pp. 9+.
Dasgupta, Gautam. "Interview: Charles Ludlam." *Performing Arts Journal*, Spring/Sum-
    mer, 1978, pp. 69+.
Disch, Thomas M. "Titus Andronicus." *The Nation*, June 20, 1987, p. 862.
Feingold, Michael. "Charles' Ark." *Village Voice*, Sept. 17, 1980, p. 80.
Gussow, Mel. "In the Ridiculous Theatrical Troupe, Ludlamania Knows No Bounds."
    New York Times, Oct. 24, 1980, p. C3.
Heide, Robert. "From the Ridiculous to the Sublime." *New York Native*, Oct. 27, 1986,
    p. 257.
Howells, William Dean. "The New Taste in Theatricals." *Atlantic Monthly*, May 1869,
    pp. 635–644.
Issac, Dan. "Charles Ludlam/Norma Desmond/Laurette Bedlam." *The Drama Review*,
    Vol. 13, No. 1 (T-41), Fall 1968, p. 105.
_____. "I Come from Ohio: An Interview with John Vaccaro." *The Drama Review*, Vol.
    13, No. 1 (T-41), Fall 1968, p. 142.
_____. "Ronald Tavel: Ridiculous Playwright." *The Drama Review*, Vol. 13, No. 1 (T-41),
    Fall 1968, p. 106.
Katz, Leon. "In Memory." *The Drama Review*, Winter 1987., p. 8.

Kaufman, David. "From the Sublime to the Ridiculous." *Interview*, Vol. xix, No. 127, Dec. 1989, pp. 77+.

Lester, Elenore. "The Holy Foolery of Charles Ludlam." *New York Times*, July 14, 1974, pp. 8+.

Ludlam, Charles. "Notes: Salammbo." *Showbill*, Nov. 4, 1985, p. 8.

MaGruder, James. "Three Gags in Ludlam." *Performing Arts Journal*, Spring/Summer 1987, pp. 30+.

Montors, Louis. "The Purpose of Playing: Reflections on a Shakespearean Anthropology." *Helios*, NS, 1980, pp. 7+.

Rabkin, Gerald. "An Introduction." *Performing Arts Journal*, Spring/Summer 1978, p. 41.

_____. "Theatre of the Ridiculous." *Performing Arts Journal*, Spring/Summer 1978.

Regelson, Rosalyn. "Up the Camp Staircase." *New York Times*, March 3, 1968, p. D14.

Samuels, Steven. "Charles Ludlam: A Brief Life." In Charles Ludlam, *The Complete Plays of Charles Ludlam*. New York: Harper & Row, 1989, p. ix.

Scheck, Frank. "20 Ridiculous Years." *Stages*, March 1986, pp. 8+.

Shepherd, Michael. "Charles Ludlam." *Christopher Street*, No. 62 (March 1982), p. 16.

Shirakawa, Sam H. "The Eccentric World of Charles Ludlam." *New York Times*, July 3, 1983, pp. H3+.

Stuart, Jan. "Sex with a Sense of the Ridiculous." *Newsday*, Nov. 15, 1991, p. 83.

Tavel, Ronald. "The Theatre of the Ridiculous." *Tri-Quarterly*, No. 6, 1966, p. 93.

Tomkins, Calvin. "Profiles: Ridiculous." *The New Yorker*, Nov. 15, 1976, pp. 55+.

Truscott, Lucian IV. "Gay Power Comes To Sheridan Square." *Village Voice*, July 3, 1969, pp. 1+.

Weaver, Neal. "Slow Burn: The Long Road to Stonewall." *LA Village View*, June 24–30, 1994, p. 32.

Weintraub, Bernard. "Thousands Line Up to View Judy Garland's Body." *New York Times*, June 27, 1969, p. 46.

Wetzsteon, Ross. "Sex Acts on Stage: Where Does Art Get Off?" *Village Voice*, March 22, 1976, p. 76.

Reviews

A.D.C. "Theatre: Big Hotel." *Village Voice*, Jan. 18, 1968, p. 26.

Barnes, Clive. "Calling All Vampires to Sheridan Sq." *New York Times*, Oct. 4, 1984, p. 50.

_____. "Galas: Tragedy Turned Comedy." *New York Post*, Sept. 26, 1983, p. 20.

_____. "Stage: An Oddly Touching Camille." *New York Times*, May 14, 1974, p. 22.

Berson, Misha. "A Moving and Funny Camille." *San Francisco Bay Guardian*, Feb. 28, 1990, p. 29.

Blau, Eleanor. "Galas." *New York Times*, Nov. 25, 1983, p. C2.

Brown, Arch. "Review: A Wonderfully Wacky Ludlam." *Villager*, March 4, 1982, p. 15.

Corliss, Richard. "Tour de Farce." *Time*, Oct. 15, 1984, p. 113.

Feingold, Michael. "The Bold Soprano." *Village Voice*, Feb. 27, 1983, p. 95.

_____. "Der Ring Gott Farblonjet: A Masterwork." *Village Voice*, April 24, 1990, p. 103.

_____. "Let Ludlam Ring!" *Village Voice*, May 9, 1977, p. 83.

_____. "Undead Awaken." *Village Voice*, Oct. 16, 1984, p. 113.

Gold, Sylviane. "Look for Gray Matter in Ludlam's Bluebeard." *New York Post*, May 9, 1975, p. 31.

Gottfried, Martin. "Bluebeard." *Women's Wear Daily*, May 11, 1970, p. 14.

_____. "Martin Gottfried Looks at New York's Ridiculous Theatre, Not Tarot-Turned." *Vogue*, June 15, 1971, p. 84.

Gussow, Mel. "Laughs Pepper Ghoulish Bluebeard." *New York Times*, May 5, 1970, p. 59.

_____. "Stage: Black-Eyed Susan Wed to 'Enchanted Pig'." *New York Times*, April 24, 1979, p. C10.

_____. "Stage: The Grand Tarot." *New York Times*, March 4, 1971, p. 28.

_____. "Stage: The Mystery of Irma Vep." *New York Post.*, Oct. 8, 1984, p. 260.

_____. "The Stage: Puppets and Pyrotechnics." *New York Times*, Oct. 26, 1974, p. 37.

_____. "The Theater: Hilarious 'Hot Ice'." *New York Times*, Feb. 11, 1974, p. 88.

Helbing, Terry. "Charles Ludlam Finds Utopia." *Where It's At*, Jan. 8, 1979, p. 20.

_____. "Taking the Veil." *New York Native*, Nov. 18, 1985, p. 43.

Kissel, Howard. "Salammbo." *Women's Wear Daily*, Nov. 8, 1985, p. 18.

Lester, Elenore. "Camille." *New York Times*, July 14, 1977, p. 8.

_____. "To Be or to Seem." *Soho Weekly News*, July 14, 1977.

Leverett, James. "Order in the Court." *Soho Weekly News*, Oct. 25, 1979, p. 48.

Loney, Glenn. "Flora Flees Fiends." *Other Stages*, Oct. 5, 1978, p. 5.

Nelsen, Don. "All Dressed Up and No Place to Go." *New York Daily News*, Nov. 15, 1985, p. 15.

Novick, Julius. "Stage Blood Is Anemic Parody." *New York Times*, Jan. 12, 1975, Sec. 2, p. 5.

Powers, Dennis. "Ludlam! The Ridiculous Theatrical Company Stalks the Primitive Child — And Audience." *Theatre Communications*, Dec. 1981, p. 4.

Rich, Frank. "Stage: Galas, New Play by Ridiculous Company." *New York Times*, Sept. 16, 1983, p. C3.

_____. "Stage: 'Le Bourgeois Avant-Garde'." *New York Times*, April 15, 1983, p. C3.

_____. "Stage: Ludlam's 'Reverse Psychology'." *New York Times*, Sept. 16, 1980, p. C1.

_____. "Theater: Ridiculous's 'Salammbo'." *New York Times*, Nov. 12, 1985, p. C13.

Sears, David. "Ludlam Stages Bluebeard." *Villager*, April 24, 1975, pp. 5+.

Simon, John. "Galas." *New York Magazine*, Sept. 26, 1983, p. 103.

Stasio, Marilyn. "Ludlam Hilarious as an Ass of the Arts." *New York Post*, June 25, 1983, p. 19.

_____. "Not So Ridiculous." *Cue Magazine*, Dec. 23–30, 1974, p. 31.

Syna, Sy. "The Secret Is Out — Campy Irma Vep Is Howlingly Funny." *New York Tribune*, Oct. 6, 1984, p. 33.

Wallach, Allan. "Charles Ludlam Takes On Flaubert." *Newsday*, Nov. 8, 1985, p. 13.

_____. "A Satirical Piece with an Apt Title." *Newsday*, Oct. 12, 1982, Part 2, p. 24.

Washburn, Martin. "Theatre: Turds in Hell." *Village Voice*, Dec. 5, 1968, p. 47.

Unpublished Works

Smith, Patrick S. *Andy Warhol's Art & Films*. Ph.D. dissertation, Michigan State University, 1986.

Wharton, Robert Thomas III. *The Working Dynamics of the Ridiculous Theatrical Company: An Analysis of Charles Ludlam's Relationship with His Ensemble from 1967–1981*. Ph.D. dissertation, Florida State University, 1985.

Index

185